Southside

Inspired by his own family history, David Alsobrook chronicles the lives of the cotton mill operatives who lived in the Southside neighborhood of Eufaula, Alabama, from the 1880s to the end of World War II. He weaves their stories together with great compassion while analyzing the rise and fall of the social division between the Southsiders and "Old Eufaula" in prose that is both rigorous and accessible. This is a valuable addition to local history and the history of the cotton mill economy of the South.

—Martin T. Olliff, associate professor of History and director of The Wiregrass Archives, Troy University Dothan

Just excellent. Deeply felt, beautifully researched and written. Eufaula's Southsiders have their bard, and a good one, in David Alsobrook.

—John Sledge, author of *Southern Bound* and *The Mobile River*

Forget dry, condescending, abstract histories of Southern milltowns! David Alsobrook presents a lively, crisply written and coherent account of this exemplary—in ways bad and good—Southern community. He artfully joins magisterial and personal perspectives in a story that stands as a model of scholarship that will serve and enlighten an array of audiences.

—Jerry Elijah Brown, dean and professor emeritus of Journalism, The University of Montana

-SOUTHSIDE-

-SOUTHSIDE-

EUFAULA'S COTTON MILL VILLAGE
AND ITS PEOPLE, 1890–1945

DAVID E. ALSOBROOK

Mercer University Press | Macon, Georgia | 2017

MUP/ H931

© 2017 by Mercer University Press
Published by Mercer University Press
1501 Mercer University Drive
Macon, Georgia 31207
All rights reserved

9 8 7 6 5 4 3 2 1

Books published by Mercer University Press are printed on acid-free paper
that meets the requirements of the American National Standard for
Information Sciences—Permanence of Paper for Printed Library Materials.

Some material is adapted and used with permission from
David E. Alsobrook, "Southside and Eufaula's Cowikee Mills Village, 1910-
1945," *Alabama Heritage* 119 (Winter 2016): 16-27.

ISBN   978-0-88146-608-9
Cataloging-in-Publication Data is available from the Library of Congress

For Oma Parish Alsobrook

and Ernest Milton Alsobrook—

Two Children of Southside

Contents

Author's Note

"Miss Oma"

I grew up in Mobile, Alabama, but spent many summer vacations and holidays in Eufaula. My parents and I were all born there. My earliest memories of my paternal grandmother, Oma Parish Alsobrook, are from the 1950s, when she lived at 534 South Randolph Street in Eufaula. At the time I was not aware that her late father-in-law, John Thomas Alsobrook, my great-grandfather, lived in that area of South Randolph Street between 1929 and 1939. My grandmother moved from South Randolph to 123 West Washington Street sometime in the mid-1950s; she remained at that address until her death in December 1969. That short stretch of West Washington Street, from the Methodist Church to Dale Road, held a lot of poignant memories for her. She spent much of her life in this portion of Eufaula that was known as Southside—the Cowikee Mill Village.

Everyone in Town called her "Miss Oma." She was employed as a weaver at Cowikee Mill No. 1 (the "Big Mill") for over forty years. Like all textile jobs, hers was physically and emotionally demanding and debilitating, yet I cannot recall her ever complaining about the work. She respected and admired Donald Comer, the owner of Avondale and Cowikee Mills. She had known him since 1909, when the Comer family acquired the old Eufaula Cotton Mill and re-named it as the Cowikee Mill. At that time, Oma was ten years old, and her parents and other Parish relatives all were mill operatives. By the time I knew her, she had lived alone for several years. The pillars of her life were Southside, the Washington Street Methodist Church, Cowikee Mills, and the Cowikee Community House. That small world nurtured and sustained her for many years.

Although the details of Oma's life were heartbreaking, she never expressed to me any feelings of bitterness or regret about anything that had happened to her or to those she loved. That was not the way she viewed the world. She wept whenever we talked about her husband, Ernest, whom she had first loved when they were children in Southside. But, despite her copious tears, she adamantly rejected the idea that God or fate had cruelly treated her.

Over the course of the years when I knew Oma, she patiently and lovingly shared her family's stories with me. She never grew frustrated with my interminable questions about who was related to whom. When we "visited" our relatives at Fairview Cemetery, she often reminded me that as long as we remember these people and tell their stories, they will never die.

We never discussed the possibility that someday I might write a book or an article about Southside. I did not tape our discussions or transcribe any notes afterward. But, I think she inherently understood that my youthful inquisitiveness might culminate in a publication based on our conversations. Willie Mae Hatfield Starnes, my maternal grandmother, frequently cautioned me about digging too deeply into family history: "If you're not careful," she sternly warned, "you'll find a few horse thieves." Oma, however, not only encouraged me to excavate our family history; she provided me with a shovel.

During my research and writing over the past four or five years, Oma and her Southside relatives and friends have never been far from my thoughts. In keeping faith with them, I have attempted to relate their stories without embellishments, so that in death they would not appear greater than they were in life.

Eufaula's Southsiders were like many other working-class families of their time—fiercely proud, independent, generous, and God-fearing. They loved life and had experienced its peaks and valleys. Like all of God's children, of course, they were imbued with many flaws and imperfections. Although the two Southside "mission" churches were very important to them, they generally were not religious zealots. Their faith was a living, breathing instrument that allowed them to navigate the treacherous waters of their lives. Despite their preachers' best efforts, many Southsiders habitually smoked, chewed, and dipped tobacco products, cursed, drank, and fought like sailors, and engaged in sex outside the sanctity of marriage. Like all human beings, they also were frequently ruled by emotion, superstition, and prejudice. Finally, Southsiders shared a deep, abiding love and loyalty for their families and friends, and they wanted their children and grandchildren to have better lives—preferably outside the mills.

I have a few cautionary notes for the reader. This book is *not* designed to be a standard historical treatise on Eufaula's textile industry. As a matter of fact, there is very little material in this book about actual mill work. This book primarily deals with the lives of textile operatives, their families, and other Southside residents. While I have sought to frame my narrative and analyses within the context of some of the definitive scholarly works on the Southern mill village experience, Southside's history is unique in many ways and defies simplistic generalizations, complex quantitative models, and comparisons with other locales. Nevertheless, much research and writing remains to be done on Southside. Although I primarily wrote this book in memory of Southsiders and their descendants, I fervently hope that something within these pages will motivate a new generation of scholars to dig deeply into the existing treasure trove of primary sources and produce additional works that further advance our knowledge of this unique place and its people.

Acknowledgments

Without the loving support and encouragement of my family, I seriously doubt that I would have written this book. Over the past forty years, my wife, Ellen Lester Alsobrook, has been the anchor and bulwark in my life and a full-time partner in every research and writing project that I have undertaken. For almost five years, despite her own pressing responsibilities, she made *Southside* one of her top priorities. Because of my near-Luddite computer and word-processing skills, she typed every word of the manuscript. But more importantly, when I was not writing, she patiently listened to my lengthy, rambling discourses on *Southside*. Afterward, she asked cogent questions that went directly to the heart of the book and then suggested how to clarify and strengthen my primary theses. Our two grown children, Adam and Meredith, have inspired me to produce *Southside* in their own ways. No parents could wish to have two finer children—they are both highly motivated, independent seekers of truth. *Southside* hopefully will give them a deeper understanding of their family's history.

In addition to my family, I have been extremely fortunate to have several close friends who have contributed significantly to *Southside* since its inception. Ginny Dunaway Young is a retired school librarian and master genealogist presently residing in Willis, Texas. Her father, J. T. Dunaway, was my grandmother Oma Parish Alsobrook's first cousin. Since her own ancestors figure prominently in the *Southside* story, Ms. Young has more than a casual intellectual curiosity in this book. From the earliest genesis of *Southside*, she understood precisely why I wanted to write this book. She subsequently guided me through the thicket of the various families' genealogies and provided timely, substantive primary and secondary material for virtually every topic. Whenever I queried her—day or night—with the most inane request, Ms. Young responded quickly and authoritatively. She also read the entire manuscript and offered incisive critical commentary.

Scotty E. Kirkland also read and critiqued *Southside* in its entirety. A Dothan native, Mr. Kirkland currently serves on the staff of the Alabama Department of Archives and History (ADAH). A gifted researcher and wordsmith, he is a rising star among our state's current generation of historians. In the midst of his own research and writing on Mobile's civil rights movement, he somehow found time to look closely at each of my chapters and provide invaluable criticisms. While Mr. Kirkland and Ms. Young applied their considerable knowledge and expertise in critiquing *Southside*, I am solely responsible for any errors in this book.

I also am deeply indebted to my friend of forty-five years, Douglas Clare Purcell, former executive director of the Historic Chattahoochee Commission (HCC). When I first mentioned my *Southside* proposal several years ago to Mr. Purcell, he immediately encouraged me to pursue it. When I initially broached this topic with him, however, I neglected to discuss how much I would rely upon his deep knowledge of Eufaula's history and would seek his counsel on a wide range of topics. Over the past three years, Mr. Purcell has responded to my withering fusillade of questions with definitive explanations, incomparable patience, and indomitable good humor. In addition to his unwavering support and research assistance, Mr. Purcell gave me very sound guidance on locating a publisher for *Southside* and introduced me to Marc Jolley and his exceptionally talented professional team at Mercer University Press.

My friend, historian Mike Bunn, another former HCC executive director, graciously read draft portions of *Southside* relating to Eufaula's antebellum era and offered detailed suggestions for revisions. He also answered several specific questions about the Civil War's impact upon the Bluff City. His excellent monograph, *Civil War Eufaula*, was one of my most informative secondary sources.

Jacob Laurence, one of my former colleagues at the History Museum of Mobile, has been a vital source of encouragement and support since *Southside*'s earliest stages. Moreover, he coordinated the preservation and digitization of all of the photographs that appear in this book. Mr. Laurence is undoubtedly one of the most talented, creative young men I have ever known—with a keen artistic eye and an innate sense of how to blend aesthetics with practicalities.

When I first embarked on this mission, several Eufaulians with deep ancestral roots in *Southside* enthusiastically responded to my call for volunteers and have been with me every single step of the way. Wendell Franklin Wentz, Jeanine and Jimmy DeVenny, June and Joe Clenney, Hallie Taylor Dalon, Janet Hatfield Scroggins, Mavis and Roy McDonald, Fred McWaters, and Yvette Benton Clark have all generously shared their Southside memories, photographs, and other family treasures with me over the past several years. Their affectionate, informative phone calls, letters, and emails have deeply inspired and strengthened me during the entire research and writing process. Other Eufaulians also have contributed immeasurably to *Southside*, each in his or her own unique way: Lawrence Hatfield, Dorothy "Dot" Hatfield, Bettie Beamon Harney, Ann Smith, Gwen Conner, Bill Davis, Emogene W. Cullifer, Mamie Beasley Ludlam, Gatra Lampley Wehle, and Wanda Strand Youngren.

I also wish to thank Mary Adams Belk of Auburn for her exceptional assistance and support in behalf of *Southside*. Her parents, Fannie Corbitt and Cleveland Adams, both grew up in Southside. Their remarkable lives and careers are important parts of this book, and I deeply appreciate the opportunity to include the Adamses in *Southside*.

A number of librarians, archivists, and researchers identified and provided a wealth of primary and secondary sources for *Southside*. Evelyn Screws of the Eufaula Carnegie Library responded expeditiously to my early request for photocopies of any secondary sources on the Cowikee Mills. The inestimable Sharon Simpson of the Barbour County Genealogy and Local History Society provided me with voluminous research material from their collections and answered my endless questions. Michael Breedlove, a recently retired ADAH archivist and author of an excellent dissertation on Donald Comer, graciously shared the fruits of his research with me. Jim Baggett, director of the Birmingham Public Library's Department of Archives and Manuscripts, greatly facilitated my examination of the Donald Comer Collection. Norwood Kerr and the entire ADAH staff provided outstanding archival assistance for my use of their vast holdings, including the Governors Administrative Files and Works Progress Administration (WPA) records. My friend and former colleague, David Stanhope, deputy director of the Jimmy Carter Presidential Library, examined federal court records on my behalf at the National Archives and Records Administration (NARA) regional branch in Morrow, Georgia, with the able assistance of archivists Maureen Hill and Guy Hall. Vicki and Tim Walch, my dear friends in Iowa City, Iowa, identified, photocopied, and collated a large cache of Depression-era correspondence relating to Alabama in the Herbert Hoover Presidential Library's collections. Archivists Matt Schaefer and Spencer Howard of the Hoover Library staff furnished expert guidance and assistance for this particular research request. Supervisory archivist Kirsten Strigel Carter and her colleagues at the FDR Presidential Library and Museum produced a substantive series of documents on the New Deal's impact on Barbour County and the Chattahoochee Valley. NARA archivists Trevor K. Plante, Dennis Edelin, and Paul Harrison located and photocopied Confederate service records for two of my great-grandfather's uncles and Donald Comer's official file for his Army service during the Philippine Insurrection. Reference librarian Patrick Kerwin, of the Library of Congress's Manuscript Division, expedited my access to a voluminous file of Barbour County WPA records that proved to be a rich primary source for *Southside*.

Finally I want to express my deep appreciation to my Auburn University family of professors and friends who have supported all of my scholarly and personal endeavors over the years: Leah Atkins, Allen W. Jones, Marlene Rikard, Jeff Jakeman, Paul Pruitt, Jr., Wayne Flynt, Marty Olliff, Jerry Brown, and David Rosenblatt.

-SOUTHSIDE-

Statue of the Reverend Morton Bryan Wharton
with inset portrait, ca. 1911.
Courtesy Gatra Lampley Wehle

Leonard Y. Dean, Jr., with unidentified young woman, ca. 1920.
Courtesy Rob Schaffeld

William Dorsey Jelks, ca. 1899–1900.
Courtesy Alabama Department of Archives and History

Crowd at Barbour County Courthouse in Eufaula
during Lester Bouyer murder trial, 23 July 1929.
Author's Collection

2nd Lt. Donald Comer, 16th Infantry Regt., US Army, prior to his transfer to the 25th Infantry Regt. in the Philippines, 1899.
Courtesy National Archives and Records Administration

Donald Comer, ca. 1938-1940.
Courtesy Birmingham, Alabama Public Library Archives

Parish-Dunaway Families, 1909.
Author's Collection

Jessie and Thomas Mallie Parish with their daughter Oma, ca. 1909.
Author's Collection

Minnie and John Thomas Alsobrook with their sons Ernest (left)
and Thomas Neville (right) ca. 1901–1902.
Author's Collection

Ernest Milton Alsobrook, ca. 1908–1910.
Author's Collection

Ernest Milton Alsobrook, ca. 1913–1915.
Author's Collection

Oma Parish (left) and Ila Mae Barlar (right), ca. 1917–1918.
Author's Collection

Oma Parish Alsobrook with son Thomas "Monzie" Alsobrook, ca. 1920–1921.
Author's Collection

Oma Parish Alsobrook, ca. 1921–1922.
Author's Collection

Jessie Lee Alsobrook and her brother Thomas "Monzie" Alsobrook, ca. 1921.
Author's Collection

D. F. "Doc" Barker, 1909.
Courtesy June Barker Clenney

D. F. "Doc" Barker and family, 1909.
Courtesy June Barker Clenney

Florida Dewar, ca. late 1890s.
Courtesy Peggy Halstead

J. T. Dunaway, ca. 1918.
Courtesy Ginny Dunaway Young

Cowikee Mill Band, October 1919.
Courtesy Ginny Dunaway Young

**Cowikee Community House Playground,
with overhead electrical lights, ca. 1935–1938.**
Courtesy Alabama Department of Archives and History

Kindergarten children with Helen Mitchell Taylor at right and
Elbert "Red" Beasley in background, 1935.

Courtesy Hallie Taylor Dalon

Kindergarten class, 1939.
Courtesy Alabama Department of Archives and History

Cowikee Mill Baseball Team, 25 June 1936.
Courtesy Jeanine Smith DeVenny

Easter egg hunt at the Cowikee Community House Playground, ca. 1935.
(Note Mill No. 1 in background.)
Courtesy Hallie Taylor Dalon

Cowikee Mill No. 1, ca. 1938–1939.
Courtesy Alabama Department of Archives and History

Operatives behind Cowikee Mill No. 1, ca. 1935–1939.
Courtesy Wendell Franklin Wentz

Troop 10 Boy Scouts with opossums and dogs;
Scoutmaster Cleveland Adams standing at right, ca. 1933.
Courtesy Alabama Department of Archives and History

Troop 10 Boy Scouts, with Thomas "Monzie" Alsobrook,
standing second from left, ca. 1937.
Author's Collection

Eufaula High School Football Team, with Coaches O. B. Carter (left) and T. J. Campbell (right), ca. 1937.

Courtesy Wendell Franklin Wentz

Washington Street Methodist Church congregation, ca. 1925–1927.

Author's Collection

Willie Mae and Amos Starnes's house, 508 South Eufaula Street, ca. 1920.
Author's Collection

John Thomas Alsobrook's house, 400 South Randolph Street, ca. 1938.
He trimmed his shrubbery after finishing his mill shift,
Monday through Saturday.
Courtesy Alabama Department of Archives and History

Battery D National Guardsmen at Camp Stewart, Georgia, 1941, (l-r) Charles Weston, Humphrey Foy, Will "Bubba" Snipes, and William Jelks Comer.
Courtesy Eufaula Tribune

War Bond rally at Eufaula High School; Frances Starnes Alsobrook
seated third from right, 17 November 1944.
Author's Collection

Mavis Barker and Roy McDonald at the Crystal Club, 1942.
Courtesy June Barker Clenney

Prologue

"The Man with His Backside to Southside"

Whom shall we consecrate and set apart as one of our great men? Sacred, that all men may see him, and, by new example added to the old perpetual precept, be taught what is real worth in man.... Whom do you set on a high column, that all men looking at it, may be continuously apprised of the duty you expect from them.[1] —Charles Francis Adams, 1907

The late nineteenth and early twentieth centuries witnessed an unprecedented proliferation of commemorative monuments and statuary throughout the United States. This movement was especially prevalent in Southern cities and towns with active chapters of the United Sons and Daughters of the Confederacy (USC and UDC).[2]

Like many other Alabama towns, in November 1904, Eufaula dedicated a statue of a solitary sentinel, in memory of Barbour County's Confederate soldiers and sailors. The local UDC chapter raised $3,000 for the thirty-five-foot shaft of polished Georgia granite. Similar monuments usually face northward, but since wartime Eufaulians anticipated an incursion of federal troops from the east via the river, this stone sentry looks in that direction.[3]

---

[1] Charles Francis Adams, quoted in Hodding Carter, "Statues in the Squares," *This Is the South*, ed. Robert West Howard (New York: Rand McNally & Company, 1959) 239.

[2] For incisive background on this topic, see, for example, Kirk Savage, *Standing Soldiers, Kneeling Slaves: Race, War, and Monument in Nineteenth-century America* (Princeton: Princeton University Press, 1997); Caroline Janney, *Burying the Dead, but not the Past: Ladies Memorial Associations and the Lost Cause* (Chapel Hill: University of North Carolina Press, 2008); Karen C. Cox, *The United Daughters of the Confederacy and the Preservation of Confederate Culture* (Gainesville: University of Florida Press, 2003); Cynthia Mills and Pamela Simpson, eds., *Monuments to the Lost Cause: Women, Art, and the Landscapes of Southern Memory* (Knoxville: University of Tennessee Press, 2003).

[3] "Confederate Monument at Eufaula, Ala.," *Confederate Veteran* 13/1 (January 1905): 12; Mike Bunn, *Civil War Eufaula* (Charleston, SC: The History Press, 2013) 118.

Located in the busy intersection of Board Street and Eufaula Avenue (U.S. Highway 431), this monument is described by one historian as "virtually inaccessible and unreachable except by the most devoted passersby or those brave enough to venture to it on foot..., its details...simultaneously hidden in plain sight, ironically difficult to access and routinely overlooked."[4] But there are two other Eufaula statues that also are frequently ignored by even the most intrepid tourists.

In January 1925, just over two decades after the UDC erected their Confederate obelisk, a "Memorial Boulder" supporting the "figure of an American Doughboy" was unveiled by the Service Star Legion at Broad and Orange streets, between the county courthouse and the post office. Memorializing Eufaulians lost in the Great War, the soldier's likeness is cast in Italian marble. He is wearing a flat steel helmet; a cartridge belt encircles his waist, and woolen leggings ("puttees") are wrapped around his calves. According to an *Avondale Sun* reporter, the doughboy's "right hand [is] holding aloft a hand grenade, the left grasping a Winchester rifle, with his strong face set in tense lines."[5] This journalist obviously was unfamiliar with the various types of combat weaponry. The soldier is carrying a .30 caliber, 1903 Springfield—the standard weapon issued to US troops during World War I. However, the inscription on the granite boulder has a far more egregious

---

[4] Bunn, *Civil War Eufaula*, 113.

[5] "Memorial Boulder Unveiled," *Avondale Sun*, 16 January 1925, 3. This Eufaula statue is one of at least five stone monuments closely resembling sculptor Ernest Moore Viquesney's original design, "The Spirit of the American Doughboy," 1920. Various versions of his statue can be found in about 140 communities across the United States. Viquesney (1876–1946) spent much of his career in Americus, Georgia. Unsigned and without a copyright date, the Eufaula doughboy cannot be definitively attributed to him. Like the four other stone figures, the Eufaula statue may have been produced by the McNeel Marble Company in Marietta, Georgia. Three pressed-copper versions of the design—all copyrighted in 1920—are located in Birmingham, Bessemer, and Anniston, Alabama, and are considered to be Viquesney originals ("Eufaula, Alabama," http://doughboysearchers.weebly.com/eufaula-alabama.html; Earl D. Goldsmith, "The Spirit of the American Doughboy," http://doughboysearchers.weebly.com/the-spirit-of-the-american-doughboy.html; "The McNeel Marble Co. Doughboys," http://doughboysearchers.weebly.com/the-spirit-of-the-american-doughboy.html; [all websites accessed on 7 October 2015]; Steven Trout, *On the Battlefield of Memory: The First World War and American Remembrance, 1919–1941* [Tuscaloosa: University of Alabama Press, 2010] 109–110, 121).

error. Written in large raised letters are the names of five Eufaula men "Who Made the Supreme Sacrifice" in World War I. Sixty-five years after the dedication ceremony, a local historian determined that five additional Eufaula soldiers, including four African Americans, had died during the Great War but went unheralded on the monument.[6]

A third statue—even farther off the beaten path than the doughboy and the Confederate sentinel—straddles the median of East Broad and North Randolph Streets, adjacent to the First Baptist Church. Hewn from Georgian and Italian marble, this impressive monument rises to a height of about twenty feet. A life-sized replica of the Reverend Morton Bryan Wharton, a nineteenth-century Baptist patriarch, stands atop the pedestal. His bareheaded figure is clad in a Victorian-era frock coat and cravat. A Wharton contemporary wrote that the statue "shows him in his familiar pose, cane in right hand, a book in the left, as he was often seen on the streets."[7] His marbleized gaze looks northward, toward the far horizon. Beneath his feet, these words are sharply chiseled:

Morton Bryan Wharton. D.D. L.L.D.
Born Orange County, Virginia, April 5, 1839.
Died Atlanta, Ga. July 20, 1908.
Preacher, Poet, Patriot, Philosopher,
Statesman, Scholar, Consecrated Christian.[8]

---

[6] Kristen E. Fischer, "Forgotten heroes left off city monument," "Lest We Forget," *Eufaula Tribune*, 10 November 2002, 3. During the Jim Crow era, the names of African Americans frequently were omitted from monuments in the South (Jacob Laurence, "'Their Names Liveth for Evermore': Remembering the Great War in Mobile," paper presented at the Alabama Historical Association Meeting, Mobile Bay's Eastern Shore, 16 April 2011).

[7] "Wharton Unveiling Is Planned to the Letter," *Montgomery Advertiser*, 29 May 1911, 10 (quote); "Wharton Monument Is Unveiled at Eufaula," *Montgomery Advertiser*, 4 June 1911, 22; "Wharton Monument," Federal Writers' Project, State Guide File, Alabama Counties-Barbour, box A15, Works Progress Administration Records, Manuscript Division, Library of Congress, Washington, DC. These records hereafter cited as FWP, State Guide File, Barbour County, box A15, WPA Records, LC.

[8] The Wharton statue originally was located closer to the First Baptist Church. The statue later was moved into the intersection on East Barbour Street, but the overhead wiring for the traffic light and utilities had to be re-configured to avoid entanglement with the Reverend Wharton's marble torso (Douglas Clare Purcell [former executive

After his death at age sixty-nine, Wharton was eulogized in the effusive style of that time: "No pastor of the city has perhaps ever en[j]oyed such universal love and esteem among all denominations.... He loved Eufaula and every citizen will cherish his memory with a fond and peculiar devotion."[9] Another tribute was even more laudatory: "No minister has ever dwelt here who worked himself more closely in the hearts of the citizens at large and he needs no earthly do[me], no monumental pile, to perpetuate his memory in the souls of the citizens of Eufaula, all of whom loved him most tenderly and devotedly."[10] Such excessively gilded adulations notwithstanding, someone among his acolytes decided that Wharton deserved a "monumental pile." Over the next three years, a concerted campaign arose to build a statue in "memory of the most distinguished citizen Eufaula ever had."[11]

The Wharton Memorial Association, anchored by the women of the First Baptist Church, energetically solicited donations for the monument. They organized elaborate fundraisers in Eufaula, Montgomery, and Cuthbert, Georgia, and sought contributions from Wharton's former congregations in Georgia, Tennessee, Kentucky, Virginia, and Maryland. By early March 1911, the requisite $1,000 for the statue was at hand.[12]

Within three months, stone craftsmen in Georgia and Italy had completed the edifice. At four thirty in the afternoon on 3 June 1911, with the First Baptist Church's sanctuary at full capacity and 3,000 Eufaulians crowding the streets outside, the dedication ceremony commenced. The front pews were jammed with Baptist dignitaries, city officials, and members of the UDC, USC, and Daughters of the American Revolution. The music and inspirational readings primarily were Wharton's own compositions, including the hymn, "My Heavenly Home," and *Pictures from a Pastorium*, the

---

director, Historic Chattahoochee Commission, Eufaula, AL] e-mail to the author, 2 July 2013).

[9] "Eufaula in Grief," *Montgomery Advertiser*, 22 July 1908, 10.

[10] "Tribute to Divine," *Montgomery Advertiser*, 28 July 1908, 8.

[11] "Wharton Benefit Planned," *Montgomery Advertiser*, 6 September 1910, 7.

[12] "Monument to Wharton," *Montgomery Advertiser*, 29 January 1909, 8; *Montgomery Advertiser*, 14 February 1909, 4; 28 October 1909, 12; "News of Eufaula," *Montgomery Advertiser*, 5 June 1910, 3; "Plan Wharton Memorial," *Montgomery Advertiser*, 31 July 1910, 3; "Wharton Benefit Planned," *Montgomery Advertiser*, 6 September 1910, 7; *Columbus (GA) Daily Enquirer*, 10 January 1911, 5; "Begin Wharton Monument," *Montgomery Advertiser*, 8 March 1911, 5.

memoir based upon his tenure at Montgomery's First Baptist Church in 1884–1891. Several of the featured eulogists were his "warm friends and contemporary pastors" during his years in Eufaula.[13]

The principal orator was Wharton's lifelong friend and college class-mate, Dr. Lansing Burrows, a pastor in Americus, Georgia, and secretary of the Southern Baptist Convention. Burrows and his fellow clergymen ex-tolled Wharton's service as a quartermaster's clerk in the Confederate Army, US consul to Sonneberg, Germany, and Baptist minister. Wharton had twice pastored the Eufaula First Baptist Church, in 1869–1871 and 1901–1908, for a total of ten years. During his two pastorates at First Baptist, sep-arated by three decades, Wharton had supervised the construction of new churches after devastating fires. When he died in July 1908, First Baptist was still being rebuilt. Protected by an honor guard of elderly Confederate veterans, his body lay in state for a full day in the sweltering heat inside the unfinished sanctuary.[14]

The eulogies concluded, Wharton's First Baptist successor, Dr. J. A. French, "paid a beautiful tribute," and Mrs. Rheta Locke sang the hymn "We Are Sitting Today in the Dear Old Church," another Wharton compo-sition. A Montgomery journalist wrote, at this point in the service, "[T]here were but few eyes not filled with tears."[15] George Legaré Comer, the beloved First Baptist Sunday school teacher and brother of Governor Braxton Bragg Comer, then presented a gold and silver loving cup to Barbour County his-torian Mattie Thomas Thompson in recognition of her leadership of the Wharton Memorial Association. Finally, the "Eufaula Rifles" Second Regi-

---

[13] "Wharton Unveiling Is Planned to the Letter," *Montgomery Advertiser*, 29 May 1911, 10.

[14] Ibid., "Wharton Monument Is Unveiled at Eufaula," *Montgomery Advertiser*, 4 June 1911, 22. For additional details about Wharton's life and career, see Thomas McAdory Owen, *History of Alabama and Dictionary of Alabama Biography*, 4 vols. (Chica-go: S. J. Clarke Publishing Co., 1921) 4:1749; Mrs. C. A. Locke, "First Baptist Church," *Eufaula Tribune*, Historical and Progress Edition, 5 December 1940, n.p.; *Macon (GA) Weekly Telegraph*, 9 February 1875, 2; 17 February 1880, 2; 25 March 1881, 9; 28 April 1881, 4; "Exercises in Troy," *Montgomery Advertiser*, 20 May 1907, 6; "Dr. Wharton Dead," *Montgomery Advertiser*, 21 July 1908, 3; "First Baptist Church," "Wharton Mon-ument," FWP, State Guide File, Barbour County, box A15, WPA Records, LC.

[15] "Wharton Monument Is Unveiled at Eufaula," *Montgomery Advertiser*, 4 June 1911, 22.

ment Band, directed by Professor S. V. DeTrinis, played the mournful funeral dirge, and "the throng filed out of the church, just as the sun set over the western hill."[16]

Outside in the gathering dusk, silently awaited "a pyramid of humanity, the sidewalks packed and carriages and automobiles lined the street."[17] Marching down the steps from the church and escorted by the band, thirty-five school children encircled the shrouded statue. Garbed entirely in white, they sang "My Heavenly Home," with sisters Sadie and Helen Cargill performing one verse as a duet. Wharton's granddaughter, Bertha Moore, and great-granddaughter, Bessie Moore Mitchell, slowly pulled the cords that released the drape from the monument. One observer noted, "[W]hen it fell every man's hat was lifted in silent reverence then a cheer, seemingly sacred, went up."[18]

At the conclusion of the event, described by a participant as "the most memorable day in Eufaula's sentimental history," Mayor Charles S. McDowell, Jr., his "every word burning with sincerity," vowed that the monument "would ever be the city's sacred trust."[19] The crowd dispersed "[a]s a cornet's notes rang 'Taps' in the still twilight."[20] A European monarch could not have been more elaborately memorialized.

People and conveyances soon disappeared from the streets surrounding the statue and the church. Electric streetlights fitfully bathed the scene in a warm, yellow-white glow. Meanwhile, only the rhythmic *clackity-clack* of the looms at the mill a half-block south, broke the silence of the night.

Despite the detailed press coverage of the entire ceremony, very little appeared in print about the crowd of 3,000 spectators outside the church. This omission seems noteworthy because reporters of that era usually published in-depth accounts about audiences at large public assemblies. For example, in October 1913, when Tuskegee Institute principal Booker T. Washington spoke for over an hour at the Eufaula court house, one journalist estimated that the crowd included "more than 6,000 Negro farmers" and "500 white citizens." He also vividly recorded the audience's reactions to

---

[16] Ibid.
[17] Ibid.
[18] Ibid.
[19] Ibid.
[20] Ibid.

Washington's remarks.[21]

Relying upon limited newspaper documentation and a single extant photograph (taken from the western side of Randolph Street) of the Wharton ceremony, one can merely speculate about the audience's composition. Were the white men, women, and children in the crowd from both Old Eufaula, north of Barbour Street, and the "Factory District," known locally as "Southside"?

In 1911, Eufaula's total population was 7,302, with approximately 2,300 people residing in Southside.[22] With well over 3,000 in attendance for the Wharton ceremony, it was clearly perceived as a significant public event. Yet, how many people were there because of their respect and adoration for the Reverend Wharton compared with those who were attracted by the excitement generated by a well-publicized community gathering? At that time in Eufaula, public events—street fairs, carnivals, circuses, parades, militia drills, concerts, and political debates—generally drew large, enthusiastic audiences. These events also were well attended by rural families from beyond the city limits. Therefore, based solely upon the traditional popularity of public events, it is quite possible that the crowd assembled outside the First Baptist Church was a mixture of residents of Old Eufaula, Southside, far-flung corners of Barbour and surrounding counties, and from neighboring Georgia across the Chattahoochee River. While questions about the crowd's make-up and motivations are quite interesting, they remain highly speculative and impossible to answer with any degree of certainty.

Given Dr. Wharton's sterling reputation as a clergyman and his unprecedented accomplishments as a "Renaissance Man" of letters, it is conceivable Eufaulians truly held him in very high regard. Moreover, in 1911, older Eufaulians were less than fifty years removed from the grisly reality of the Civil War. The presence of a number of surviving Confederate veterans (some disfigured by their wounds) also served as a poignant reminder of what Eufaulians considered to be the nobility of the "Lost Cause." Consequently, Wharton's Confederate service—albeit as a noncombatant—added another layer of heroic patina to his legendary aura. In life, he personally

---

[21] "B.T. Washington Speaks to Thousands of Farmers," *Montgomery Advertiser*, 6 October 1913, 6.

[22] *Alabama Official and Statistical Register, 1911* (Montgomery, AL: Brown Printing Company, 1912) 216, 221.

burnished his veteran's image by actively participating in Confederate commemorative ceremonies.[23]

Virtually everything written about the Reverend Wharton during his life and afterward portrayed him as an exemplary man of faith, intellect, and compassion. An overly simplistic summation of his life and ministry would be that he loved *everyone* in Eufaula, and they felt the same way about him. Yet, one of the most intriguing and challenging aspects of historical study is that it seldom conforms to such neat, comfortable, reassuring assessments.

History, like our individual lives, is full of inconsistencies, unpredictable twists and turns, and anomalies that often frustrate scholars' most prodigious efforts. Moreover, historians frequently discover that both unquantifiable evidence and raw factual data can carry equal weight as to our understanding and interpretation of the past. Each successive generation of both scholars and participants reassesses and reinterprets history based upon specific experiences, biases, and, most importantly, perceptions.

Southside's rich oral tradition, based upon a cross-generational sharing of stories, customs, and folk wisdom, contributes a jarring retort to the hagiographical tributes to the Reverend Wharton. From the early 1900s through the late 1950s, several generations of Southsiders perceived *and* believed that they had been treated wretchedly by Old Eufaula. And after 1911, the Wharton statue evoked decidedly bitter emotions among mill families. For them, it was far more than celebratory marble. It was a symbol of their systematic exclusion from Eufaula's mainstream. Therefore, they sardonically referred to Wharton's marble figure as "The Man with his Backside to Southside."[24]

By the time Wharton returned in 1901 for his second tenure as Eufaula's First Baptist preacher, Southside's residents had developed a re-

---

[23] Bunn, *Civil War Eufaula*, 108–110; "Dr. Van Hoose's Speech," *Montgomery Advertiser*, 28 April 1907, 13; "Veterans Hold Annual Reunion in Eufaula," *Montgomery Advertiser*, 26 July 1911, 10; "Eufaula Host to Thousands," *Montgomery Advertiser*, 13 August 1910, 5.

[24] Although this scalding sobriquet for Wharton's statue does not appear in printed historical sources, it apparently had become embedded in the Southside vernacular and oral tradition prior to the Great War. As a child in Eufaula in the late 1940s and early 1950s, I frequently heard my middle-aged and elderly Southside relatives use this nickname for the statue. They never mentioned Wharton by name. When pressed for additional details, they usually responded, "This shows you what they think about us."

markable degree of independence and solidarity, primarily because of the establishment of two "mission" churches. Beginning in the early 1890s, the Eufaula Methodist and First Baptist Churches had conducted fundraising campaigns to build and support two houses of worship in Southside. Their efforts financed the founding of the Washington Street Methodist Episcopal Church, South, and the Second Baptist Church. Both of these new congregations organized Sunday school programs, Bible study clubs, and missionary aid societies and competed for members from among the mill population. In short, these new churches became deeply immersed in Southside's social fabric. Despite their humble origins and dependence upon itinerant circuit preachers, the two Southside missions thrived over the years and still exist today as Washington Street United Methodist Church and Parkview Baptist Church.[25]

The mission churches' founding members, however, harbored no illusions about the downtown congregations' magnanimity, which further isolated mill families within the confines of Southside. Eufaula Methodist and First Baptist congregates cheerfully filled their collection plates to fund the Southside mission churches because they did not want to worship with people from "below the railroad tracks."[26]

Even if Dr. Wharton had evinced an interest in Southside proselytizing after 1901, his First Baptist predecessor, J. G. Bow, had completed much of that task a decade earlier. Yet, in the early 1900s, Wharton and his Baptist colleagues openly expressed their frustrations in attempting to recruit members from among "the factory population in the state."[27] In 1902, one of Wharton's associates in Troy professed that factory and mill workers were "largely or wholly country Baptists [who] moved to town" and would con-

---

[25] Douglas Clare Purcell, "A History of Eufaula First Methodist Church, 1834–1989," unpub. typescript, 1989, 14; Oma Alsobrook, "A Brief History of Washington Street Methodist Church," unpub. typescript, 1956, 1–3, both in author's possession; A. E. Barlar, "Washington Street Church," *Eufaula Tribune*, Historical and Progress Edition, 5 December 1940, 7; Eugenia Persons Smartt, *History of Eufaula, Alabama* (Birmingham, AL: Roberts & Sons, 1933) 124–25; Parkview Baptist Church groundbreaking photograph, *Avondale Sun*, 13 February 1950, 4; "Parkview Baptist Church Centennial, 1895–1995," unpublished typescript, 1995, 2–13, in author's possession.

[26] Wendell Franklin Wentz email to author, 21 February 2015.

[27] "Baptist Convention Meets in New Decatur," *Montgomery Advertiser*, 25 June 1902, 5.

tinue as such with "their own churches and their own pastor, but they would not attend the city churches where they felt the bars of society up against them."[28] Wharton fully concurred with this sentiment. At the State Baptist Convention in 1902, he cited several specific examples in Columbus and Augusta, Georgia, and in other cities where "factory people will not mix with others. They feel the contrast is too great."[29]

Like his own First Baptist congregation and the Eufaula Methodist members, Wharton was satisfied with mill workers having their own churches. He did not say they were unwelcome at his church, but by placing the onus upon them for refusing to "mix with others," he implied that Southsiders were better off where they were. While he apparently felt no personal animosity toward mill families, Wharton shared Old Eufaula's class consciousness regarding the residents of the "Factory District." Thus, after his death, Wharton's statue became a convenient target for Southsiders who seethed with anger over perceived ill treatment at the behest of Old Eufaula.

Other Eufaulians often validated Southsiders' bitter perceptions. Highly respected historian and educator Robert H. "Bootie" Flewellen, who wrote unsentimentally about his hometown, forcefully argues that Southsiders were "victims of a social ostracism practiced by Eufaula citizens who by virtue of education, wealth, and economic status considered themselves the elite, the upper crust of society."[30] More specifically, he adds that mill workers and their kin were condescendingly labeled as "'southsiders or 'lint heads' or worse,[and] they were excluded or rejected by the well-to-do and were never accepted in 'high society.'"[31]

While Flewellen's impassioned commentary is an important supplement to the Southside narrative, individual examples of discrimination and ostracism provide deeper insight into such abuses. John Timothy Dunaway was a talented musician who grew up on Dale Road before World War I. He was one of the few members of his family who did not enter the mills as a child laborer. He performed as a teenaged trombonist in the first Cowikee Mill Band in 1918–1919 and in the 1920s traveled with Hobart "Puss"

---

[28] Dr. A. B. Campbell, quoted in ibid.

[29] Dr. M. B. Wharton, cited in reporter's words in ibid.

[30] Robert H. Flewellen, *Along Broad Street: A History of Eufaula, Alabama, 1823–1984* (Eufaula, AL: City of Eufaula, 1991) 186.

[31] Ibid.

Hortman's orchestra, famous for its Southern venues. Near the end of his life in 1979, Dunaway spoke of competing for a tenor soloist's part in a school operetta as a boy in Eufaula. With a beautiful tenor's range and a natural ear for music, he seemed ideal for the role; however, in the presence of his classmates, the music teacher—probably Agnes Wilkinson, the school superintendent's wife—abruptly announced, "J. T., I wish I could choose you, but I can't—you're from the Southside."[32] Although this incident had occurred more than sixty years earlier, he never forgot those hurtful words.

J. T. Dunaway's experience was not unique. Several Eufaula public school teachers always seemed to find something to criticize about the mill children—their hair, teeth, speech, and clothing. The children sometimes failed to comprehend that they were being shabbily treated, but their parents fully understood. On one memorable occasion in the early 1950s, Pete Head found a pair of overalls he liked at the Wentz Market on South Eufaula Street. His father, William Head, the Eufaula High School band director and a former mill hand, vehemently refused to purchase the overalls despite Pete's anguished pleas. William Head had worn overalls when he toiled as a young man in the mills and wanted to protect his son from being stereotyped as a Southsider because of his choice of wardrobe.[33]

In preferring overalls for school and play, many Southside boys simply were emulating their fathers, uncles, and older brothers who were mill hands. Regardless, one ironclad clothing rule existed in Southside—whenever anyone appeared in public, his or her garments were expected to be impeccably neat, clean, pressed, and free of any holes or patches.[34]

---

[32] Ginny Dunaway Young (J. T. Dunaway's daughter) email to the author, 15 February 2013.

[33] Author's telephone conversation with Wendell Franklin Wentz, 31 January 2014; Wendell Franklin Wentz email to the author, 29 September 2015. Before and after his Army service during World War II, William Head was the Cowikee Mill band director.

[34] I vividly recall one day in 1974 when I arrived at Willie Mae Starnes's (my maternal grandmother's) front door at 508 South Eufaula Street. I was clad in a stained T-shirt and a pair of ragged, cut-off jeans with holes and patches in the seat. My grandmother was shocked and appalled at my appearance and sternly reprimanded me for dressing "like a hobo." When I attempted to explain that my clothing was "quite stylish," she responded, "Your people don't dress like that." When my father later explained the reasons for my grandmother's reaction, he told me that as a boy in Southside he did not

Class distinctions between Old Eufaula and Southside extended beyond obsessions with clothing and appearance. Some Old Eufaula residents who could not trace their ancestral lineage directly to the town's "pioneer settlers" became the most insidious enforcers of the unwritten discrimination policies aimed at Southsiders. Albert Sidney Dozier, Jr., born in Georgia in 1889, moved to Eufaula in 1919 with his wife, Sarah, and their two young daughters. The son of a grocer in Columbus, Georgia, Dozier opened his own store in the 1920s at the corner of East Broad and North Randolph Streets, just barely within Old Eufaula's boundaries. During their early years in town, the Doziers boarded with another family on West Barbour Street. The grocery prospered, even during the Great Depression. Around 1930, the Doziers purchased a home on North Randolph Street. Within a decade, they owned a larger, more comfortable residence on North Eufaula Street. Albert Dozier served as president of the school board and the Kiwanis Club. The ladies of Old Eufaula tapped Sarah Dozier for membership in one of the town's most prestigious literary societies, the Symposium Club. By 1940, the Doziers were financially secure, well-established residents of Old Eufaula.[35]

Because of the proximity to their homes in Southside, mill families routinely shopped in the retail stores on Broad and North Randolph Streets. However, Albert Dozier not only discouraged these citizens from patronizing his grocery; he cussed and then ejected any Southside youngsters who dared to enter the premises.[36] One Southsider, whose father and grandfather also were grocers, had heard about Dozier's behavior and later recalled, "He looked down upon those children, and he was not the only one."[37]

Incredibly, some Southsiders who left the mill settlement quickly

---

own a large wardrobe, but every article of clothing was always washed before he could appear in public.

[35] 14th–16th US Census, 1920–1940, Schedule No. 1, Population, Barbour County, Alabama, National Archives and Records Administration, Washington, DC; this archival depository hereafter cited as NARA; "Mr. And Mrs. Albert Dozier to Make Future Home in Eufaula," *Columbus (GA) Ledger*, 3 December 1919, 2; Dozier to Head Club," *Macon Telegraph*, 7 January 1930, 13; "Symposium Club Holds Meeting," *Columbus Daily Enquirer*, 8 February 1937, 2; "Engagement of Miss Mary Dozier to George S. Thomas Announced," *Columbus Daily Enquirer*, 11 January 1938, 3.

[36] Wendell Franklin Wentz email to the author, 9 January 2015.

[37] Wendell Franklin Wentz email to the author, 30 September 2015.

adopted the exclusionary elitism of Old Eufaula. Helen Jones, the daughter of Mr. and Mrs. C. T. Jones, graduated from Eufaula High School in the early 1930s and clerked for several years in the grocery on Dale Road owned by her uncles, Jim and John R. "Bob" Hatfield. In July 1934, she married Birmingham native Robert Hornsby in a quiet ceremony at the Washington Street Methodist Church parsonage. The young couple initially lived with her parents on South Eufaula Street and then moved in 1938 to Riverside Drive on the Bluff.[38] The Hornsbys now were securely ensconced within Old Eufaula.

But Eufaula was a small town in which secrets were impossible to keep, and gossip spread like wildfire. Even the most casual comment could feed the flames. In mid-October 1944, Helen Hornsby informed an acquaintance that her children were not allowed to swim at the Cowikee Mill Community House "because *all* classes went in the pool, and she was afraid [they] would contract some kind of disease."[39] After hearing this story, a teller at the Eufaula Bank and Trust immediately wrote to her husband, serving overseas in the US Navy: "I know you remember Robert and Helen Hornsby—she was Helen Jones and was born and raised over here. Now that Robert is sort of getting somewhere with the Power Company, they've gotten the big head something awful, and feel themselves way above South Side!"[40] The bank teller's husband, a star athlete at Eufaula High School who learned how to swim at the Cowikee Community House pool, briefly replied, "Helen must be losing her mind. I know a lot of healthy people that went swimming there. Ahem."[41]

Helen Hornsby's provocative remarks quickly made the rounds throughout Southside. Mild-mannered Eddie Mae Cox Brown, whose husband also was a sailor in the Pacific, was so upset by the story that she decided to confront Helen Hornsby. Since her parents did not have a telephone, she strolled across South Eufaula Street to make her call at the home of Amos and Willie Mae Starnes. According to the Starnes's daughter, Mrs.

---

[38] "Hornsby-Jones," *Avondale Sun*, 14 July 1934, 6; "Personals," *Avondale Sun*, 23 May 1938, 5.

[39] Frances Starnes Alsobrook to Thomas Alsobrook, 19 October 1944, in author's possession.

[40] Ibid.

[41] Thomas Alsobrook to Oma Alsobrook, 5 November 1944, in author's possession.

Brown "called Helen up and wanted to know what she meant by saying such a thing and Helen denied it—Eddie Mae really told her off...[and] said she was glad Robert was getting to stay home and help raise his children, but he shouldn't make them feel that they are better than the ones whose husbands are overseas."[42] The Eufaula telephone exchange still utilized party lines during World War II; by the end of the conversation, the Hornsby tale had been disseminated even more widely and grew larger with every subsequent retelling.

Perhaps the strangest aspect of Eufaula's social caste system was the manner in which it ensnared those who did not live in Southside or work in the Cowikee Mills. During the early 1940s, Lois Segars and several other young women boarded with Mrs. Emma Greathouse on the Bluff. Each Sunday Segars and her friends walked from Riverside Drive down to the Second Baptist Church on Hunter Street. They frequently encountered strangers along the way who remarked, "Y'all are from the other side of the tracks." Segars and several of the other women were employed at the Infant Socks Mill on Barbour Street adjacent to Cowikee Mill No. 1. That fact, combined with their church affiliation seemingly relegated them to Southside social status. Many years later, Segars commented, "But, God doesn't pay attention to those things."[43]

These anecdotal snapshots provide glimpses into the manner in which Old Eufaula elites categorized and excluded Southsiders. Such discrimination relied upon stereotyping mill families as another variety of "poor whites," locked by heredity and circumstances into a repetitive cycle of poverty, ignorance, immorality, alcoholism, and violence.[44]

While a cursory examination of Southsiders lends some credence to this viewpoint, through more detailed research, a richer mosaic emerges of individuals with deep family loyalties, an abiding code of personal honor, and great tenacity and resiliency in the face of adversity. Historian Robert Flewellen asserts that Southsiders "generally were good citizens who organized their own churches, traded in neighborhood stores, worked hard, and

---

[42] Frances Starnes Alsobrook to Thomas Alsobrook, 19 October 1944, In author's possession.

[43] "Parkview Baptist Church Centennial, 1895–1995," 9.

[44] Flewellen, *Along Broad Street*, 186; Wayne Flynt, *Poor but Proud: Alabama's Poor Whites* (Tuscaloosa: University of Alabama Press, 1989) 106–107; W. J. Cash, *The Mind of the South* (New York: Alfred A. Knopf, 1941) 295–96.

paid their taxes…they had little use for 'poor white trash' and blacks in general, but…had a will to survive and a desire to provide better things for their children."[45] Wendell Franklin Wentz, a Southsider who came of age after World War II, became intimately acquainted with mill families who patronized his father's meat market. He believes that "the best people in Eufaula resided south of the railroad tracks.… [T]hey paid their bills and they kept their word."[46] Wentz, however, readily admits that Old Eufaula also produced its share of men and women of inestimable honor: "Several people whose paths I crossed put steel in my backbone, and [attorney] Lee Clayton [Jr.] was one of those men."[47] He also praises Eufaula Bank and Trust president L. Y. "Yank" Dean, III, as "a friend to cotton mill workers" who consistently loaned money to them because "he knew they were hard-working and honest."[48]

Several generations of mill families endured a relentless onslaught of ostracism, proscription, and subjugation. But they quietly bore all of their burdens with a stubborn dignity. No statue ever commemorated their contributions to the progress and betterment of Eufaula. From their establishment in the 1880s, through two world wars and the Great Depression, Eufaula's cotton mills formed a bulwark against financial collapse and widespread poverty. Yet, today, visitors to Eufaula will discover few extant architectural relics associated with the mills and these workers—Washington Street Methodist Church, the Cowikee Community House Band Hall, and the crumbling ruins of Mill No. 3 on South Randolph Street. Most of the mill hands' homes were razed or relocated many years ago. It is as if the mill settlement and its people never existed.

Southsiders never expected to be memorialized with a statue comparable to the Confederate sentinel, the doughboy, or the Reverend Wharton. Nevertheless, on 25 April 2013, several descendants of those anonymous, long-dead Southsiders who coined the nickname for the Wharton monument, proudly assembled on West Barbour Street for the dedication of the Historic Chattahoochee Commission's marker that commemorates the establishment of Cowikee Mills and the existence of the nearby workers' vil-

---

[45] Flewellen, *Along Broad Street*, 186.
[46] Wendell Franklin Wentz email to the author, 7 May 2014.
[47] Ibid.
[48] Wendell Franklin Wentz email to the author, 21 February 2015.

lage.[49] This handsome marker's brief inscription of eighty-nine words succinctly summarizes the history of Eufaula's cotton mills and the village.

But what of the mill workers and their families? Many of them rest in antebellum Fairview Cemetery on a high bluff overlooking Lake Eufaula's tranquil backwaters. Southsiders who lived and toiled together now are reunited in burial plots sheltered by ancient magnolias, oaks, and cedars. Ironically, their graves are intermingled among the ornate tombs of Old Eufaula's founders and "pioneer families," illustrious political leaders, and men and women of wealth and influence. The Reverend Morton Bryan Wharton's mortal remains also are interred at Fairview. In this peaceful garden of stones, the class warfare that once tore the two Eufaulas asunder has never existed. However, one piece of unfinished business still remains. No substantive history of the mill village and its people currently exists. More specifically, Southsiders' stories in their own voices have seldom been heard. This book focuses on their lives outside the mills—their hopes and dreams, joys and sorrows. In illuminating these voices we also will explore Southsiders' roles in creating a new Eufaula.

---

[49] "Cowikee Mill Historically Marked," *Eufaula Tribune*, 1 May 2013, 9A. The marker stands on the site of Cowikee Mill No. 1, which was razed in 2009.

Chapter 1

Confluence:
History, Myth, and Memory in Eufaula

We only remember what is pleasant and approved by God...
—Eugenia Persons Smartt, 1933

Celebrated in history, poetry, and legend, the Chattahoochee River is key to any exploration of Eufaula's past. The river provided sustenance and a means of transportation for the region's aboriginal people, who fished and traversed its swirling waters. In the early nineteenth century, the first white settlers were attracted by the natural beauty and the potential bounty of the river and adjoining countryside. Martha Crossley Rumph, whose family lived in the small village of Irwinton before 1834, later wrote, "Oh! The beauty of the bluff scenery..., the silvery glittering silent river with its green fringed banks and natural curve, and the boats at the wharf, lowland and plantation beyond.... [I]t is strange that any true artist should wander farther for one of nature's choicest pictures."[1]

In the early 1830s, Irwinton—located near the site of "Eufaula," an ancient Creek town—was a remote frontier outpost in East Alabama. Irwinton served as a portal for hundreds of land-hungry settlers, speculators, and adventurers who were probing the Chattahoochee River Valley. Under the subterfuge of the Treaty of Cusseta, whites illegally occupied Creek lands. Skirmishes over land ownership between these new émigrés and Native Americans escalated in 1836 into the brief, ferocious, Second Creek War. US troops stationed fifty miles upriver at Fort Mitchell occasionally were deployed to Irwinton to eject the illegal settlers and fight the Creeks. By 1837, the majority of the Creeks had been subdued, forcibly removed to the West, and whites in Irwinton returned to a semblance of normalcy.[2]

---

[1] Martha Crossley Rumph, quoted in Flewellen, *Along Broad Street*, 15.

[2] Ibid, 5–7, 21–25; Mike Bunn and Douglas Clare Purcell, "Eufaula to Host Annual Meeting," program, *Alabama Historical Association 66th Annual Meeting* 28/1 (Spring 2013): 5; Smartt, *History of Eufaula*, 12–14, 17–19; Albert Burton Moore, *History of Ala-*

Sited upon a towering bluff above the river, Irwinton by the late 1830s had a population of only about 500. The small settlement, however, had become a rising entrepôt, linking East Alabama by steamboat with Columbus, Georgia, and Apalachicola, Florida, on the Gulf of Mexico.[3] In 1843, with their town on a meteoric commercial trajectory, Irwinton's leaders decided to reclaim the old Creek name, "Eufaula," which suggested "something of an earlier age" or "told of other times." Although the specific reasons for this name change have been lost to history, local inhabitants perhaps sought to honor their frontier heritage even as they looked optimistically to the future.[4]

During the two decades before the Civil War, Eufaula became one of the most prosperous towns on the river. Cotton exports and slave labor fueled the town's economic engine. Large cotton consignments from outlying plantations reached Eufaula's wharves by oxcart and wagon and were shipped downriver, ultimately bound for textile mills in New England and Great Britain. Returning steamers delivered foodstuffs, dry goods, finely crafted furniture, and agricultural supplies for the burgeoning population in and around Eufaula. In this fashion, the river connected the Bluff City with ports along the Gulf Coast and the Atlantic Seaboard and in Great Britain. Except during the Civil War's Union blockade, with only a few minor modifications, this reciprocal trading pattern remained in place well into the twentieth century.[5]

Wealth accumulated from cotton profits dramatically transformed Eufaula during the antebellum era. In the 1840s and 1850s, planters, cotton

---

bama (Tuscaloosa: Alabama Book Store, 1951) 30–32, 165–68; Mike Bunn email to the author, 18 January 2016; Douglas Clare Purcell email to the author, 28 January 2016.

[3] Flewellen, *Along Broad Street*, ix, 5; Smartt, *History of Eufaula*, 16–17.

[4] Bunn, *Civil War Eufaula*, 18, 130 (130n.4); Bunn and Purcell, "Eufaula to Host Annual Meeting," 5. Local legend suggests that the name change resulted from the frequent misdirection of mail to Irwinton, Georgia. Merchant Edward B. Young, who had lost a sizable amount of money in this manner, led the local campaign for reclaiming the town's original Creek name.

[5] Bunn and Purcell, "Eufaula to Host Annual Meeting," 5; Flewellen, *Along Broad Street*, ix, 33; Smartt, *History of Eufaula*, 36; Bunn, *Civil War Eufaula*, 19; "All About Eufaula," *Macon Weekly Telegraph*, 5 November 1869, 1; "600 Bales Go to Eufaula," *Montgomery Advertiser*, 24 September 1911, 18; *Columbus Daily Enquirer*, 23 January 1917, 3; 4 February 1917, 2; 26 April 1917, 4.

factors, warehousemen, and other merchants associated with the booming trade in "White Gold," built impressive homes and patronized local mercantile firms, purchasing household goods for their families and slaves. Physicians, attorneys, and bankers swelled the ranks of a nascent elite upper class. Known for their ostentatious lifestyles, Eufaula's antebellum "nabobs," while creating a vibrant economy, also nurtured the town's growing reputation as the "social metropolis of east Alabama." Festive soirees, balls, dinner parties, and barbeques flourished during the heady antebellum era.[6]

Beneath its genteel societal facade, Eufaula also was a political hotbed during the tumultuous decade before the Civil War. Actively encouraged by Alabama's secessionist "fire-eater," William L. Yancey, a small coterie of wealthy Barbour County lawyers founded the "Eufaula Regency," an informal coalition dedicated to a pro-slavery, states' rights philosophy. With strong ties to the Southern Rights Associations, the Regency disseminated its message through the pages of Eufaula's *Spirit of the South*. During the 1850s, this loosely organized "brotherhood" publicly supported the pro-slavery cause. In 1856, for example, Jefferson Buford's abortive expedition to protect pro-slavery settlers in the Kansas Territory gained national notoriety for the Regency. The Regency's political hegemony reached its zenith in 1860–1861, when several members were in the vanguard of Alabama's secessionist movement, including John Gill Shorter, who was elected governor.[7]

With the outbreak of hostilities in 1861, Regency members were among the first Barbour County men to rally to the Confederate colors. Several of these early volunteers entered the enlisted ranks, such as forty-one-year-old James L. Pugh, who vacated his congressional seat and joined the Eufaula Rifles. By the war's end, three Barbour County residents with Re-

---

[6] Bunn and Purcell, "Eufaula to Host Annual Meeting," 5–6; Flewellen, *Along Broad Street*, 33; Bunn, *Civil War Eufaula*, 19–21.

[7] Anne Kendrick Walker, *Backtracking in Barbour County: A Narrative of the Last Alabama Frontier* (Richmond, VA: Dietz Press, 1941) 165; Mattie Thomas Thompson, *History of Barbour County, Alabama* (Eufaula, AL: privately printed, 1939) 254; Bunn, *Civil War Eufaula*, 23–33, 41–45; Moore, *History of Alabama*, 244–47; Mike Bunn, "'Equality in the Union, or Independence Out of It' The Eufaula Regency and the Secessionist Movement in Alabama," *Alabama Hermitage* 121 (Summer 2016): 22-27; Mike Bunn email to author, 18 January 2016. Regency members included Alpheus Baker, Jefferson Buford, John Gill Shorter, Edward C. Bullock, Henry D. Clayton, L. L. Cato, John Cochran, and James L. Pugh.

gency affiliations had risen to the rank of general: Alpheus Baker, Henry D. Clayton, and Cullen A. Battle. Altogether, the county mustered 1,500 to 2,000 Confederate troops—a half-dozen infantry companies, several artillery batteries, and at least one cavalry unit. These soldiers suffered high casualty rates, exemplified by the Barbour Light Artillery, which lost almost 50 percent of its original complement of 140 men. As the war dragged on and the grim casualty figures mounted, recruitment efforts to fill the decimated ranks became problematic. By 1864–1865, the majority of the county's able-bodied men of military age—volunteers and draftees—had gone to the regular Confederate forces or the state militia. Barbour County's combat veterans who miraculously survived the war, including the grievously wounded, returned home to a place, that, like themselves, had been changed forever.[8]

As in much of the state, Eufaula and Barbour County escaped the widespread destruction that the war inflicted upon Virginia, Georgia, and the Carolinas. When General Benjamin H. Grierson's Union cavalry reached Eufaula in late April 1865, the officers were billeted in a local hotel; the 4,000 troopers encamped across the river near Georgetown. During their four months in Eufaula, his men reportedly conducted themselves with remarkable discipline and decorum. Other than their destruction of whiskey stores and confiscation of rations (both from the Confederate commissary on Broad Street), the cavalrymen did not disturb any local property. The Grierson incursion contrasted sharply with General William T. Sherman's "March to the Sea" in 1864 which is remembered for its indiscriminate pillaging and burning of plantations, farms, and homes.[9]

Although Eufaula was being spared the torch, the home front experience was hardly felicitous for those who lived through it. The war wreaked irreparable damage upon Eufaula's cotton-centric economy. A few local

---

[8] Flewellen, *Along Broad Street*, 76–77; Bunn, *Civil War Eufaula*, 50–53, 59, 108; Mike Bunn emails to the author, 17 November 2015, 18 January 2016; Smartt, *History of Eufaula*, 65–67, 69–72, 74–77.

[9] Smartt, *History of Eufaula*, 79–80; Flewellen, *Along Broad Street*, 88–89; Bunn, *Civil War Eufaula*, 91–106. During Grierson's march from Clayton to Eufaula, some thefts of livestock and damage to private property occurred. Grierson's men suffered only one casualty near Clayton—a sniper took the life of Private Joseph C. Marlin, Company K, 2nd New Jersey Cavalry. Shortly after this incident, the troopers received the news of President Abraham Lincoln's assassination. Grierson restrained his soldiers from seeking revenge for the deaths of Marlin and Lincoln.

merchants managed to ship their cotton upriver to Columbus and by rail to Savannah, but with tons of cotton rotting on wharves and in warehouses, most of the town's planters, factors, and bankers were reduced to poverty and despair. Regardless of rare infusions of goods aboard vessels that ran the Union blockade off Apalachicola, Eufaula experienced acute shortages of clothing, shoes, coffee, tobacco, spices, medicines, needles, and paper.[10]

Beyond these financial losses and consumer deprivations, the war left civilians and combatants with deep but invisible wounds. Four seemingly interminable years of worry about the safety of their loved ones on distant battlefields and daily fears of an imminent Union invasion had driven many Eufaulians to the brink of nervous exhaustion. Many of the returning veterans who appeared to be physically sound were nursing psychological injuries. Future generations of physicians later would diagnose such wounds as shell shock, combat fatigue, and post-traumatic stress disorder.[11]

The war left other legacies for Eufaulians. The Civil War was the only major armed conflict in US history in which thousands of Americans ended up on the losing side. Consequently, defeated Southerners were forced to deal with the war's unprecedented economic, social, political, and psychological impact. Confronting the bitter realities of defeat prompted a variety of responses. Perhaps the most extreme reaction came from men like Joseph Ridley Buford and Irving Miller, who immigrated with their families to the "Confederados" colony in Brazil and never returned to Barbour County. Other local ex-Confederates grudgingly signed their loyalty oaths and remained in Eufaula. Leonard Y. Dean, Jr., Joseph Porter, and John G. Archibald devoted their remaining days to publicly reminiscing about their combat service and attending Confederate reunions and commemorative events that honored fallen comrades and the "Lost Cause." In the 1920s, one elderly veteran in Southside sat for hours each day on his front porch, loudly

---

[10] Bunn, *Civil War Eufaula*, 62–72; Flewellen, *Along Broad Street*, 82, 85.

[11] Glenn Feldman, *The Irony of the Solid South: Democrats, Republicans, and Race, 1865–1944* (Tuscaloosa: University of Alabama Press, 2013) 22; Bunn, *Civil War Eufaula*, 49, 55–59, 108, 110; Smartt, *History of Eufaula*, 88–89. Eufaula historian Eugenia Smartt compiled a lengthy, grotesque catalogue of serious combat injuries suffered by local troops, accompanied by a briefer inventory of men who were "slightly wounded." However, she omitted even a suggestion of the psychological impact of their horrific experiences under fire.

damning the "Yankee blue-bellies" all to hell.[12]

The presence of many "old soldiers" who survived into the 1920s and 1930s, along with the establishment of local chapters of the United Confederate Veterans and Sons and Daughters of the Confederacy ensured that a narrative of the "Lost Cause" would be enshrined securely, albeit sometimes inaccurately, in Eufaula's historical annals and collective memory. The "Lost Cause" became another constant in Eufaula, as steadfast as the rolling waters of the Chattahoochee River. Silent film footage in 1913 of aging Confederate and Union veterans tearfully embracing during the fiftieth anniversary of the Battle of Gettysburg re-affirmed Southerners' fervent belief in the "Myth of the Lost Cause." Their soldiers never lacked courage under fire and dedication to the Confederate cause. These flickering images of the emotional camaraderie among the old foes at Gettysburg indelibly stamped the validity of the Myth into many Southern hearts and minds.

According to the Myth's basic thesis, the North triumphed through the deployment of its superior volumes of manpower and material, *not* because its troops exhibited greater valor in combat or dedication to the Union cause than their courageous adversaries who fought for states' rights. And a subtext to this portion of the Myth posits that the South did not fight to preserve slavery.[13]

---

[12] Feldman, *The Irony of the Solid South*, 22; Flewellen, *Along Broad Street*, 93; Bunn, *Civil War Eufaula*, 109–110; "Eufaula Observes Memorial Day," *Avondale Sun*, 2 May 1936, 3. Several of my Southside relatives recalled this unnamed Confederate veteran and his steady streams of profanity.

[13] Modern historians did not coin the term "Lost Cause." One of its earliest usages in print appeared in Edward A. Pollard, *The Lost Cause: The Standard Southern History of the Confederates*, published in 1866. The influential editor of the *Richmond Examiner*, Pollard produced a pro-Confederate account of the war and its causes and an unapologetic defense of slavery. For further reading on the "Lost Cause," see Gary W. Gallagher and Alan T. Nolan, eds., *The Myth of the Lost Cause and Civil War History* (Bloomington: Indiana University Press, 2000); Rollin G. Osterweis, *The Myth of the Lost Cause* (Hamden, CT: Archon Books, 1973); Gaines M. Foster, *Ghosts of the Confederacy: Defeat, the Lost Cause, and the Emergence of the New South, 1865 to 1913* (New York: Oxford University Press, 1987); David W. Blight, *Race and Reunion: The Civil War in American Memory* (Cambridge: Harvard University Press, 2011); David Goldfield, *Still Fighting the Civil War: The American South and Southern History* (Baton Rouge: Louisiana State University Press, 2002); W. Stuart Towns, *Enduring Legacy: Rhetoric and Ritual of the Lost Cause* (Tuscaloosa: University of Alabama Press, 2012).

Journalist Mark Perry, citing an "iconic restatement" of the Myth embedded in Harper Lee's novel *Go Set a Watchman*, argues that expunging slavery from the historical equation leads to an "audacious claim": "[V]irtuous southerners died chivalrously defending a culture of benevolent masters set amidst a society of swaying magnolias and mint juleps. That this South was not defined by chains and overseers and mixed-race children, but by Tara and Twelve Oaks."[14] Perry bitterly concludes that the Myth effectively hid "the unutterable truth that 260,000 southerners died defending the indefensible."[15]

In a gentler, more nuanced critique than Perry's, historian Alan T. Nolan categorizes the Myth as "an American legend," akin to sagas such as *Beowulf* and the *Song of Roland*. Nolan asserts that within this context the Civil War emerges as an "essentially heroic and romantic melodrama, an honorable sectional duel, a time of martial glory on both sides, and triumphant nationalism."[16] In Nolan's estimation, "The victim of the Lost Cause legend has been *history*, for which the legend has been substituted in the national memory.[17]

The Myth, in its various explicit and symbolic forms, became deeply ingrained in the post-1865 psyche of Eufaula and the entire benighted South. Most significantly, the Myth served as an addictive, amnesiac balm for Southerners' recurring nightmares of war, defeat, and personal loss. During and immediately after Reconstruction, when the last "foreign troops" were withdrawn from the South, the Myth gained even greater leverage. The Myth weighed most heavily upon small towns like Eufaula which had invested so much of its blood and treasure, and where virtually every family, regardless of social or economic status, had been ravaged by the war.

After 1875, politicians, editors, businessmen, and ministers evoked the Myth whenever it served their purposes. According to one political aphorism of that era, "A wooden leg or a battered eye acquired on a Virginia battlefield enhanced a candidate's chances more than the possession of actual

---

[14] Mark Perry, "Dissecting the Myth of the Lost Cause in Montgomery, Alabama," *Politico*, August 2015, http://www.politico.com/magazine/story/2015/08/south-lost-cause-confederacy-alabama-120914 (accessed 30 November 2015).

[15] Ibid.

[16] Alan T. Nolan, "The Anatomy of the Myth," in *The Myth of the Lost Cause*, ed. Gallagher and Nolan, 267.

[17] Ibid., 268.

qualifications."[18] Colonel William Calvin Oates, a former Eufaula Regency affiliate, lost his right arm in combat serving with the 15th Alabama Infantry. Early in his post-war political career, Oates carefully perfected the technique of speaking in right oblique profile to his audiences. This maneuver usually achieved the desired effect. During the 1894 gubernatorial campaign, a grizzled old Confederate veteran confessed to Oates that he supported Populist Reuben F. Kolb, but could not vote against the "empty sleeve." Kolb also was a decorated and wounded Confederate combat veteran, but he had survived the war with his limbs intact. While a Confederate service record was a basic prerequisite in any political candidacy for at least twenty-five years after the war, a disfiguring wound usually assured a victory. Colonel Oates, the "one-armed hero of Henry County," whose primitive left-handed scrawl also reminded voters of his personal sacrifice to "the cause," was elected governor in 1894.[19]

Despite the impact of such emotional appeals in the political arena, the reminiscences of ordinary Confederate soldiers were equally important in the Myth's perpetual enshrinement in Eufaula. Historian Mike Bunn, who has written extensively about the war's dramatic impact on the Bluff City, offers an incisive commentary about the nexus between local Confederate chroniclers and the Myth:

> Vicariously, city residents lived the war over again through the stories they heard, experiencing its tragedy in a new but profoundly personal way that was passed down to their children and beyond.... Perhaps the veneration of these heroes and the stories they told helped civilians make sense of the chaos that had wrecked so many families and disrupted the lives of everyone so that the cause became, on some level, worthy of the struggle.[20]

Although the communal sharing of "war stories" produced some positive therapeutic results, particularly for the veterans, this process depended

---

[18] Francis Butler Simkins, *A History of the South* (New York: Alfred A. Knopf, 1963) 312.

[19] William Warren Rogers, *The One-Gallused Rebellion: Agrarianism in Alabama 1865–1896* (Baton Rouge: Louisiana State University Press, 1970) 277; Moore, *History of Alabama*, 632–33; William Warren Rogers, "Reuben F. Kolb: Agricultural Leader of the New South," *Agricultural History*, 32/4 (1958): 109–110; Reuben F. Kolb, "Biographical Memoranda," 1910, Kolb Biographical File, Alabama Department of Archives and History (ADAH), Montgomery, AL.

[20] Bunn, *Civil War Eufaula*, 110.

heavily upon selective memory. Paying tribute to her Confederate ancestors in 1933, Eufaula historian Eugenia Persons Smartt evinced no desire to "re-vive...bitter memories which God had permitted to fade out from manly and fraternal hearts. We only remember what is pleasant and approved by God; valor, fidelity, self-devotion, and glorious loyalty to our native land."[21] Such self-induced historical amnesia may have exorcised some lingering wartime demons, but it also created a nostalgic, delusional romanticism about the past.[22]

This emotional yearning for a return to a "simpler time" was particular-ly disingenuous in association with slavery. Shortly after the war, during his occupation of Eufaula, General Benjamin Grierson presciently observed, "[T]he wealthy classes...clutch on to slavery with a lingering hope to save at least a relic of their favorite yet barbarous institution for the future."[23] Grier-son was neither an abolitionist nor a missionary; he was merely a war-weary citizen soldier who had performed his duty and was eager to return home, but his brief assessment of white Southerners' racial mind-set and postwar goals proved to be remarkably prophetic. Grierson erred in his assumption that only "the wealthy classes" sought to preserve a vestige of slavery as a means of maintaining social control and order in the South.

The vast majority of Southern whites after 1865, including Eufaulians, adamantly rejected any suggestion of racial equality for former slaves. The Myth's omission of slavery as a primary *casus belli* reinforced an intransigent brand of racism, cloaked in paternalism and sentimentality. Seen through the Myth's racially distorted lens, slaves were universally loyal to their be-nevolent owners and their families. Accordingly, even after freedom, African Americans remained happy, child-like, ignorant, and indolent; only their former masters, overseers, and *other whites* truly understood these "wayward souls" and how to "manage" them.[24]

---

[21] Smartt, *History of Eufaula*, 89.

[22] See Matthew A. Speiser, "Origins of the Lost Cause: The Continuity of Region-al Celebration in the White South, 1850–1872," *Essays in History*, Corcoran Department of History, University of Virginia, 2011, http://www.essaysinhistory.com/articles/2011/6 (accessed 30 November 2015).

[23] General B. H. Grierson, quoted in Bunn, *Civil War Eufaula*, 106.

[24] Cash, *The Mind of the South*, 131; Flewellen, *Along Broad Street*, 94, 109, 132; Caroline E. Janney, "The Lost Cause," *Encyclopedia Virginia*, http://www.encyclopedia-virginia.org/lost_cause_the (accessed 30 November 2015); Howard N. Rabinowitz, *Race*

This stereotypical image of African Americans gradually was absorbed into the Myth's crowded pantheon of iconic symbols—the Confederate flag, the grey uniforms, "Dixie," and other "sacred relics" associated with the "Lost Cause." Whites responded emotionally to these symbols and the Myth's other accoutrements, particularly the hagiographical adoration for Confederate heroes, manifested by elaborate commemorative events and the erection of ornate statuary honoring the dead. Now joining the Myth's images of the brave Confederate soldier at war and his long-suffering family on the home front was a caricature of the "loyal plantation darky."[25]

This twisted stereotype endured for more than sixty years after Appomattox. When Sol Mitchell, a Cowikee Mills night watchman, died in 1924, his *Avondale Sun* obituary included these words:

> He was a faithful old "slave-time" negro, . . . born and reared around Eufaula. When he was a small boy, his "ole marster" gave him to his young master, Mr. Avery, and during the [W]ar between the States he served his young master. When Mr. Avery was killed in the Battle of Gettysburg, Sol was with him,...bringing his dead master's sword and other personal belongings back home with him. Although his face was black (he was a full-blooded African), his heart was white, and we are sure that at the final Judgement Day, old Sol will be there, waiting to greet us. Would that there were many more like him![26]

Festooned with specific allusions to the "Lost Cause," Mitchell's obituary embodied a basic theme in the Myth's depiction of African Americans—"Good Negroes" had always remained loyal to their white owners and would be their faithful servants even unto death. Such "tributes" for black Eufaulians appeared in print at least through the late 1930s. Just a year be-

Relations in the Urban South, 1865–1890 (New York: Oxford University Press, 1978) 25–30.

[25] David S. Williams, "Lost Cause Religion," *New Georgia Encyclopedia*, http://www.georgiaencyclopedia.org/articles/history-archaeology/lost-cause-religion; "War and Reunion—The Lost Cause in Southern Memory," Tennessee Virtual Archive, Tennessee State Library and Archives, http://teva.contentdm.oclc.org/cdm/landingpage/collection/p15138coll4 (both websites accessed 30 November 2015).

[26] "Faithful Worker Dies," Sol Mitchell's obituary, *Avondale Sun*, 10 October 1924, 8. Mitchell, one of the few African Americans on the Cowikee Mills payroll at that time, was hired by Donald Comer around 1909 after his family purchased the old Eufaula Cotton Mill property.

fore African Americans would be asked to risk their lives in the defense of democracy against the Germans and Japanese, Ransom Mason's obituary in the *Eufaula Tribune* labeled him as an "'Uncle Remus' type of Southern darky."[27]

The confluence of paternalism, nostalgia, and sentimentality within the Myth itself guaranteed that racial stereotyping was not only accepted, but embraced by white Eufaulians. However, to be fair, documented cases exist in the Works Progress Administration's "Slave Narratives" and "Life Histories" of paternalistic relationships between African Americans and whites in Eufaula, that, while they were not based on any semblance of equality, revealed mutual affection, admiration, and respect.[28]

This postbellum paternalistic legacy undoubtedly helped shape Eufaula's future racial history and the town's own version of segregation that was evolving rapidly by the end of Reconstruction and was firmly in place by the 1890s. "Jim Crow" in Eufaula rested solidly upon one basic premise— the lowliest, poorest white farmer, laborer, and cotton mill operative was racially superior to any African American.[29] This racial imperative united white Eufaulians for nearly a century after the Civil War. Despite their differences over a myriad of political, social, and economic issues, whites stood together on all racial matters.

As in other small Southern towns, Eufaula implemented and enforced Jim Crow primarily without the adoption of segregation ordinances or other legal codifications. Local customs and traditions—buttressed with intimida-

---

[27] "Old Black Joe," Ransom Mason's obituary, *Eufaula Tribune*, Historical and Progress Edition, 5 December 1940, n.p. The fact that this obituary appeared in the *Tribune*'s "Historical and Progress Edition" obviously is rich with irony.

[28] Bunn, *Civil War Eufaula*, 75–80; "A Faithful Servant," Lizzie McGowan life history, interviewed by Gertha Couric, 31 December 1938, Federal Writers' Project, Life Histories/Stories (Ex-Slave Tales), Short Stories, Barbour County, box SG022774, Works Progress Administration Files, Alabama Department of Archives and History (ADAH), Montgomery, AL. These records hereafter cited as WPA Files, ADAH. Lizzie McGowan was born in Barbour County around 1865. Between 1885 and 1935, she was employed as a servant in the home of Islay and Harmon Lampley. Gertha Couric, the WPA employee who interviewed Lizzie McGowan, was well acquainted with her and the Lampley family members. This interview offers a remarkably revealing glimpse into postbellum personal relationships between blacks and whites in Eufaula.

[29] Cash, *The Mind of the South*, 109; Flewellen, *Along Broad Street*, 94.

tion and threats of violence—proved to be more than adequate in subjugating and controlling the town's African Americans. By the early 1890s, even in the absence of *de jure* Jim Crow measures, Eufaula's segregation net was fully tightened. Alabama's 1901 constitution, with its complex web of electoral "reforms," such as the poll tax and the literacy test, removed the majority of blacks (and many whites) from participatory democracy. These draconian statewide measures simply added another layer of racial proscription and control to segregation in Eufaula.[30]

The town's deeply rooted paternalism softened some of Jim Crow's brutality—at least initially. Both races co-existed peacefully by adhering to the proscribed traditional rules of "live and let live." Not surprisingly, the heaviest burden of racial reconciliation and accommodation fell upon African Americans' shoulders. Black Eufaulians pursued jobs that whites traditionally had despised and avoided—as laborers, gardeners, cooks, house servants, chauffeurs, draymen, liverymen, laundresses, and barbers.[31] As long as African Americans were not perceived by whites as competitors for more skilled jobs, peace and tranquility prevailed in Eufaula.

However, a more virulent strain of racism evolved in the late 1870s and metastasized across the South. Whites became increasingly obsessed with the absolute necessity of protecting the "purity of Southern womanhood" from sexual assaults by "black brutes." Although the precise origins of this obsession are difficult to trace, historian Wayne Flynt offers one cogent explanation: "Lurking only slightly beneath the psychological surface of white society was a belief that black males lusted after white women. Blacks would take their revenge for centuries of injustice by raping and ravishing."[32]

This so-called "rape complex" became an unchallenged justification for

---

[30] J. Morgan Kousser, "*Strange Career* and the Need for a Second Reconstruction of the History of Race Relations," in *Dixie Redux: Essays in Honor of Sheldon Hackney*, ed. Raymond Arsenault and Orville Vernon Burton (Montgomery, AL: New South Books, 2013) 406–408; Dewey W. Grantham, *Southern Progressivism: The Reconciliation of Progress and Tradition* (Knoxville: University of Tennessee Press, 1983) 47–48, 112–18; Derrick A. Bell, Jr., "The Racial Imperative in American Law," in *The Age of Segregation: Race Relations in the South, 1890–1945*, ed. Robert Haws (Jackson: University Press of Mississippi, 1978) 12–17.

[31] See Cash, *The Mind of the South*, 318; Robert Higgs, "Race and Economy in the South, 1890–1950," in *The Age of Segregation*, 108.

[32] Flynt, *Poor but Proud*, 213. See also Cash, *The Mind of the South*, 117–19.

torturing and murdering African Americans. Among many Southern white males of all social classes, a perception grew that the threat of lynching offered the only viable preventative measure for all black criminality, particularly rapes. Beginning in the late 1870s, sensationalized press accounts of rapes, murders, and other heinous crimes, allegedly committed by African Americans, further inflamed whites. Equally graphic stories about lynchings also filled the pages of newspapers from coast to coast.[33]

William Dorsey Jelks, the editor of the *Eufaula Daily Times* between 1880 and 1898, frequently weighed in with editorials on these incendiary topics. Jelks, who later served as a state senator and governor, seldom minced words as to his racial views. In an editorial in 1882, titled "Mr. Nigger," he characterized the African American as an "ignorant devil, . . . a foul blot, [and] a blight upon the land.[34] In 1885, Jelks wrote that any black man who assaulted a white woman "with a view to outraging her person," should be forewarned "that his neck will be broken without the benefit of judge, jury, or clergy." He added that if a sheriff's posse determined the "wretch in hand" was guilty, he should be "hanged on the spot" to spare taxpayers the expense of incarceration. He also angrily brushed aside as "sentimentalists" and "sticklers for the law" any reformers who opposed vigilante justice for accused black rapists: "It is a cure and an effective one, too, for the guilty brutes, and it does suppress the evil as far as they are concerned."[35]

Although Jelks periodically revisited this topic in his commentaries, and his *Daily Times* printed lengthy accounts of lynchings elsewhere in Alabama and the South, local incidents of mob violence were seldom men-

---

[33] Cash, *The Mind of the South*, 123, 201, 309, 311, 385; Flynt, *Poor but Proud*, 213; Rabinowitz, *Race Relations in the Urban South*, 52–54; August Meier and Elliott Rudwick, *From Plantation to Ghetto* (New York: Hill and Wang, 1970) 193; August Meier, *Negro Thought in America, 1880–1915: Racial Ideologies in the Age of Booker T. Washington* (Ann Arbor: University of Michigan Press, 1969) 161. Many journalists in the late nineteenth century merely reflected the racist tenor of the times. Between 1895 and 1908, a spate of racist literature appeared: Thomas Dixon's trilogy, *The Leopard's Spots*, *The Traitor*, and *The Clansman*; Charles Carroll's *The Negro a Beast*; and Robert W. Shufeldt's *The Negro: A Menace to American Civilization*.

[34] Jelks editorial, *Eufaula Daily Times*, 21 March 1882, quoted in David Ernest Alsobrook, "William Dorsey Jelks: Alabama Editor and Legislator" (MA thesis, West Virginia University, 1972) 139. Hereafter cited as Alsobrook, "W. D. Jelks" thesis.

[35] Jelks editorial, *Eufaula Weekly Times and News*, 21 July 1885, quoted in ibid, 142.

tioned. Jelks preferred to address this topic in the abstract, rather than after a lynching in his own community. He reserved some of his harshest invectives for Northern journalists who condemned the South's shocking record of mob violence. In June 1881, after a local sixteen-year-old African American was lynched, Jelks wrote, "We can direct our own affairs.... If our civilization has taught us to so far respect the virtue of innocent girlhood as to meet [sic] out immediate punishment upon the head of the violator of her person we failed to see any reason for a complaint...."[36]

Jelks was only twenty-four years old when he purchased the *Eufaula Daily Times* in fall 1880. He penned some of his most vitriolic editorials on the "Negro Question" before he turned thirty. Since he grew up in Union Springs during Reconstruction, Jelks's racial philosophy had been molded by the bitter social and political milieu of that place and time in the Black Belt. After 1900, perhaps out of political necessity, Jelks slightly ameliorated some of his racial views, but he never apologized for his provocative remarks on lynching.[37]

Over the years, Jelks saw no need to issue a *mea culpa* for his youthful journalistic indiscretions. The majority of white Alabamians agreed with his racial philosophy; his *Daily Times* commentaries mirrored his readers' beliefs. Moreover, by the time he embarked on his political career in the late 1890s, public sentiment strongly favored the disfranchisement of African Americans, and the 1901 constitution accomplished that goal. Consequently, Jelks had no fear of alienating African Americans who would be ineligible to vote in future elections. As governor, Jelks was obligated to adopt an official anti-lynching stance. Privately he never deviated very far from his racial views, solidified during his formative years in Union Springs and Eufaula.

In 1905, Jelks candidly told a reporter he realized that mobs frequently lynched innocent blacks accused of rape, but "for this crime against women

---

[36] Jelks editorial, *Eufaula Weekly Times and News*, 16 June 1881, quoted in ibid.

[37] For additional details about Jelks's life and career and the evolution of his racial views, see William Dorsey Jelks, "The Acuteness of the Negro Question: A Suggested Remedy," *North American Review* 184 (15 February 1907): 389–95; David E. Alsobrook, "William D. Jelks (1901–1907)" *Encyclopedia of Alabama* (online), http://www. encyclo-pediaofalabama.org/article/h-1438 (accessed 17 November 2015), hereafter cited as "William D. Jelks," *EOA* online; David E. Alsobrook, "William Dorsey Jelks," in *Alabama Governors: A Political History of the State*, ed. Samuel L. Webb and Margaret E. Armbrester (Tuscaloosa: University of Alabama Press, 2001) 140–46.

no Southern judge, court, or governor can expect to convict those who have avenged the wrong."[38] While accurately recognizing the difficulty in the South of winning convictions in court against lynchers, he shockingly suggested that retribution for the rape of a white woman justified the death of an innocent African American. Any reforms instituted at the state level to protect prisoners from mobs would be left to Jelks's successors in the governor's mansion after 1907.[39]

Even a cursory assessment of Jelks's life, and his careers as an editor and governor, is vital in exploring one of the most neglected areas of Eufaula's history—racial violence. Jelks's editorial views and gubernatorial decisions did not directly precipitate lynchings. But neither his rhetoric nor actions were salubrious contributions to any civil public discourse on race when the old accommodationist, conciliatory paternalism was rapidly disintegrating.[40] Moreover, without paternalism as a bulwark, the confluence of the racially charged politics of Reconstruction, the persistence of the "Myth of the Lost Cause," and the rising tides of visceral racism and sensationalized journalism, by the end of the 1870s, formed a "perfect storm" conducive to mob violence. This savage storm slammed into the South on multiple fronts— and the small, bucolic Bluff City on the Chattahoochee River would not escape its fury.

One of the first documented lynching cases in Barbour County after Reconstruction occurred in December 1879. Two teenaged Irish immi-

---

[38] *Mobile Daily Herald*, 19 March 1905, quoted in David Ernest Alsobrook, "Alabama's Port City: A Study of Mobile during the Progressive Era, 1896–1917" (PhD diss., Auburn University, 1983) 155. Hereafter cited as Alsobrook, "Mobile" diss.

[39] Ibid., 154–155, 165–68, 172–73; "William D. Jelks," *EOA* online. As governor between 1901–1906, Jelks did not respond decisively to Alabama mayors' and sheriffs' requests for state troops to protect prisoners from lynch mobs. A few months before he left office in autumn 1906, Jelks vacillated in deploying the state militia in Mobile to protect two young black prisoners, who subsequently were lynched. Although Jelks primarily blamed the lynchings on local African Americans who sheltered criminals, he had failed miserably in fulfilling one of his most important constitutional duties as governor.

[40] See Allen Day Grimshaw, "A Study in Social Violence: Urban Race Riots in the United States" (PhD diss., University of Pennsylvania, 1959) 80. Sociologist Grimshaw argues that racial violence usually occurs during times of the greatest pressure upon a society's "accommodationist structure." The so-called "classic period of lynching" (c. 1895–1910) coincided with whites' attempting "to re-establish the disrupted, and in memory, sentimentalized pattern of superordination and subordination."

grants, Edward Harvey and James McGeever, employed as traveling dry goods salesmen, stopped briefly in Eufaula. After depositing $180 in a bank, they proceeded northward into Russell County. When the two young men failed to return after several days, Eufaulians feared foul play and organized a search party. Two "suspected negroes" confessed that they had murdered Harvey and McGeever and had dumped their bodies in the Chattahoochee's muddy waters. Neither the salesmen's corpses nor any personal possessions were recovered. Nevertheless, a large posse of "white and colored men,....including many from Eufaula, assembled about twenty miles north in Russell County and lynched the two African Americans, described by one press account as "sullen, indifferent and defiant."[41]

By the time of this lynching, several basic "rules of engagement and conduct" governing the mob clearly were in effect and repeatedly surfaced in future episodes of vigilantism in the Eufaula area. First, while actual physical evidence of a crime was not an absolute prerequisite for action, confessions from the accused suspects should be obtained, if possible. Second, to pre-serve "order" in the community, retribution should be conducted swiftly and efficiently—preferably far away from town.

In June 1881, Josh Shorter, a sixteen-year-old African American, was accused of an "atrocious assault on a respectable white girl," aged twelve. Although the alleged rape was committed in Eufaula, an armed mob "carried the boy over to the Georgia side of the river, despite the protests of the sheriff." Young Shorter, tearfully pleading for his life, swore never to repeat such an act, but the lynchers "strung him up, and he died without a groan."[42]

In both the 1879 and 1881 lynchings, given the dearth of detailed doc-umentation, one wonders about the "confessions" attributed to the suspects. Newspaper accounts of lynchings in that era typically included assurances that prisoners had made "full confessions." Extracting admissions of guilt—whether through intercessions by clergy or through physical force, threats, or at gunpoint—created a facade of legitimacy for lynchings as "legal execu-tions." Many mob victims literally had nooses snugged tightly around their

---

[41] "Judge Lynch," *New York Herald*, 23 December 1879, 4.

[42] "Lynching A Negro," *New York Herald*, 10 June 1881, 4; Flewellen, *Along Broad Street*, 190. This lynching sparked a wave of editorial protests in Northern newspapers, leading to William D. Jelks's fiery response in the *Eufaula Daily Times*. His newspaper identified the alleged rapist as "John Shorter," aged nineteen, and his alleged victim as fourteen years old.

necks when they were given a final opportunity to confess.[43]

Although journalists and other "witnesses" (including mob members) conscientiously preserved lynching victims' final words, newspaper narratives and official records often omitted pertinent details, such as specific geographical locations and the decedents' full names.[44] Such inaccuracies in the documentation of lynchings have frustrated scholars for over a century. In regard to Eufaula, with mounted vigilantes roaming back and forth across the Chattahoochee River—usually with their victims in tow—the site of a particular lynching seldom was reported accurately. In a number of instances, a corpse's location when discovered would be listed as a lynching site. Always fearful of negative publicity, Bluff City leaders breathed collective sighs of relief whenever the press reported lynchings in Baker Hill, Midway, or on the Batesville Road, rather than "near Eufaula."

Nevertheless, during the 1880s and 1890s, lynchings were on the ascendancy in Barbour County. Each barbaric episode grew increasingly more ritualistic and gruesome, epitomized by the shooting and burning of African American Edgar Onlu near Eufaula in April 1893.[45] With the dawn of the new century, mob violence in the area did not dissipate precipitously. However, during the first decade of the twentieth century, the number of failed lynchings steadily increased. This figure may indicate that by 1910 lawmen had become more resourceful in thwarting lynchings.[46]

---

[43] See, for example, details of a lynching in Mobile in 1906 described in Alsobrook, "Mobile," diss., 167.

[44] See, for example, Monroe N. Work, "Lynchings in Alabama," 18 February 1921, 2–6, attached to R. R. Moton to Mrs. M. B. Owen, 21 February 1921, Tuskegee State University Publications, Alabama Department of Archives and History (ADAH), Montgomery, AL.

[45] Ibid., 5; "Burned at the Stake," *Montgomery Advertiser*, 14 April 1893, 1; "A Murderer Shot and Burned," *Kansas City (Mo) Times*, 15 April 1893, 2. Onlu confessed to murdering Jeff D. Burnett, a twenty-year-old white shopkeeper in Quitman County, Georgia. According to the newspaper accounts, Onlu was from Jacksonville, Florida, and was traveling with "a band of gypsies." A mob of fifty or sixty whites and African Americans captured Onlu about six miles from the scene of Burnett's murder. While Onlu probably died in Georgia, the exact location was not provided in the press reports.

[46] "They Strung Him up to Tree," *Atlanta Constitution*, 5 January 1907, 9; "Hanged and Riddled," *(Bryan, TX) Eagle*, 6 January 1907, 1; "Black Brute Swings," *(Newport News, VA) Daily Press*, 5 January 1907; "Hundreds Hunt Black Murderer," *Montgomery Advertiser*, 10 March 1910, 1; "Fugitive Outwits Dogs and Posse," *(New Orleans, LA)*

During the progressive era, reformers began to push back against the horror of lynching. National opponents of racial violence, including large numbers of women, applauded the efforts of charismatic reformers like Ida B. Wells-Barnett, who launched vigorous anti-lynching campaigns.[47]

Like many other Southern chief executives, Alabama's governors were reluctant to speak out against lynchings. Beginning in the early 1890s, Tuskegee principal Booker T. Washington secretly lobbied each successive governor in behalf of a state anti-lynching program and other issues of vital concern to African Americans. Washington's concerted efforts elicited mixed results until after 1907, when former governor Thomas Goode Jones, sitting as a US District Judge, and his gubernatorial successors, Braxton Bragg Comer and Emmett O'Neal, creatively used federal and state laws in combating mob violence.[48]

Ironically, the 1901 constitution, which disfranchised thousands of black Alabamians, included an obscure statute that became an effective legal weapon against racial violence. Since Reconstruction, state laws had empowered county sheriffs to use armed force, including the militia, to protect prisoners and repel mobs. But the penalties for sheriffs failing to safeguard prisoners from lynchings were relatively light and rarely enforced. Section 139 of the new constitution, however, clearly stipulated that if a prisoner was killed or "suffer[ed] grievous bodily harm" because of "the neglect, connivance,

---

Times-Picayune, 11 March 1910, 3.

[47] Karen Rutherford, "Ida B. Wells-Barnett," The Mississippi Writers Page, http://mwp.olemiss.edu//dir/wells-barnett_ida/; Tyina Steptoe, "Barnett, Ida Wells (1862–1931), The Black Past: Remembered and Reclaimed," http://www.blackpast.org/aah/barnett-ida-wells-1862-1931 (Both websites accessed 18 Decemer 2015); see also, Linda O. McMurry, *To Keep the Waters Troubled: The Life of Ida B. Wells* (New York: Oxford University Press, 1998).

[48] Louis R. Harlan, *Booker T. Washington: The Making of a Black Leader, 1856–1901* (London: Oxford University Press, 1975) 231–32, 255–56, 300–302, 308–10; and Harlan, *Booker T. Washington: The Wizard of Tuskegee, 1901–1915* (New York: Oxford University Press, 1983) 240–44; Charles Flint Kellogg, *NAACP: A History of the National Association for the Advancement of Colored People*, 2 vols. (Baltimore: Johns Hopkins University Press, 1973) 1:211, 234; Alsobrook, "Mobile" diss., 173, 186; Thomas Goode Jones to Booker T. Washington, 5 April 1907; Booker T. Washington to R. R. Moton, 27 May 1911; Booker T. Washington Papers, Manuscript Division, Library of Congress, Washington, DC; *United States v. Powell*, 112 US 564 (1908) affg.151 Fed. 648 (CCND Ala. 1907).

cowardice, or other grave fault of the sheriff," he could be impeached and removed from his position.[49] This procedure would effectively end a sheriff's career as an elected public official. Between 1909 and 1911, the sheriffs of Mobile and Bullock County both forfeited their badges after being impeached and convicted under this statute.[50]

Sheriffs throughout Alabama—especially in rural, isolated counties like Barbour—were now on notice that their jobs were in jeopardy if they capitulated to a mob. In an impassioned appeal to one South Alabama sheriff, Governor B. B. Comer wrote,

> I want our officers to show that under any or all circumstances when present they can vindicate the law.... I am anxious for you to show that you can care for a prisoner...in your charge a week or six months, if need be, to make it perfectly plain that the State of Alabama, through its proper officers must not be over-awed or show the white feather.[51]

In June 1909, Comer's new anti-lynching policy was put to a stern test in Eufaula. On 6 June, African American Laurence Davis was accused of attempting to rape Lizzie Thomas, a young white telephone operator in Eufaula. On that quiet Sunday afternoon, safely locked in the county jail, Davis was scheduled to be arraigned and charged on the next day. However, unbeknownst to Davis, over the next twenty-four hours, his life would lay in the hands of a small cadre of brave, resourceful local lawmen and National Guardsmen.

Deputy Sheriff Virgil Crawford, aged fifty-eight, was the officer in charge of the jail in Eufaula. His boss, Sheriff R. B. Teal, was at his home in Clayton, about twenty miles away. Other than an unusual number of "men in buggies" on the streets around the jail and courthouse, Eufaula's main business district seemed to be typically quiet on that particular Sunday.[52]

---

[49] James J. Mayfield, *The Code of Alabama*, 3 vols. (Nashville, TN: Marshall & Bruce Company, 1907) 3:105.

[50] Alsobrook, "Mobile" diss., 181–87; David E. Alsobrook, "Mobile's Solitary Sentinel: U. S. Attorney William H. Armbrecht and the Richard Robertson Lynching Case of 1909," *Gulf South Historical Review* 20/1 (Fall 2004): 6–27.

[51] Governor B. B. Comer to John S. Drago, 17 August 1910, quoted in Alsobrook, "Mobile" diss., 185–86. Comer frequently used this term ("white feather") in his correspondence with sheriffs and other lawmen. The "white feather" was a traditional symbol of cowardice, particularly prevalent in English literature in the late nineteenth century.

[52] "Eufaula Soldiers Drive Mob from the Jail Doors," *Montgomery Advertiser*, 8 June

Teal and Crawford were "tipped off" about "preliminary plans for a lynching"—several local residents had acquired a rope, sledge hammers, and "a big piece of timber." Upon receiving this timely warning, Sheriff Teal immediately left Clayton by buggy for Eufaula. Meanwhile, Deputy Crawford double-locked all of the jail's doors. Although he desperately tried to deputize other citizens to join him in defending the jail, only two men volunteered. Shortly after five that afternoon, a "drunken mob" of about 180 men gathered in front of the jail. As fifteen to twenty vigilantes battered down the jail's outer door, Crawford frantically telephoned for assistance from the town's National Guard company, the Eufaula Rifles.[53]

Since many of their soldiers usually attended worship services on Sunday evenings, Colonel E. H. Graves and Captain Kenneth B. McKenzie dispatched non-commissioned officers to the nearby churches to sound the alarm for riot duty. Throughout the evening, small squads of armed Guardsmen arrived at the jail. Graves and McKenzie stationed most of their men in positions directly facing the mob and also posted riflemen on the jail's landing and in the courthouse's windows. After briefing B. B. Comer in Montgomery by telephone, Graves delivered the governor's orders to his troops: "Protect the prisoner—shoot if you must, but protect the prisoner."[54]

The Guardsmen met each surge of the mob at the shattered doorway with rifle butts and the threat of bayonets. In the steamy gloom on the jail's landing a "cussin' match" erupted between vigilantes and Guardsmen who "recognized each other." The diminutive Junius B. Couric, "hardly as tall as his rifle," stood face-to-face with the mob on the landing. After one "big young fellow" reviled Couric as "little and dried up," "Junie" defiantly shouted back, "That's all right, you big stiff, I'm here doing my duty and if you put your foot on this landing—if you even touch it I'll drill you through with a bullet." Standing nearby, Colonel Graves warned, "If a man tries to cross this line, push him back. If he keeps coming, run him through with your bayonet."[55]

Mayor Charles McDowell, Jr., stood in the midst of the vulgar, sweat-

---

1909, 1–2.

[53] Ibid. Surprisingly, the jail's telephone lines had not been cut, perhaps evidence of a lack of preparation by the mob's leaders.

[54] Ibid.

[55] Ibid, 1.

soaked throng on the landing and loudly announced that the evidence against Davis was "strong enough" to produce a "speedy trial." McDowell pleaded with the men to go home, but an eyewitness noted that "the mob was still ugly." Next came a fortuitous moment in the melee that probably saved many lives.

As Captain McKenzie struggled to clear a jammed cartridge from a soldier's Springfield, the rifle accidentally discharged with a deafening roar, the spent round lodging harmlessly in the ceiling. The single rifle shot immediately silenced the angry mob. At that point, emerging from the dark street, "a well known man in whom the mob had confidence," exclaimed, "Boys, they have got all of the military here—plenty of them. They are too many for you. You had better go home."[56] The mob quickly dispersed, abandoning "the rope with which Davis was to be hanged, several sledge hammers and other trophies." The exhausted troops of the Eufaula Rifles stood vigil in the silent jailhouse for the rest of the long night.[57]

By skillfully deploying their troops and using several very clever feints, Graves and McKenzie had disguised the fact that the company probably never reached its full strength during the assault on the jail. On 7 June 1909, they launched one final deceptive maneuver to protect Davis. The troops, along with Teal, Crawford, and their prisoner, boarded a westbound train, ostensibly heading to Montgomery. However, before reaching Union Springs, the engineer braked his locomotive on an isolated stretch of track. A waiting surrey, manned by armed deputies, rushed Teal, Crawford, and Davis on "a fast drive" to the Clayton jail.[58] Relying upon speed, precise timing, stealth, and luck, this daring, audacious subterfuge had worked to perfection.

The men who stood resolutely between the mob and Laurence Davis earned sterling accolades from state officials and the press. The *Montgomery Advertiser* lauded Sheriff Teal for "us[ing] every resource at his command, even to calling upon the military.... [I]t was demonstrated at Eufaula that...if he is brave enough..., a sheriff can protect a prisoner from a mob."[59] When asked by a reporter if he would shoot his own friends who were vigi-

---

[56] Ibid., 1–2.
[57] Ibid.
[58] Ibid.
[59] "Wholesome Effect," editorial, *Montgomery Advertiser*, 10 June 1909, 4.

lantes, Teal grimly replied, "The man who would join a mob to lynch my prisoner is no friend of mine. I'd fire on any man who would go into a mob to do me that wrong."[60]

The incident at the Eufaula jail in June 1909 proved that disciplined, well-armed troops, commanded by experienced officers and lawmen, could prevent lynchings. Two years later, mob violence again exploded in Eufaula. Unfortunately, Teal and Crawford were not on duty, and the Eufaula Rifles were not mustered. As a result, the outcome was tragically different.

On the evening of 11 February 1911, Iver Peterson, an eighteen-year-old African American, allegedly attempted to rape Mrs. E. A. Hudson near Cherry Street in Old Eufaula. Mrs. Hudson, described as "a prominent woman of Eufaula…in social and church circles," claimed that Peterson accosted her in the dark around seven o'clock as she returned to her home on North Eufaula Street. After her piercing screams "attracted several of her neighbors to the scene in a few moments…, the negro had fled."[61]

An account of this story that has survived within Eufaula's African-American community suggests that Peterson was the victim of an unfortunate case of mistaken identity. As a child in the early 1920s, David Frost, Jr., overheard his parents discussing the tragic story of Iver Peterson, who was waiting in the dark that night for his girlfriend, the "Hegley girl [who] worked for some white people on Cherry Street." Frost recalled, "[A] white girl came out of the house…, walking straight toward him like his girlfriend had been doing and he did not know she was white…. [H]e said, 'Here I am.' …So she screamed, which frightened the Peterson boy and he ran away."[62] Despite the lack of any physical evidence of a struggle, such as cuts, bruises, abrasions, and torn clothing, Mrs. Hudson's claim was enough to launch a manhunt.

After Peterson was identified as Mrs. Hudson's alleged attacker, policemen and citizens scoured the neighborhood through the night. Around eight o'clock on the morning of 12 February 1911, they apprehended the young man at his father's residence, located in the rear of Congressman Henry D. Clayton, Jr.'s property on North Eufaula Street. The arresting

---

[60] Sheriff R. B. Teal quoted in ibid.

[61] "Eufaula Mob Lynches Negro," *Dothan (AL) Eagle*, 13 February 1911, 1.

[62] David Frost, Jr., *Witness to Injustice*, ed. Louise Westling (Jackson: University Press of Mississippi, 1995) 5.

officer, Constable William N. Beverly, was a sixty-five-year-old Confederate veteran who had served as a boy in the Barbour Light Artillery. Fearing that his prisoner would be lynched if he remained in Eufaula, Beverly quickly devised a plan to transfer Peterson to the Clayton jail. Joseph W. Spencer, proprietor of a local garage, volunteered to drive Beverly and Peterson to Clayton. Around nine o'clock that morning, at "the eight mile post" outside of town, "twenty of the most prominent citizens of Eufaula" surrounded the automobile and dragged Peterson into the woods by the highway. They hanged him from a tree and riddled his suspended body with bullets.[63]

In retrospect, the Iver Peterson lynching probably was the most enigmatic case of racial violence in Eufaula's history. Despite accurately assessing the volatile atmosphere at the time, Constable Beverly did not enlist support from the governor's office, the National Guard, or the sheriff. He also failed to provide additional security for the potentially dangerous journey from Eufaula to Clayton. One elderly, inexperienced constable, who had been on duty for barely a month, did not present a serious impediment to twenty heavily armed adversaries who brazenly intended to murder Peterson in broad daylight. Regardless of his failure to prepare adequately for an imminent lynching, Beverly was not punished by the state in 1911. He was still serving as a constable at the time of his death in 1917.[64]

Perhaps the "prominent citizens" in the mob were too influential or powerful for anyone to oppose. Unlike the telephone operator Lizzie Thomas, whom Laurence Davis allegedly threatened in 1909, Mrs. Hudson was an elite "society woman" of Old Eufaula. An attempted assault upon her by an African American likely was perceived as a direct attack upon the very heart of Old Eufaula's social order. More than the honor and virtue of one woman

---

[63] Ibid., 5–7, 45; "Eufaula Mob Lynches Negro," *Montgomery Advertiser*, 13 February 1911, 1; "Gubernatorial Appointments," *Montgomery Advertiser*, 4 January 1911, 5; *Smartt, History of Eufaula*, 76; Ginny Dunaway Young email to the author, 12 December 2015, with attached biographical material on Beverly. According to David Frost, Jr.'s account, Dr. Walter S. Britt was one of the mob's primary leaders and fired the first shots into Peterson's body. Two other members of the mob specifically identified by Frost's parents were Seth Speight and Harry McCullohs, both of whom later became peace officers in Eufaula. No corroborating documentation apparently exists for these allegations.

[64] In contrast to this episode, two months later, in April 1911, after an African-American prisoner in the custody of the sheriff in Union Springs was lynched, that county official was subsequently impeached and convicted for his negligence.

were on the line—a public act of retribution was required to restore Eufaula's social and racial equilibrium. Therefore, a very disturbing possibility exists—this particular mob may have included Eufaula lawmen, National Guardsmen, and well-heeled civic and commercial leaders.[65] This obviously bold supposition, however, offers a plausible explanation as to why Constable Beverly faced the mob alone on the road to Clayton in February 1911.

Iver Peterson's lynching, in comparison with the failed assault on the Eufaula jail in 1909, clearly showed that only a well-coordinated, armed force—preferably troops—could defeat a large, frenzied mob. State and local officials and peace officers seemingly learned this lesson from the 1909 and 1911 episodes in Eufaula. Peterson's brutal murder was one of the only two recorded lynchings in Alabama in 1911. Over the next decade, the state's number of lynchings continued to decrease. After 1921, documented cases of attempted lynchings actually surpassed those that were completed in Alabama between 1926 and 1929.[66] The long battle against the scourge of mob violence was being won at the point of a bayonet.

During the 1920s in Barbour County, courageous, innovative lawmen successfully foiled several lynchings. For example, in August 1921, posses with bloodhounds tracked accused murderer Alford Culver from Henry County into Eufaula. The search parties finally apprehended the black suspect, hiding at the bottom of a forty-foot well. Deputies briefly held Culver in the Clayton jail and then shipped him to Montgomery, only minutes ahead of a mob. Through the cooperative efforts of deputies and policemen from multiple jurisdictions, another lynching in Barbour County was narrowly averted.[67] But the fact that the prisoner had survived without protection from the National Guard probably created a false sense of security among lawmen.

The bitter lessons of 1909 and 1911 were, however, periodically forgotten. In January 1922, Willie Jenkins, a decorated black World War I veteran, was accused of "insulting a white woman" in Batesville, about twelve miles northwest of Eufaula. With a mounted band of outlaws in hot pursuit,

---

[65] On the participation of lawmen in Southern lynchings, see Alsobrook, "Mobile" diss., 176–78, 181–83; see Cash, *The Mind of the South*, 309–10.

[66] Ibid., 307; Work, "Lynchings in Alabama," 1–2, 15; Alsobrook, "Mobile" diss., 186; Geoffrey Perrett, *America in the Twenties: A History* (New York: Simon & Schuster, 1982) 88.

[67] "Negro Lodged in Montgomery Jail," *Montgomery Advertiser*, 1 August 1921, 3.

Jenkins fled by train to Georgetown. Evading sheriff's deputies, the mob retrieved Jenkins and carried him back across the river. His mutilated body later was found by the road in Batesville.[68] Once again, the National Guard had not been mobilized, with the same murderous result as in 1911.

By the late 1920s, Alabama governors seldom hesitated in calling out the National Guard whenever mob violence was threatened. In July 1929, after lurid, sensationalized newspaper coverage of a murder and rape a few miles from Eufaula, decisive action by Governor Bibb Graves very likely prevented extensive bloodshed.

On 10 July 1929, Jack Hines, a white twenty-eight-year-old mechanic, was murdered on a deserted country road about four miles north of Eufaula. His female companion, Beatrice Clark, aged eighteen, was raped, shot, and left for dead. Bleeding profusely from a shotgun wound in her left arm, she walked down the railroad tracks to Eufaula and reported that an unidentified African American was the perpetrator and had escaped in Hines's Chevrolet.[69]

After a week-long manhunt, police officers arrested Lester Bouyer, alias "Charlie Harris," a black thirty-eight-year-old saw mill worker, north of Montgomery. Bouyer confessed to the murder and the rape. After the news of Bouyer's capture reached Eufaula, "two crowds of masked men" began searching all automobiles entering the town.[70] They obviously were looking for Bouyer, whose trial would be held in Barbour County.

The situation on the ground in Eufaula by 21 July was deteriorating rapidly. The Associated Press warned of "a highly inflamed public mind in southeast Alabama and southwest Georgia."[71] "[A]though no disorders have been reported,...feeling was at a high pitch against the negro, especially in

---

[68] Frost, *Witness to Injustice*, 12–19; "Negro Lynched; Insulted Woman, Sheriff Asserts," *Atlanta Constitution*, 12 January 1922, 14; "Negro Alleged to Have Insulted White Woman Is Lynched," *(Biloxi, MS) Daily Herald*, 11 January 1922, 1; "Probe Lynching of Negro in Alabama," *Boston Herald*, 12 January 1922, 11.

[69] "Boy Killed, Girl Wounded by Negro," *Clayton (AL) Record*, 12 July 1929, 1; "Shotgun with Which Jack Hines Was Killed Was Stolen from Georgia Negro Home," *Eufaula Daily Citizen*, 12 July 1929, 1; "Name of Murderer of Jack Hines Now Known," *Eufaula Daily Citizen*, 15 July 1929, 1.

[70] "Negro Confesses to Hines Murder," *Clayton Record*, 19 July 1929, 1.

[71] "Spirit Negro away to Take Him to Trial," *Manitowoc (WI) Herald-Times*, 23 July 1929, 1.

the cotton mill districts."[72] Circuit Judge J. S. Williams and other local officials notified Governor Graves that Barbour County lacked enough manpower to protect Boyer during a trial in Eufaula or Clayton. Graves responded, "There will not be a lynching in Alabama if I can prevent it."[73]

On 22 July, Graves mobilized two National Guard infantry companies in Birmingham, with orders to protect Bouyer "at any hazard." These 200 troops would be accompanied by a special squad of twenty state police officers. General Walter E. Bare, the National Guard's commanding officer, dispatched an advance contingent of fifty soldiers ahead to Eufaula to establish a security cordon around the courthouse. As the train carrying the main force of Guardsmen with Bouyer left Kilby Prison in Montgomery at dawn on 23 July, Bare released a terse statement to the press: "We have been called upon by the government to protect this negro during his trial; that protection will be given."[74]

When the train arrived in Eufaula at eight o'clock, a crowd of 1,500 people waited at the depot. Wearing steel helmets and with fixed bayonets, the Guardsmen filed briskly from the train and marched Bouyer three blocks to the courthouse. Fifty soldiers and twenty-five policemen ushered the prisoner into the court room and remained there during the two-hour trial. About 150 Guardsmen were stationed outside the building, where at least 3,000 spectators had gathered. After meeting his court-appointed defense attorney for the first time, Bouyer pled guilty. The prosecution called three witnesses, including Beatrice Clark, whose left arm was heavily bandaged. She identified Bouyer and related the details of Hines's death. The rape indictment was not pursued during the trial. After ten minutes' deliberation, the jury returned a guilty verdict for murder. Before sentencing, Bouyer requested that his execution be expedited without any delays. Judge J. S. Williams sentenced him to death by electrocution within thirty days at Kilby Prison. Escorted back to the depot by the Guardsmen, Bouyer was back in his cell on death row in Montgomery before two o'clock on 23 July. Only

---

[72] "Militia to Guard Negro Murderer," *Miami (OK) Daily News-Record*, 22 July 1929, 1.

[73] "Call Soldiers to Guard Negro," *Boston Herald*, 29 July 1929, 17; "Alabama Governor Orders State Troops to Protect Prisoner," *New York Age*, 27 July 1929, 1.

[74] Soldiers Sent to Guard Negro during Hearing," *Richmond Times-Dispatch*, 23 July 1929, 10; "Spirit Negro away to Take Him to Trial," *Manitowoc Herald-Times*, 23 July 1929, 1 (Bare quote).

thirteen days had elapsed since the fateful night he had encountered Hines and Clark outside Eufaula. Bouyer died in the electric chair at 12:26 a.m. on 27 August 1929.[75]

In the wake of the Bouyer trial, Governor Bibb Graves was highly commended in newspapers across the region and nation for preventing a lynching. However, Graves was no civil libertarian; he was primarily concerned about the adverse publicity that would befall the state if Bouyer died at the hands of a mob. A negative image of Alabama would damage Northern business investments and lead to greater federal involvement in the state's racial affairs. Two years later, although he refused to pardon the Scottsboro Boys, Graves again mobilized the National Guard to prevent their lynchings.[76]

While African-American journalists also applauded Graves's use of the National Guard in protecting Bouyer, they universally criticized the lack of an adequate defense attorney and swift implementation of the death penalty after a guilty plea.[77] The influential *Pittsburgh Courier* editor wrote, "Governor Graves has proved to the world that lynching can be avoided.... [T]he legal defense was missing, ...but there was no illegal lynching and a step forward has been made."[78] The Bouyer trial represented only a slight, incremental progression toward the eradication of mob violence. Nevertheless, regardless of his underlying motivations for protecting the life of one African-American prisoner, Graves may have prevented "a carnival of sadism" in Eufaula that characterized the lynching of Claude Neal in Marianna, Florida, in 1934.[79]

---

[75] "Negro Slayer Is Brought Safely to Eufala [*sic*] Ala.," *Kingsport (TN) Times*, 23 July 1929, 1, 4; "Negro Tried and Sentenced to Chair All in Two Hours," *Jefferson City (MO) Post-Tribune*, 23 July 1929, 1; "200 Troops Guard Negro at Trial," *Reading (PA) Times*, 24 July 1929, 3; "Murderer of Jack Hines Given Death Sentence," *Clayton Record*, 26 July 1929, 1; "Negro Murderer to Pay Penalty Today," *Clayton Record*, 23 August 1929, 1; "Bouyer Goes to Chair for His Crime," *Clayton Record*, 30 August 1929, 1.

[76] See Feldman, *The Irony of the Solid South*, 103, 109–10.

[77] E. W. Norton, a white attorney from Clayton, Bouyer's court-appointed lawyer, did not request a change of venue despite the obvious local bias against the defendant in Barbour County. See "Alabama Slayer Given Physical, No Legal Aid," *Pittsburgh Courier*, 3 August 1929, 4.

[78] Ibid.

[79] Feldman, *The Irony of the Solid South*, 107–108. For further details on the Neal

This episode was a defining moment in Eufaula's lengthy history of racial violence because it did not degenerate into a full-blown riot or massacre.
The Bouyer trial—brought to a resolution literally at bayonet's point—did
not mark an end to racism or racial animosity in Eufaula. One can argue
with some validity that the inflammatory press stories about Bouyer's crimes,
trial, and electrocution actually exacerbated racial tensions over the short
term and then also played an integral part in perpetuating hatred and dis-
trust between blacks and whites in Eufaula.

Perhaps this spectacle of 200 armed troops peacefully subduing a potentially bloodthirsty mob of 3,000 resonated on some level within the town.
Without overly dramatizing this point, it appears that Eufaulians instinc-
tively understood the unique importance of what they had witnessed. An
anonymous photographer snapped a blurred image from a second-story window on Broad Street of the Guardsmen surrounding the courthouse and
facing the mass of spectators. The World War I doughboy's statue also was
in the photographer's frame. With his flat steel helmet and Springfield rifle,
the stone soldier closely resembled the young Guardsmen arrayed below
him. And somewhere in the crowd at the courthouse that day was an eight-
year-old Southside boy who never forgot what he saw—silent, determined
soldiers with loaded rifles and fixed bayonets staring down a crowd full of his
friends and relatives. At the time this youngster lacked a full understanding
of why those troops were there, but he realized that this was no ordinary day
in Eufaula.[80]

On balance, despite almost five decades of documented mob violence,
Eufaula's racial history was not significantly different from the experiences of
other small towns in the Alabama Black Belt and Wiregrass during the Jim
Crow era. The bitter legacies of the Civil War and Reconstruction generated
fertile soil for the seeds of racism, which in turn produced a rigidly segregat-

---

lynching, see James R. McGovern, *Anatomy of a Lynching: The Killing of Claude Neal*
(Baton Rouge: Louisiana State University Press). Neal, an accused black rapist and murderer, was carried by a mob from the jail in Brewton, Alabama, over the state line to Marianna, Florida, where he was tortured and lynched. Large numbers of spectators assembled in Marianna to view Neal's corpse.

[80] This photograph probably was taken by H. E. Maugans, who had been recording
images of downtown Eufaula since the early 1900s. This young boy was my father,
Thomas Neville Alsobrook (1920–1996), who clearly remembered that particular day in
Eufaula.

ed, intolerant society.

Perhaps the Bluff City's racial narrative would have played out differently if a few of the more enlightened residents of Old Eufaula and Southside, who privately were horrified by Jim Crow's inherent evils and brutality, had publicly voiced their outrage. Fearing ostracism and retribution, they silently acquiesced, thereby allowing Eufaula's systemic racist contagion to fester unabated for several generations. The first positive racial changes in Eufaula—like melting glaciers—finally appeared after the passage of a century and the advent of the "Second Reconstruction" of the modern civil rights era.[81] But, even then, the long shadows of the "Myth of the Lost Cause" and unresolved issues from Jim Crow's "bad old days" cast a heavy pall over attempts at racial reconciliation.

Any substantive history of Eufaula includes some events and topics that are not necessarily "pleasant and approved by God," despite Eugenia Persons Smartt's assertion in 1933. The story of Eufaula's rise from a desolate frontier outpost to an antebellum jewel on the Chattahoochee and the heroic sagas of the Civil War's combat and home front experiences constitute vital elements in the town's rich historical tapestry. However, analyses of racial bigotry, brutality, and violence—guaranteed to elicit discomfort—also are essential in seeking a deeper understanding and appreciation of Eufaula's diverse history. As historian Robert Flewellen masterfully reveals in *Along Broad Street*, Eufaula's story did not end in 1865. It continued on, with issues of race, caste, and class flowing together, mixing history, memory, and myth, just as the nearby river absorbed soil and sediment from its tributaries.

Eufaula's "Cotton Mill Campaign" in the late 1880s inaugurated a new chapter in the Bluff City's history that lasted for over a century. This new industrial order initially presented a sizable challenge to Old Eufaula's leaders—how to control, without alienating, a large, "untamed" group of textile workers whose labor was essential to commercial prosperity. The resolution

---

[81] Mary Ellen Gale, "The Movement Comes to Wallace's Home" and "How Not to Desegregate the Schools—Without Really Trying," both in *(Montgomery, AL) Southern Courier*, 27–28 November 1965, 4; Larry Scott Butler, "Diary of an Alabama SCOPE Volunteer—Larry Butler," Summer 1965; Larry Scott Butler, "A Short History of the Freedom Movement in Barbour County, Alabama," 10 December 1965, both in author's possession; Frank Sikora, "Unrest simmers at Eufaula in wake of shooting of two blacks," *Birmingham News*, 20 April 1983, 13A; Peyton McCrary, "Minority Representation in Alabama," in *Dixie Redux*, ed. Arsenault and Burton, 380.

to this dilemma lay in yet another cynical manipulation of the race issue. For both the elites of Old Eufaula and Southside's mill families, the Civil War and the "Myth of the Lost Cause" reverberated over the years with an identical steady drumbeat. These two disparate groups also shared a core belief in the racial superiority of whites over African Americans.

Therefore, even after decades of ostracism and discrimination at the hands of Old Eufaula, Southsiders apparently failed to see any similarity between their plight and that of African Americans and refused to admit that they shared any commonality with an "inferior race." Whether they were conscious of it or not, the confluences of race, class, and the Lost Cause mythos shaped the orbit of Southsiders' daily lives in ways both apparent and unseen. Granted, they did not occupy the lowest rung of the social ladder, but neither were they on an equal footing with the Bluff City's "pioneer families." Consequently, long before the first bolt of finished cloth came forth from Eufaula's cotton mills, the place in society of textile operatives and their kin was completely circumscribed and solidified. With the Jim Crow racial imperative in full bloom, Southsiders merely shrugged their shoulders and genuflected toward Old Eufaula, comfortable in their ingrained belief that they still were superior to African Americans.

Chapter 2

"Phoenix" Rising on the Chattahoochee: Eufaula's Rebirth as a Cotton Mill Town

We hear rumors of a cotton factory noised upon the streets, and hope ere long to report they have ripened into a reality.
—Macon Telegraph, *12 April 1884*

In fall 1869, a Georgia journalist visiting Eufaula for the first time since the end of the Civil War observed, "The progress of the 'Bluff City' is wonderful both in population and material wealth."[1] Without citing any data about business transactions, he marveled at the "lively and cheering" daily commercial activity—"[T]he principal streets are thronged and literally jammed with wagons..., bringing in the fleecy staple and returning laden with goods from the enterprising and intelligent merchants."[2] He was particularly impressed with Eufaula's business infrastructure: fifty to sixty mercantile houses, retail shops, grist mills, two hotels, three cotton warehouses, three banks, a foundry, and two spacious livery stables.[3]

This ebullient writer's grandiloquent assessment belied the reality of some very troubling economic deficiencies hidden beneath the town's attractive veneer. "King Cotton" still reigned supreme atop Eufaula's financial hierarchy to be sure, but the antebellum era's bountiful supply of "free labor" had vanished. Moreover, the war had eviscerated the land-based system of collateral and credit and distant trading partnerships—arteries of Eufaula's economic life blood. A year after the exuberant reporter's appraisal of Eufaula's commerce, another visitor recorded a very different financial outlook. "Dul[l]ness iterated and reiterated only would describe the situation now," he gloomily wrote, except for two or three days of the week, "when the country comes to town, and Broad and Eufaula streets bristle with wag-

---

[1] "All About Eufaula," *Macon Weekly Telegraph*, 5 November 1869, 1.
[2] Ibid.
[3] Ibid.

ons and other vehicles."[4]

During the late 1860s and early 1870s, despite a general "dullness" in business and fluctuating cotton prices, several prominent Eufaula exporters, including John Wesley Tullis, J. G. Guice, and Harmon Lampley, rolled the dice, gambling that investments in "White Gold" were still worth the risks. They shipped large cotton cargoes north on the river to Columbus, Georgia, and south to Apalachicola, Florida. After docking in these two ports, their cotton was purchased by Columbus's Eagle and Phenix Mills and by faraway textile plants in New England and Great Britain. The Vicksburg and Brunswick and Montgomery and Eufaula Railroads in the 1870s soon re-placed wagons in transporting cotton shipments into Eufaula.[5]

Cotton exporters Tullis, Guice, and Lampley exemplified a new breed of ambitious entrepreneurs who rebuilt Eufaula's economy after 1865. Sever-al dozen of these audacious "men on the make" arose in Eufaula. First and foremost, they were shrewd, energetic businessmen who primarily sought to turn a profit and enrich themselves and their families. But in the course of improving their own personal financial prospects, they ensured that Eufaula would rise from the bitter ashes of defeat. Beyond their exceptional business acumen, these men shared a searing life experience—they were Confederate combat veterans.[6]

Regardless of their actual ranks during the war, even the lowliest enlist-ed man among them later was accorded the honorary title of "Captain," "Major," or "Colonel." So it was with John Wesley Tullis, who established Eufaula's first cotton mill. He was dubbed "Captain" although he never had risen above the rank of first lieutenant in the Confederate Army.

Born in the Edgefield District of South Carolina in 1839, Tullis as an infant moved with his family to Macon County, Alabama. He spent his boyhood on the family's farms in Macon and Pike counties. In 1861, stand-ing just over six feet, the blue-eyed, sandy-haired Tullis at age twenty-two looked optimistically ahead to his life as a gentleman farmer in Pike County. In April 1861, he enlisted in Hardaway's Battery in Montgomery, Alabama.

---

[4] "Letter from Eufaula," *Macon Weekly Telegraph*, 10 May 1870, 2.

[5] Smartt, *History of Eufaula*, 112; Flewellen, *Along Broad Street*, 96, 98, 139, 156–57.

[6] For biographical sketches of several of these men, see Smartt, *History of Eufaula*, 256, 263–64, 276, 283, 296; Flewellen, *Along Broad Street*, 96–99, 202–203.

This unit primarily included recruits from Russell, Macon, and Tallapoosa counties. Tullis subsequently served as an artillery lieutenant in all of the major campaigns in Northern Virginia. "His [left] foot was shot away at the ankle" at Gettysburg. After nine months as a prisoner of war, Tullis was exchanged and "invalided" back to Columbus, Georgia. From September 1864 until the end of the war, he commanded a home guard artillery unit in Columbus. During the last months of the war, Tullis purchased a cotton warehouse, which he sold in autumn 1866, and relocated to Eufaula.[7]

A year after he arrived in the Bluff City, Tullis married Mary C. Woods, the daughter of Clayton R. Woods, an influential local businessman. Tullis partnered with his wife's family in several successful commercial enterprises. By the mid-1870s, Tullis had established a large cotton purchasing and exporting company. His close friend, Harmon Lampley, soon joined him as a full partner. Over the next thirty-five years, John W. Tullis & Co. dominated the wholesale cotton trade in Eufaula. In 1879, in recognition of Tullis's professional expertise and personal popularity, local merchants elected him as president of the Eufaula Cotton Exchange. He carved out time from his demanding schedule to serve on the Eufaula School Board and as a trustee of several railroads with local connections. He was a Gilded Age Midas; everything he touched turned to gold. His investments simultaneously produced personal profits and upgrades in Eufaula's infrastructure. In 1884, for example, he built the first coal gas plant in Eufaula—the only one at that time in Southeast Alabama. Via his Eufaula Gas Works' pipeline, the downtown business district and residences north of Broad Street soon were brightly illuminated, and gas stoves began to replace wood-burners in Old Eufaula. However, these improvements did not reach Southside until at least a decade later.[8]

---

[7] "John Wesley Tullis," in Owen, *Dictionary of Alabama Biography*, 4:1688–89; J. W. Tullis's "Application For Artificial Limb," 12 June 1876; J. W. Tullis, entry No. 257, Census or Enumeration of Confederate Soldiers Residing in Alabama, 1907, in Alabama Confederate Pension and Service Records, Alabama Department of Archives and History (ADAH), Montgomery, AL; Willis Brewer, *Brief Historical Sketches of Military Organizations Raised in Alabama during the Civil War* (Montgomery, AL: Alabama Department of Archives and History, 1966) 697–98.

[8] Flewellen, *Along Broad Street*, 29, 98, 156, 180–82, 202; Smartt, *History of Eufaula*, 127; "Death Claims Captain Tullis," *Montgomery Advertiser*, 19 December 1909, 10.

Tullis's ascendancy as a leader of Eufaula's civic-commercial elite close-ly followed a pattern witnessed in towns from Virginia to Texas. As with antebellum "Captains of Commerce"—planters, cotton factors, and other members of the landed gentry—the mantle of leadership rested comfortably upon the shoulders of ex-Confederates such as Tullis who exhibited excep-tional talent in civic and business affairs. Wounded combat veterans such as Leonard Y. Dean, Jr., J. G. Guice, and Tullis did not need to produce evi-dence of their leadership credentials. Those Eufaulians who literally had followed men like them into the "cannon's mouth" became their most devot-ed disciples. Eufaula's first postbellum generation of "Cotton Men"—imbued with a deep sense of *noblesse oblige*—felt duty-bound to lead in peace time as they had during the war.[9]

Tullis and his friends inherently understood that their hegemony as leaders was contingent upon confidently demonstrating that they had sound fiscal plans and policies to weather the storm after the Panic of 1873 and "boom and bust" cycles in cotton prices. Further complicating matters, by the late 1870s, Eufaula's heavy investment in railroad bonds had brought the town to the brink of financial collapse. Additionally, even with cotton ex-ports booming, Eufaula's bank loans largely were tied up in advances to planters on their future crops.[10]

By 1879 both the Vicksburg and Brunswick and Montgomery and Eufaula railroads were bankrupt and had been sold to satisfy bondholders' demands. The rapidly expanding Central of Georgia Railroad absorbed both of these lines; they later became vital transportation links for Eufaula's fledg-ling textile mills. Nevertheless, in 1930 Eufaula was still burdened with heavy indebtedness from these original railroad bond issues.[11] Moreover,

---

[9] Cash, *The Mind of the South*, 113–14; Broadus Mitchell and George Sinclair Mitchell, *The Industrial Revolution in the South* (Baltimore: Johns Hopkins University Press, 1930) 147–48.

[10] Broadus Mitchell and George Sinclair Mitchell, *The Industrial Revolution in the South*, 147; Flewellen, *Along Broad Street*, 99, 119, 138–39, 146–47, 156–57. By 1878, cotton prices had dropped to ten cents per pound and trended steadily downward for twenty years, reaching below five cents in 1898. See Cash, *The Mind of the South*, 152; John W. Tullis to G. Gunby Jordan, 31 October 1898, SPR744, Alabama Department of Archives and History (ADAH), Montgomery, AL.

[11] Flewellen, *Along Broad Street*, 157; Smartt, *History of Eufaula*, 111; Moore, *Histo-ry of Alabama*, 499, 523, 533–35.

local banks' addiction to loans on cotton advances continued unabated until the international market collapsed after the outbreak of the Great War.

Possible deliverance from Eufaula's systemic financial deficiencies appeared in the guise of a "Cotton Mill Campaign," organized in the 1880s by local civic and commercial leaders. A frothy brew of three "isms"—evangelicalism, paternalism, and hucksterism—had driven similar promotional campaigns throughout the South's textile region. Often obscured by excessive hoopla and hokum, these crusades generally emphasized that cotton mills would provide steady employment, moral uplift, and personal fulfillment for hundreds of unskilled, displaced poor white farmers, while integrating the impoverished, agricultural South into the nation's industrial mainstream.[12]

The campaign's evangelical and paternalistic components frequently overlapped. Charismatic clergymen such as the Reverend Robert G. Pearson barnstormed across the South, preaching the virtues of a hybrid gospel blended from disparate beliefs in "the sureties of salvation and the rewards for living the sanctified life."[13] He challenged his audiences to inject "a spiritual dimension" into "the everyday New South World of locomotives, business, credit, and debt." Preaching at revivals across North Carolina in autumn 1887, Pearson spoke emotionally of local communities' moral

---

[12] Broadus Mitchell and George Sinclair Mitchell, *The Industrial Revolution in the South*, 74–75; Broadus Mitchell, *The Rise of Cotton Mills in the South* (Baltimore: Johns Hopkins University Press, 1921) 130–37, 151–57, 160–231; Cash, *The Mind of the South*, 180–83.

[13] Gary R. Freeze, "God, Cotton Mills and New South Myths: A New Perspective on Salisbury, North Carolina, 1887–1888," (quote by Freeze) in *The Adaptable South: Essays in Honor of George Brown Tindall*, ed. Elizabeth Jacoway, Dan T. Carter, Lester C. Lamon, and Robert C. McMath, Jr. (Baton Rouge: Louisiana State University Press, 1991) 53; "Evangelist Pearson in Mobile," *Charlotte (NC) News*, 18 March 1891, 1; "Rev. R. G. Pearson," *Charlotte (NC) Observer*, 23 February 1893, 4; "Rev. R. G. Pearson Coming," *Birmingham Age-Herald*, 11 January 1896, 8. Born in Mississippi in 1847, Pearson graduated in 1876 from the Cumberland Presbyterian Seminary in Lebanon, Tennessee. By the end of the 1890s, he had toured many of the states in the South. One of the highlights of his career was an appearance with Dwight L. Moody at the Chicago World's Fair in 1893. Pearson visited Alabama on at least three occasions between 1891 and 1896. In January 1896, he spoke in Birmingham, just one year before Braxton Bragg Comer established his central Avondale Mill. It is not known if Comer attended this revival.

obligations to build cotton mills for the spiritual and material salvation of poor whites.[14]

Eufaula's campaign, however, was much more secular than spiritual and lacked the paternalistic appeals that characterized Pearson's sermons. Although a devout Methodist, Tullis's primary motivation in building a cotton mill was pecuniary rather than evangelical or paternalistic. He was a dedicated, hard-driving businessman; for him, profits superseded the need for social welfare programs. Also, the leading booster in the campaign, William Dorsey Jelks, editor of the *Eufaula Daily Times*, shared Tullis's business sentiments and later professed that he was "not a member of any church."[15] Jelks and Tullis knew each other well from their service together on the Eufaula School Board. Jelks's father had died in a Confederate Army hospital in Richmond in 1862. Therefore, the impressionable, young journalist probably viewed Tullis, the wounded Confederate hero, with considerable awe and respect.[16]

Jelks, through his impassioned commentaries in the *Eufaula Daily Times*, served as Tullis's voice in behalf of a cotton mill. In a relentless editorial series that ran for over six years, Jelks extolled Eufaula's impressive assets: $2 million accrued annually in cotton receipts, four "fast passenger trains daily," the churches, the Shorter Opera House, the Union Female College, hosiery and flour mills, the Barbour Machine Works, the Ross Carriage Factory, a bottling works, and John P. Foy's Oil and Fertilizer Company.[17]

In spring 1882, fifty-four merchants and private citizens, including Stouten Hubert Dent, R. J. Woods, William Petry, A. H. Merrill, and Tullis, successfully petitioned the city council to acquire a parcel of land on Union Street as the site for "a cotton factory." In May the council sold the land to the Eufaula Cotton Manufacturing Company for $100 and granted a tax exemption for eight years. Jelks quickly congratulated Tullis and his associates for "set[ting] the seal of prosperity and greatness upon the communi-

---

[14] Freeze, "God, Cotton Mills, and New South Myths," 54.

[15] Flewellen, *Along Broad Street*, 170–71, 183–84; W. D. Jelks, "Biographical Memoranda," 1901, Jelks Biographical File, Alabama Department of Archives and History (ADAH), Montgomery, AL; Alsobrook, "W. D. Jelks" thesis, 6–7.

[16] Alsobrook, "W. D. Jelks" thesis, 3–4, 15.

[17] Flewellen, *Along Broad Street*, 170, 183.

ty."[18]

The editor's accolades proved to be premature. Tullis's company announced that the mill's construction would be postponed until spring 1883. Then, without any explanation, the project was abandoned. Although he grew increasingly frustrated with this venture's failure, Jelks never wavered in his fierce advocacy for a cotton mill in Eufaula.[19] However, because of his close association with the project, Jelks had to endure editorial sniping from other newspapers. In April 1884, one of his journalistic rivals in Georgia gently ridiculed the failure: "We hear rumors of a cotton factory noised upon the streets, and hope ere long to report they have ripened into a reality."[20]

Nevertheless, despite Jelks's frustration and impatience, by the mid-1880s, several local economic developments undoubtedly provided him with some optimism about the future. In 1884, cotton exports continued to average about 100,000 bales per year. Two new compresses were constructed to facilitate the movement of cotton during the busy marketing season. The Central of Georgia built one of these compresses and unveiled plans for "a large and beautiful passenger depot at the foot of Broad Street." Eufaula's wholesale merchants reported a sizable increase in their trade in groceries and dry goods, "reaching a territory never supplied by us in the past."[21]

During an era when the debilitating effects of the Panic of 1873 still lingered, these recent economic trends encouraged Eufaula's civic and commercial boosters. The Central of Georgia's solid confidence in the town's future was especially noteworthy. One newspaper in 1884 also revealed concrete evidence that the local housing industry was on the rise:

> Eufaula's future seems brighter than ever before. Real estate is enhancing in value, and holders seem disposed to cling to what they have and purchase more. Several handsome residences are now being built, and scores of neat tenement homes are under course of erection. One favorable indication is that each house is applied for by renters before it is finished.[22]

---

[18] Ibid., 184.

[19] Ibid., 183–84.

[20] "Eufaula, Ala.," *Macon Telegraph*, 12 April 1884, 3.

[21] Ibid. This reference to the opening of new wholesale markets suggests that ongoing railroad construction by the Central of Georgia in Southeast Alabama and Southwest Georgia was paying dividends for Eufaula's tradesmen.

[22] Ibid.

Although this writer neglected to specify the location of these "neat tenement homes," they very likely were in Southside and would be occupied by mill families in the coming decades.

Finally, in spring 1888—more than six years after Eufaula's first campaign for a cotton mill—everything seemed propitious for a successful venture. The newly incorporated Eufaula Cotton Mill Company, led by Tullis, Stouten Hubert Dent, and a half-dozen other directors, purchased twenty acres of land for $6,000 from banker John McNab. Located at the corner of Eufaula and Barbour Streets, the future mill site commanded a prominent position on the southwestern periphery of the business district. The Eufaula and East Alabama Railroad (later acquired by the Central of Georgia) curved along the lower quadrant of the property. The Central of Georgia later laid a spur line to the mill's yard and loading docks. South of the tracks lay the area that became the Southside mill settlement.[23]

Initially capitalized at $50,000, mill stock sales proceeded briskly, and that figure soon was doubled. In June 1888, Tullis proudly announced that he had ordered components for 120 looms and 3,744 spindles. With the basement excavated and the foundation laid, by early July, the brick walls of the two-story structure were erected. Within seven months, under Tullis's careful scrutiny, the exhausted construction crew had completed their work. On 19 December 1888, Tullis fired up the mill's steam boilers and equipment for the first time. Like a child whose Christmas gifts failed to arrive on time, Tullis regretted that the brass steam whistle was not yet on hand. He wanted its shrill blasts to roust slumbering Eufaulians from their warm beds like a herald to his new venture. Two hundred curious spectators assembled at the mill on 3 January 1889 to view the clattering machinery in action. Eufaula officially had entered the cotton mill age.[24]

Tullis's vision was now a reality. Almost overnight the Eufaula Cotton

---

[23] "Eufaula, Ala.," *Macon Telegraph*, 20 June 1888, 3; Flewellen, *Along Broad Street*, 184–85; Smartt, *History of Eufaula*, 127–28. The other members of the original board of directors included several prominent businessmen and attorneys: Leonard Y. Dean, A. H. Merrill, George Legaré Comer, M. M. Berringer, G. W. Guice, and W. N. Reeves.

[24] "Down at Eufaula," *Columbus Daily Enquirer*, 7 July 1888, 3. "Eufaula, Ala.," *Macon Telegraph*, 11 July 1888, 3; "Southern Development," *(New Orleans, LA) Times-Picayune*, 4 September 1888, 4; "Eufaula's Cotton Mill Starts," *Macon Telegraph*, 29 December 1888, 2; Flewellen, *Along Broad Street*, 184–85; Smartt, *History of Eufaula*, 127–28.

Mill became a profitable business enterprise. In fall 1889, Tullis's first ac-
counting report to the mill's stockholders prompted them to consider dou-
bling the plant's production capacity. William Jelks argued that the stockholders' report proved conclusively "that cotton mills pay better, when well-
managed, than anything else and our future is made much brighter by the
great possibilities that lie in them. We want and expect Eufaula to become a
great town."[25]

Tullis seldom disappointed his stockholders. During its first decade in
operation, the mill paid large dividends to investors twice a year. In 1892
alone, the mill's net profits were $19,583. The board of directors raised the
plant's stock capital in 1893 to $150,000. With his surplus capital fund top-
ping $40,000, Tullis tripled his number of looms and spindles.[26] Remarka-
bly, the Eufaula Cotton Mill's most prosperous years coincided with another
national financial crisis, the Panic of 1893.

During his sixteen years as the mill's president, Tullis focused on production figures for cotton cloth and stockholders' dividends. On his watch,
the mill produced an average of 110,000 yards of finished white cotton cloth
each week. Tullis also divided his time between mill operations and his lucrative job as a cotton exporter. As a result, he devoted less time and energy
to the needs of his mill operatives. Other than a small library on the mill
property, Tullis did not provide any educational or recreational programs for
his employees and their families.[27]

However, in 1892, Tullis hired a thirty-eight-year-old superintendent
who paid closer attention to daily management of the mill and its workers.
George T. Marsh, a New York native, was described by a contemporary as
"a whole souled, wide-awake hustler…[who] knows his business like a child
does its catechism."[28] Meticulous, hard-working, and convivial, Marsh
quickly earned the respect of Tullis and the workers. Marsh also inaugurated
a tradition for all of the superintendents who followed him. Although he

---

[25] M. C. White, "Eufaula, Ala.," *Columbus Daily Enquirer*, 7 May 1899, 12; Flewellen, *Along Broad Street*, 185; Jelks editorial, *Eufaula Daily Times*, 20 September 1889,
cited in Alsobrook, "W. D. Jelks" thesis, 161n.103.

[26] M. C. White, "Eufaula, Ala.," *Columbus Daily Enquirer*, 7 May 1899, 12; *Charlotte Observer*, 29 March 1893; Flewellen, *Along Broad Street*, 200.

[27] M. C. White, "Eufaula, Ala.," *Columbus Daily Enquirer*, 7 May 1899, 12; Flewellen, *Along Broad Street*, 185.

[28] M. C. White, "Eufaula, Ala.," *Columbus Daily Enquirer*, 7 May 1899, 12.

deeply immersed himself in the life of Southside, Marsh, by virtue of his title, also had an entrée into Old Eufaula. He was a founding member of the Washington Street Methodist Church in 1894 and served as a Sunday school superintendent. But he also was elected to the city council in 1896 from the third ward and sat on the board of the Union Female College.[29] Thus, from the 1890s on, mill superintendents held "dual citizenship" in the two Eufaulas. Although Marsh's sojourn in Eufaula was relatively brief, he made a significant imprint upon the mill and the town.[30]

But Marsh's boss left a more substantial legacy. Tullis met the challenges of the commercial world in the same manner that he faced combat— with courage and fortitude. After losing his leg at age twenty-three, he easily could have spent the rest of his life as an embittered casualty of war. But he took the high road and became one of Eufaula's most influential entrepreneurs. During his thirty-nine years in Eufaula, he consistently turned every business opportunity into a long-term success. In October 1905, Tullis moved to Montgomery and launched a wholesale hardware company in partnership with three of his sons. Like all of his previous business enterprises, this company flourished. A week before Christmas in 1909, Captain John Wesley Tullis, Eufaula's original "Cotton Mill Man," suffered a cerebral hemorrhage while taking a bath and died within two hours. He was seventy years old.[31]

Most of Tullis's posthumous tributes omitted one significant fact about his illustrious Eufaula career. In addition to building the Bluff City's first textile plant, Tullis also was indirectly responsible for the establishment of the second cotton mill. During the 1880s, John P. Foy, along with his three brothers and Robert Anderson Ballowe, founded two very profitable businesses—a cottonseed oil and fertilizer plant and a grocery. In 1893, buoyed by Tullis's success, the Foy brothers, Ballowe, George Legaré Comer, and several of their friends, filed incorporation papers for the Chewalla Cotton

---

[29] Ibid.

[30] 13th–15th US Census, 1910–1930, Schedule No. 1, Population, Montgomery County, AL, NARA; Ginny Dunaway Young email to author, 8 January 2016, with biographical information about George T. Marsh (1854–1934). Marsh moved from Eufaula to Montgomery in the early 1900s. He was employed as a mill superintendent in Montgomery for a number of years, but near the end of his life, he worked as a coal dealer.

[31] "Death Claims Captain Tullis," *Montgomery Advertiser*, 19 December 1909, 10.

Mill, to be located alongside the Central of Georgia Railroad tracks on South Randolph Street. Chewalla managers copied Tullis's template on a slightly smaller scale—with an initial capitalization of $50,000, 100 looms, 3,000 spindles, and about 75 operatives. Chewalla also would produce white goods, specializing in finely woven sheeting.[32]

With extensive interaction among the managers of the two mills, Chewalla appeared to be poised to follow Tullis's pathway to early commercial success. Unfortunately, on 26 December 1894, barely a year after its opening, the Chewalla Mill was partially destroyed by a boiler explosion. "Flying brickbats and fragments of iron" also severely damaged John P. Foy's cotton-seed oil and fertilizer plant.[33] Over the next thirty years, the rebuilt Chewalla Mill suffered through at least two bankruptcies and multiple changes of ownership. New managers twice changed the mill's name—from Chewalla to Glenola, and then to Marcella.[34] Despite the best efforts of Foy, Ballowe, G. L. Comer, B. B. McKenzie, and a host of other commercial leaders, the mill never approached the level of productivity and profitability of Tullis's plant.

Although it fared better than Chewalla during the 1890s, after 1900, the Eufaula Cotton Mill also encountered financial difficulties. In June 1903, in response to a scarcity of cotton and a decline in the market's demand for its finished products, the mill closed for two months. Tullis managed to stabilize the mill, and it was fully operational by the time he retired two years later. However, the Panic of 1907 plunged the mill into bankrupt-

---

[32] "Eufaula's Enteerprise [sic]," Macon Telegraph, 7 June 1893, 1; letterhead, Eufaula Oil and Fertilizer Company, letter of recommendation for John F. Dunnaway [sic] by R. A. Ballowe, 28 April 1892, Ginny Dunaway Young Collection; M. C. White "Eufaula, Ala.," Columbus Daily Enquirer, 7 May 1899, 12; Smartt, History of Eufaula, 127–28; Flewellen, Along Broad Street, 203.

[33] Smartt, History of Eufaula, 128.

[34] "Cotton Mills Suspend," Montgomery Advertiser, 7 January 1910, 7; "Comer's Mill Pays," Montgomery Advertiser, 15 January 1910, 5; Charlotte News, 22 October 1910, 2; 14 November 1910, 2; 4 February 1911, 2; "Business Troubles," Montgomery Advertiser, 25 June 1910, 8; "Mills Will Re-Open," Montgomery Advertiser, 21 October 1910, 13; "Mill in Eufaula to Resume," Montgomery Advertiser, 7 January 1911, 6; Montgomery Advertiser, 13 July 1914, 6; "Glenola Cotton Mill Is Bought by Philadelphia Man," Montgomery Advertiser, 20 June 1918, 2; "Cotton Mill Is Sold to Atlanta Concern," Avondale Sun, 11 January 1924, 3; "Marcella Mills Sold," Avondale Sun, 22 May 1925, 7; Smartt, History of Eufaula, 128, 276.

cy. At this critical juncture, in 1908, the Comer family paid $45,000 to acquire this "busted mill" for inclusion in its vast Avondale textile empire.[35] Governor Braxton Bragg Comer, Avondale's founder and president, entrusted salvaging the Eufaula Cotton Mill to his son, James McDonald "Donald" Comer.

In 1909, in his early thirties, the tall, frail, bespectacled Donald Comer had only a rudimentary knowledge of the textile industry. Prior to "volunteering" for the Eufaula job, he had planned to devote his life to managing his family's Barbour County plantation and the Avondale Mills. Soft-spoken and self-effacing, he suffered from lifelong chronic illnesses, including asthma and recurring attacks of malaria, which he originally contracted during his Army service in the Philippine Insurrection. Given his bad health, introverted demeanor, and limited management experience, the young Comer appeared to be a poor candidate for retrofitting a failed cotton mill in a small, isolated Alabama town. Subsequent developments, however, proved the wisdom of his father's decision.[36]

Comer immediately recognized that the seventy-five veteran operatives he had inherited with the Eufaula Cotton Mill property were treasured assets. Many of these experienced spinners, weavers, and loom mechanics formed the working core of the newly named Cowikee Mill and spent the rest of their days on Comer's payroll. Eddie Cox, Bennie Morgan Clark, James "Doc" Hughes, James Wesley Gill, Clara Gill Blackmon, Thomas Mallie Parish, John Thomas Alsobrook, and others were dexterous, versatile operatives, and they eagerly embraced even the most menial, grueling tasks.[37]

Within a year of his arrival in Eufaula, Comer oversaw the installation of new "finishing machinery" which enabled the mill to produce colored

---

[35] "Plant at Eufaula Will Be Idle till September," *Columbus Ledger*, 24 June 1903, 6; "Alabama Mills to Curtail," *Charlotte Observer*, 27 November 1907, 2; "Comer's Mill Pays," 15 January 1910, 5; "Donald Comer Writes," *Avondale Sun*, 5 August 1946, 4; 20 June 1955, 5.

[36] David E. Alsobrook, "Southside and Eufaula's Cowikee Mills Village, 1910–1945," *Alabama Heritage* 119 (Winter 2016): 20.

[37] Ibid. It is not known why Comer selected "Cowikee," a Creek name, for his new mill. It is believed that "Cowikee" means "carrying water" (Mike Bunn email to the author, 11 February 2016).

chambrays, checks, and striped ginghams, rather than plain white cloth.[38] Three decades later, weaver John Thomas Alsobrook vividly recalled this conversion process: "Old machinery was torn down and new put in. I helped wear the new out, then personally took a sledge hammer and beat the skeletons so they could be thrown out the window."[39] When Comer later converted the Cowikee Mill from steam to electrical power, he demanded similar herculean efforts from his workers and consistently rewarded them with promotions and bonuses.

Although Comer's supervisors frequently rose from the Cowikee operatives' ranks, he also recruited seasoned workers as foremen and superintendents from Avondale Mills and other textile plants in Georgia and the Carolinas. Between 1909 and 1944, Eufaula's Cowikee Mills had only two senior superintendents, Robert Dallas Jones and Owen Franklin Benton, both of whom Comer personally hired from textile companies in the Carolinas. Comer also rotated his most experienced foremen throughout the Avondale and Cowikee Mills. He was particularly adept at identifying and developing young operatives with management potential, such as Eufaulians Tyson Smith and Cleveland Adams, who entered the mills during their high school days.[40]

After World War I, with his work force well established, Comer expanded his Cowikee operations beyond Eufaula to Union Springs and Ozark. In 1929, he purchased Eufaula's defunct Chewalla-Glenola-Marcella Mill and absorbed it into his company. Each Cowikee Mill received a numerical designation based on its acquisition date. The two Eufaula plants

---

[38] "Add New Machinery," *Montgomery Advertiser*, 24 September 1910, 5; *Charlotte News*, 14 November 1910, 2.

[39] Tom Alsobrook family life history, "Fifty-two Years in the Cotton Mill," interviewed by Gertha Couric, 13 October 1938, folder 18, Federal Writers' Project Papers #3709, Southern Historical Collection, Wilson Library, University of North Carolina, Chapel Hill, NC. This collection hereafter cited as FWPP, SHC, UNC.

[40] For details on the lives and careers of superintendents Jones and Benton, see "R. D. Jones, Former Superintendent, Dies at Eufaula," *Avondale Sun*, 27 April 1929, 1, 6; "Who's Who With Avondale Mills, Owen Franklin Benton," *Avondale Sun*, 14 June 1930, 12; "Cowikee Mills General Supt. Dies in Eufaula," *Avondale Sun*, 7 February 1944, 1, 4; "Owen F. Benton, Mill Executive, Dies in Eufaula," *Columbus Daily Enquirer*, 27 January 1944, 3. Benton achieved the distinction of serving as superintendent of all four of the Cowikee mills.

thus were Cowikee Mill No. 1 (the "Big Mill") and No. 3 (the "Little Mill"), with No. 2 in Union Springs and No. 4 in Ozark.[41] Comer's modesty was legendary; he seldom claimed personal credit for his mills' accomplishments. Whenever Comer spoke about programs he was particularly fond of, such as the workers' profit-sharing plan, he always provided his managers with an opportunity to take a victory lap. But he was very proud that in Eufaula, Union Springs, and Ozark, "All four of these little mills were busted when we bought them and closed down. We have made them decent places for decent people to work."[42] By 1940, these four "little mills" employed about 1,200 people, with 50 percent allocated to the two Eufaula plants. In less than thirty years, through innovation, perseverance, and hard work, Comer had added three new jewels to the Avondale Mills crown.[43]

"Mr. Donald," as he was affectionately known to his mill families, was a practical, hard-headed businessman, who, very much like Captain Tullis, was highly motivated to earn profits in the textile industry. However, unlike his predecessor, Comer paid very close attention to the needs of his employees and their families. Although he loved traveling the globe and consulting with governors, legislators, and presidents, Comer preferred to be "at home" in Barbour County among "his people"—farmers and mill workers. He had a genuine respect and affection for these people who worked on his family's land and in the Comer mills.

Although he vociferously objected to the term "paternalism," Comer was a particularly adroit practitioner of it. His own brand of paternalism evolved from his family's philanthropic ideas and sense of *noblesse oblige* and his own deep religious faith. In 1929, a close friend wrote to Comer: "You and your family, in the tender sympathy and human understanding of your people have revealed a new aspect of the human relationship between the operator and operatives."[44] Although union organizers continually accused

---

[41] "Cowikee Mills Big Factor in Section's Life," *Eufaula Tribune*, Historical and Progress Edition, 5 December 1940, n.p.

[42] "Donald Comer Writes," *Avondale Sun*, 5 August 1946, 4.

[43] "Cowikee Mills Big Factor in Section's Life," *Eufaula Tribune*, Historical and Progress Edition, 5 December 1940, n.p.

[44] Mary M. McCoy to Donald Comer, 12 June 1929, "Athens College," folder 7.45.31, box 45, James McDonald Comer's Avondale Mills office files, Department of Archives and Manuscripts, Birmingham Public Library, Birmingham, AL. This collec-

Comer of trying to "buy off" his employees with welfare services, he never ceased in his efforts to improve the quality of their lives. After World War I, with the establishment of the Cowikee Mills Community House in Eufaula, Comer provided a wide range of educational, recreational, and social programs for his employees and their families. As in the other Comer textile plants and mill settlements, the Community House was an architectural symbol of his paternalism.[45]

While Donald Comer exhibited a greater personal interest in his workers' welfare than Captain Tullis, both were totally dependent upon the men, women, and children who toiled in Eufaula's cotton mills. Some of Tullis's employees already were living in the local community when he opened the Eufaula Cotton Mill in 1889. But many new mill hands were, in the parlance of that era, peripatetic "strangers" from elsewhere in Alabama and the South. They had learned about Tullis's new cotton mill from newspapers, labor agents, relatives, and friends. Beginning in the late 1880s, destitute farmers and restless itinerant textile workers ("floaters") from Georgia, the Carolinas, and the Alabama Black Belt and Wiregrass regions migrated to Barbour County to seek mill jobs in Eufaula.[46]

The first wave of Southside mill families descended upon Eufaula by train, wagon, horse, and even on foot. Since the Central of Georgia ran four or five trains a day into Eufaula, those "strangers" who could afford the price of a ticket chose the railroad. Frightened and homesick, they reached the Bluff City with their meager possessions crammed into battered trunks, valises, and cardboard suitcases. The gangly, rawboned teenager John Thomas Alsobrook and his mother, Henrietta, arrived in Eufaula sometime in the late 1880s. He never knew his father and had worked since childhood alongside Henrietta in a textile mill in Early County, Georgia. Since John Thomas's birth in 1871, they had lived a hand-to-mouth existence with Henrietta's brothers in Georgia and in Newton, Alabama, a small town on the rail line in Dale County. Two of Henrietta's brothers in Newton, Eldridge and Landon Alsobrook, had been wounded during their service with the 39th Alabama Infantry Regiment. For the fatherless John Thomas, these two

---

tion hereafter cited as Donald Comer Papers, BPLA.

[45] Alsobrook, "Southside and Eufaula's Cowikee Mills Village," 22. For further details about Comer's paternalism and workers' programs, see chs. 4 and 5.

[46] Ibid., 20–21.

young uncles were the most dominant male figures during his formative years.[47]

When John Thomas and Henrietta Alsobrook arrived in Eufaula from Newton, no relatives or friends greeted them at the depot. Embarking on their new lives in Eufaula, they undoubtedly were excited and optimistic because they no longer had to depend on family charity for their survival. Both were skilled operatives, whom Captain Tullis desperately needed. The Alsobrooks would make their own way in the years to come, among their "adopted" family members in the mill and in Southside.

The Alsobrooks, like other new Southside residents, were only vaguely aware of their ancestral roots. The Civil War and its aftermath were the defining elements of their history. The majority of white Southsiders— including the Alsobrooks, Dunaways, Parishes, Snipeses, Hatfields, Gills, Gillises, Barkers, and Blands—tranced their lineages to eighteenth-century English, Scottish, and Irish immigrants who had moved westward from Virginia and the Carolinas. Primarily Baptists and Methodists, these émigrés eked out a hardscrabble existence as small farmers and laborers in rural areas across the South. Survivors of the Civil War and Reconstruction and two decades of economic upheaval, newly arrived Southsiders were a "broken," disinherited people, desperately searching for a fresh start in this small town along the Chattahoochee.[48] As one social worker later noted, "When the first whistle blew, people flocked to the light from barren places. These cotton mills were established [so] that people might find themselves and be found."[49]

To support the influx of mill families, by the mid-1890s, Southside had

---

[47] Ginny Dunaway Young, "Ancestors of David Ernest Alsobrook," and "2013, family history, unpub. typescript, in author's possession; 10th US Census, 1880, Inhabitants Schedule, 1140th Militia District, Early County, Georgia, NARA; Compiled Service Records, Landon C. Alsobrook and E. N. Alsobrook, both in Company D, 39th Alabama Infantry Regiment, War Department Collection of Confederate Records, Record Group 109, NARA.

[48] Young, "Alsobrook Family History," and "Dunaway-Parish Family History," 2013, both in author's possession; Broadus Mitchell and George Sinclair Mitchell, *The Industrial Revolution in the South,*" 117–18, 147.

[49] John W. Speake, quoted in Lois MacDonald, *Southern Mill Hills: A Study of Social and Economic Forces in Certain Textile Mill Villages* (New York: Alex L. Hillman Publishers, 1928) 17.

become a self-contained town within a town, with its own grocers, butchers, carpenters, blacksmiths, liverymen, seamstresses, and craftsmen. Although designated as Eufaula's "Factory District," Southside in reality was not a true "company town" in which schools, churches, and workers' housing were designed, built, and owned by the mills. Southside thus avoided the regimented, monotonous architectural schematics of the other Alabama mill villages. Depending upon the sizes of their families, Eufaula's mill operatives lived in an eclectic assortment of homes—from sprawling, faded Victorians to compact "prettily painted" cottages and bungalows. Thanks also to Donald Comer's innovative home-loan program, many Southsiders became property owners for the first time in their lives.[50]

During the 1920s, the steady growth in home ownership and retail businesses, accompanied by the expansion of the Community House's services solidified Southside's self-sufficient identity. Eufaula's population grew from about 7,000 to 9,000 between the two world wars. Roughly 1,500 to 2,000 people resided in Southside—approximately 25 percent of Eufaula's total population. During that era, Eufaula's two cotton mills employed about 600 workers.[51] Even those Southsiders who were not on the Comer payrolls had connections to the mills through relatives, friends, and the Community House. Since Southside families patronized retail stores outside the mill village, they contributed heavily to Old Eufaula's economic prosperity.

Although its boundaries were never rigidly delineated, Eufaula's mill settlement occupied approximately 130 to 150 acres, bordered north to south by Barbour and Boundary Streets, and east and west by Randolph Street and Dale Road. The bulk of mill families lived inside this rectangular area—bracketed by the two mission churches. Some operatives' homes lay outside of Southside, along Barbour, Orange, and Union Streets. These neighborhoods all were within convenient walking distance of both mills, the churches, retail stores, and the Community House.[52]

---

[50] Alsobrook, "Southside and Eufaula's Cowikee Mills Village," 21–22.

[51] Ibid.; "Cowikee Mills Big Factor in Section's Life," *Eufaula Tribune*, Historical and Progress Edition, 5 December 1940, n.p.; *Alabama Official and Statistical Register, 1915* (Montgomery, AL: Brown Printing Company, 1915) 313, 320; *Alabama Official and Statistical Register, 1923* (Montgomery, AL: Brown Printing Company, 1923) 298, 306, 339; *Alabama Official and Statistical Register, 1951* (Alexander City, AL: Outlook Publishing Co., n.d.) 401, 435.

[52] Douglas Clare Purcell emails to the author, 25 October 2015. I am indebted to

"Below the tracks" often was used derisively by Old Eufaula's elites to pinpoint the mill settlement's location. However, the Central of Georgia Railroad actually encircled Southside in an oblong loop. With mill families also scattered beyond Southside's periphery, the tracks represented a symbolic, rather than a physical, line of demarcation between the two Eufaulas.[53]

The presence of Eufaula's large African-American population adds another significant historical metric to any analysis of Southside's geography and demographics. By 1910, over 60 percent of Barbour County's population were African Americans, including a sizable number of farmers. Factoring in the loss of several hundred black residents during the "Great Migration" to the North before World War I, African Americans in the town of Eufaula between 1920 and 1940 probably averaged around 55 to 60 percent of the total population. In contrast to residential patterns in many larger towns and cities in Alabama and the entire South, African Americans in Eufaula were not rigidly segregated in one or two neighborhoods.[54]

At least a decade before World War I, African Americans lived in "pockets" within Southside neighborhoods—with their largest concentration on the Bluff on Union and South Livingston Streets, along Boundary Street and Dale Road, and on Davis Street in "Comer Town," just west of South Eufaula Street.[55] These black residential patterns generally were still in place in the late 1940s. One Southsider who grew up in Comer Town after World War II recalls, "I guess the blacks were just scattered all about…, lived right next to us on Davis Street, and the white [Baptist] preacher on the other

---

Mr. Purcell for his cartographical expertise and his estimates on the approximate size of Southside.

[53] Alsobrook, "Southside and Eufaula's Cowikee Mills Village," 22.

[54] *Alabama Official and Statistical Register, 1915,* 313, 317, 320; "Exodus of Alabama Negroes Alarming," *Salisbury (NC) Evening Post,* 28 September 1916, 1; Edmund Haynes, "Conditions Among Negroes in the Cities," *Annals of the American Academy of Political and Social Science* 49 (September 1913): 105–19; Rabinowitz, *Race Relations in the Urban South,* 97–124. The newspaper article cited above indicated that by 1916 the "Great Migration" of African Americans had "reached Eufaula and Barbour County, and nearly every train to Montgomery carried a delegation of anywhere from 25 to 50 of them."

[55] 13th–16th US Census, 1910–1940, Schedule No. 1, Population, Barbour County, Alabama, NARA. This description of African-American residential patterns is based on an analysis of US Census records between 1910 and 1940.

side of us in the parsonage."[56] According to Wendell Franklin Wentz, who delivered groceries in the early 1950s from his family's meat market to homes throughout Southside, blacks and whites "lived elbow to elbow in many places."[57] Whites and African Americans in Southside peacefully co-existed but did not socialize; both races lived there out of economic necessity. Wentz later was amazed at adult Southsiders' reactions to African Americans:

> Children that grew up in that environment were used to blacks living next to them. When these same children grew up, graduated from college and moved to Montgomery, Birmingham, Columbus, Atlanta, etc., they protested when a black family moved into their communities, and hell, they lived next door to them in Eufaula. It was the damnedest thing I have ever witnessed…, and there they were howling, fussing, cussing, and screaming when a black moved within two blocks in the city.[58]

African Americans also lived in Old Eufaula. In several instances—probably a legacy of the era when their ancestors were enslaved—blacks owned small patches of property directly behind antebellum mansions. On one strip of land between Eufaula and Colby Streets, African Americans tilled gardens and raised livestock, in Wendell Wentz's words, "right there in the back yards of the rich folks."[59] Wentz, however, argues that such racially diverse neighborhoods actually were chimerical distortions that camouflaged the reality of segregation: "[T]here were three Eufaula[s].… One was white, one was black, and one was Southsiders who were the mill workers, and they were classed about [on] the same level as blacks."[60]

Wentz's "Three Eufaulas" was one of the residual legacies of the Bluff City's transformation into a New South cotton mill town. When Captain John Wesley Tullis and his associates prophesied in the 1880s that cotton mills would be Eufaula's salvation, they failed to foresee that a bitter divisiveness based on race and class would accompany the financial renaissance. By the time Donald Comer came to Eufaula in 1909, mill workers and their families already had been stereotyped and categorized as a particular genus

---

[56] Anonymous email to the author, 6 November 2015.
[57] Wendell Franklin Wentz email to the author, 6 November 2015.
[58] Ibid.
[59] Ibid.
[60] Wendell Franklin Wentz email to the author, 30 September 2015.

of "poor whites" and subjected to two decades of discrimination and ostracism. To his credit, Comer did all within his power to nurture and protect his mill families and to restore their sense of self-worth. Nevertheless, the daily rigors of life and survival in Southside within the caste system would severely test even the heartiest of souls. What transpired was not idyllic in any sense, but it ultimately became an important part of Eufaula's historical narrative.

Chapter 3

Like Threads in a Skein:
Southside's Families and Friends

Each of them has a story all his own.... Like a smooth-running river
that flows on and on. But under the surface the current flows. Sometimes
swift and angry and bitter.
—"Listen to the Loom" by Margaret Billingsley, 1953

By the mid-1890s, Southsiders had settled into a steady routine of living and working within Eufaula's proscribed system of caste, class, and race. Regardless of age, sex, or occupation, everyone had been absorbed into the rhythmical pulse of daily life in the mill village. Like martial bugle calls, the mills' shrill steam whistles announced the dawn and close of each day and the changing shifts. Their staccato melody echoed northward, past the First Baptist Church, along Randolph, Broad, and Eufaula Streets, and finally to the serene "City of the Dead," Fairview Cemetery, where Southsiders and Old Eufaulians slept side-by-side. Competing with the cacophony of whistles from locomotives, riverboats, and circus calliopes, the mill's clarions reminded Old Eufaulians that their venerable Bluff City was in the midst of a challenging, new industrial age.

For these scions of Eufaula's "pioneer families," Southside was akin to a foreign country or "Indian territory." From their perspective, all Southsiders were "factory people," even if they had never spent a single day at the looms. Yet, Old Eufaula desperately needed Southside's mills to drive the town's new economic engine. But what of the mill workers and other Southside residents? Although they also were essential to future financial prosperity, their presence threatened Old Eufaula's traditional social equilibrium.

In 1903, a Eufaula journalist ventured into Southside, "to see what was over there," suggesting the exploration of a mysterious uncharted land mass inhabited by an alien people. He was astounded to discover many neat, well kept homes, shops, and churches. He also offered this assessment of Southsiders: "[A]s a whole those are clever and energetic people and have been great factors in building up Eufaula and the vicinity."[1] However, his adding "as a whole" to this supposedly complimentary description of mill villagers was very revealing.

Old Eufaula awkwardly struggled to create a *lingua franca*, a "common language," for communicating with Southside. But seemingly earnest efforts to parley southward consistently struck discordant notes, illustrated by a *Eufaula Times and News* comment in 1917:

> [T]hose who live beyond the railroad in the southside of the city are not paupers or objects of charity. *They are as a general rule, with but few exceptions*, hard working self respecting people who are as good citizens as there are in Eufaula. They should justly resent a patronizing and condescending attitude toward them or any insinuation that they are residents in a pauperized section of the city.[2]

For Southsiders, such sermonettes drove a deeper wedge between themselves and Old Eufaula and intensified their desire to be totally self-sufficient. Sequestered inside the mill settlement, they turned inward and focused upon their basic material, emotional, and spiritual needs. But mill village life was neither idyllic nor romantic.

The epicenters of life in Southside were the two cotton mills. By all accounts, cotton mill jobs epitomized drudgery—monotonous, grueling, physically and mentally debilitating, and extremely hazardous. When interviewed by the Federal Writers' Project staff near the end of the Great Depression, Eufaula textile operatives spoke proudly but not affectionately about their jobs. Some even expressed a wistful desire to return to the land as farmers, thereby speaking volumes about the brutality of mill work.[3]

The dangers of the cotton mill rivaled coal mines and steel plants. Heavy machinery with exposed gears, teeth, belts, pulleys, and rollers threatened mill operatives' lives and limbs. Prior to the conversion from steam- to electrically powered looms, equipment mounted in the ceilings frequently

---

[1] *Eufaula Times and News*, n.d., c. 1903, quoted in Flewellen, *Along Broad Street*, 226.

[2] *Eufaula Times and News*, n.d., c. January 1917, quoted in ibid, 242. Italics added for emphasis by the author.

[3] For example, see B. T. Clements life history, "Three Workers of Cowikee Cotton Mill," interviewed by Gertha Couric, 13 October 1938, folder 10; and Tom Alsobrook family life history, 13 October 1938, folder 18, both in FWPP, SHC, UNC.

fell and maimed or killed people as they worked.[4] In mill card rooms, where razor-sharp machine blades combed dirt and other debris from cotton sheets, accidents ranged from lacerations to the traumatic removal of fingers, nails, and hands.[5] An Avondale Mill carding foreman claimed in 1935 that a mechanical malfunction rarely caused an accident, but "when one does occur it would seem that someone was sure to get killed." He described the terrifying moments following an equipment failure: "It is a fearful sight to see one of the belts on these high-speed machines break or come off and whip and curl like a snake…[and] a pulley…jump off a shaft and come across the floor like a cannonball."[6]

Beyond such obvious dangers, the mill workplace itself was an incubator for disease. For example, in the Eufaula and Chewalla Cotton Mills, workers shared common water buckets and dippers, and the only toilet facilities were fetid, vermin-infested outhouses—so-called "sanitary privies." Since many mill hands chewed tobacco and dipped snuff, weaving room floors were slathered with expectorate.[7]

Before the installation of automatic looms, weavers threaded yarn through shuttle eyes by mouth. Operatives referred to this process as "suck-shuttle time." Mrs. Clifford McLeod Anderson, a weaver in the Eufaula Cotton Mill, acquired her snuff habit to facilitate spitting wads of lint onto

---

[4] Jennings J. Rhyne, *Southern Cotton Mill Workers and Their Villages* (Chapel Hill: University of North Carolina Press, 1930) 10; Jacquelyn Dowd Hall, James Leloudis, Robert Korstad, Mary Murphy, Lu Ann Jones, and Christopher B. Daly, *Like a Family: The Making of a Southern Cotton Mill World* (Chapel Hill: University of North Carolina Press, 1987) 49; "Eufaula Man Injured," *Montgomery Advertiser*, 16 November 1910, 6. "Safety First," *Avondale Sun*, 14 December 1935, 1; 10 May 1937, 13.

[5] "Safety First," *Avondale Sun*, 4 November 1933, 1; Hall et al., *Like a Family*, 49, 82–83.

[6] Leonard E. Pittenger, "Accidents in the Card Room, Their Causes and Prevention," *Avondale Sun*, 16 February 1935, 1, 12.

[7] Rhyne, *Southern Cotton Mill Workers*, 10; Pat Keller, "The End of an Era: Milltown Life from 1914 to 1978," *Alabama Life* 1/1 (June—July 1978): 43; W. H. Oates, *Annual Report of the Factory Inspector of the State of Alabama For the Year Ending December 31st, 1912* (Montgomery, AL: Brown Printing Company, 1913) 19–21; Mrs. Lee Snipes [Carrie Belle Parish Snipes] life history, "Three Workers of Cowikee Cotton Mill," interviewed by Gertha Couric, 13 October 1938, folder 10; Nancy Nolan life history, "Mill Workers," interviewed by Gertha Couric, 20 October 1938, folder 13; both in FWPP, SHC, UNC.

the floor. She insisted that her physician recommended snuff as a hookworm preventative. Coated with thick layers of dried saliva, the shuttle eyes were not sanitized between shifts. After purchasing J. W. Tullis's mill, the fastidious Donald Comer was appalled by these filthy conditions in the weave room. He found that the placement of cuspidors adjacent to the looms failed to solve this problem.[8]

Operatives frantically struggled to maintain their footing upon slippery layers of coagulated tobacco juice and machine oil and grease. To keep the yarn pliant and fire retardant during the weaving process, textile engineers introduced humidification devices such as steam jets and sprinklers into the working environment. In the absence of adequate ventilation and air conditioning, weave rooms' temperatures hovered between seventy-five and eighty-five degrees, with a relative humidity of about sixty percent. Saturated with excessive heat and moisture, weave rooms produced numerous "slip and fall" accidents. Overheated, poorly lubricated looms also fired broken shuttles like shrapnel throughout the crowded workspace. Thus, some of the most hideous facial injuries in millwork resulted from "kissing the shuttle."[9]

In scenes reminiscent of Dante's *Inferno*, weavers labored for ten to twelve hours in this oppressively hot, humid, and noisy maelstrom. Some of the first scientific studies of mill workers' health in the 1920s determined that weavers were particularly susceptible to respiratory diseases—bronchitis, pneumonia, and tuberculosis. Female weavers also died of tuberculosis at a much higher rate than their male colleagues and at a higher rate than women who worked outside the mills. And at least eighty years before medical researchers discovered byssinosis, or "brown lung," mill operatives were inhaling large daily doses of cotton dust that would cause permanent disabili-

---

[8] Mr. and Mrs. James C. Hughes life history, interviewed by Gertha Couric, 20 October 1938, folder 11; Mr. and Mrs. Sam Anderson life history, interviewed by Gertha Couric, 21 October 1938, folder 12, both in FWPP, SHC, UNC; "Donald Comer Discusses Textile Work Tasks in Daily News Record," *Avondale Sun*, 6 October 1934, 1; Donald Comer, "Cotton Textile Mfg. During Last Fifty Years," *Avondale Sun*, 16 June 1952, 7.

[9] Elizabeth L. Otey, "Women and Children in Southern Industry," *Annuals of the American Academy of Political and Social Science* 153 (January 1931): 164–65; George V. S. Michaels, "Safegaurding [*sic*] Textile Employees," *Southern Textile Bulletin* 1 (20 April 1911): 5; Thomas Alsobrook to Oma Alsobrook, 8 October 1944, in author's possession.

ties and premature deaths.[10]

Eufaula mill workers who were spared from life-threatening maladies still experienced recurring illnesses that were directly attributable to their jobs. One Cowikee operative who moved to Florida before 1920, later recalled, "There used to be more sickness and death, and queer complaints there [Southside] than I ever saw anywhere else, in all my life."[11] She also commiserated with her niece, a young Cowikee weaver, who had chronic tonsillitis:

> I believe people have that ailment worse in Eufaula than any where else. I had it when we lived there so bad until my tonsils rose and festered like any other rising. I'd have burning fevers and hurt so bad from head to feet until I could hardly bear the pain. I had it so much until my tonsils shrank away to less than half their normal size, but I've never had it since I left there.[12]

During the 1920s and 1930s, Eufaula's mill employees logged extensive sick leave hours because of tonsillitis. Although, by that time, infected tonsils could be removed surgically, without antibiotics, these operations could be life threatening. In October 1934, five-year-old Jesse Reaves, Jr., the only child of Jesse and Alma Dunaway Reaves, died of pneumonia after a tonsillectomy. Physicians and social workers alike cited a lack of rigorous exercise and poor dietary habits as the primary causes of tonsillitis, bronchitis, and more serious respiratory diseases, including tuberculosis, among the Southern mill population. Close observers of the textile industry remained oblivious (at least publicly) to any direct correlation between the daily absorption of heavy concentrations of cotton lint into operatives' lungs and respiratory diseases.[13]

After finishing lengthy shifts in the mills, Eufaula's operatives were too exhausted for any kind of strenuous exercise regimen. While their diets were not carefully balanced, they were varied. Mill families consumed plentiful

---

[10] Otey, "Women and Children in Southern Industry," 165; Hall et al., *Like a Family*, 53, 81–82, 84; Flynt, *Poor but Proud*, 104, 112.

[11] "Aunt Lula" to "My Dear Niece" [Oma Parish Alsobrook], 17 January 1927, in author's possession.

[12] Ibid.

[13] "Jesse Reaves, Jr., Dies at Hospital Sunday Morning," *Avondale Sun*, 20 October 1934, 14; see, for example, Gilbert T. Rowe, "Cotton Mills of the South," *Charlotte Observer*, 2 August 1903, 7.

portions of salt pork, potatoes, and cornbread, along with fresh vegetables, eggs, and poultry from their backyard gardens and chicken coops. Many Southsiders also raised dairy cows and hogs. Therefore, their primary grocery purchases were sugar, syrup, flour, coffee, and beef, which was considered to be a luxury item.

Southside women usually prepared two meals a day. A typical pre-dawn breakfast consisted of fried or scrambled eggs, grits, bacon or sausage, biscuits or "hoecakes" (fried dough patties), and coffee. Fried or broiled fish roe (eggs) also became a popular breakfast delicacy. Menus for the noon meal, "dinner," featured a variety of choices: fried chicken, pork loin, or fish; collard or turnip greens; squash, rutabagas, okra, peas, butter beans, green beans, carrots, tomatoes, corn, white or sweet potatoes, cornbread, and buttermilk. A favorite Southside dessert was a small fried pie—dried apples or peaches enfolded in a greasy, crispy-brown envelope of dough. For "supper," the evening meal, re-heated dinner leftovers were served, usually with bowls of "pot-likker," a yellow-brown broth skimmed from the residue of collards or turnips.[14]

Southside diets generally provided enough carbohydrates, vitamins, minerals, and proteins to ensure relatively good health. However, high-cholesterol lard, butter, and salt pork were essential ingredients in food preparation. Therefore, while Southside's pellagra cases gradually declined after 1920, high blood pressure and heart disease steadily increased. Sedentary lifestyles, combined with heavy alcohol and tobacco usage, guaranteed that many Southsiders' lives would be terminated prematurely by strokes, heart attacks, and cancer.[15]

---

[14] Otey, "Women and Children in Southern Industry," 165; Mr. and Mrs. Sam Anderson life history, 21 October 1938, folder 12; Tom Alsobrook family life history, interviewed by Gertha Couric, 13 October 1938, folder 18, both in FWPP, SHC, UNC. This description of Southside culinary practices also is based upon my own memories of meals prepared by my maternal grandmother's cook, "Tildie" Jones, in the 1950s and 1960s.

[15] Hall et al., *Like a Family*, 150–51; Otey, "Women and Children in Southern Industry," 165; Flynt, *Poor but Proud*, 173–77; "Miss Curran Has Pellagra," *Montgomery Advertiser*, 18 September 1911, 8; Mr. And Mrs. W. S. Nolan life history, interviewed by Gertha Couric, n.d., c. 1938, Federal Writers' Project, Life Histories/Stories (Ex Slave Tales), Short Stories, Barbour County, box SG022774, WPA Files, ADAH; "Vital Statistics," 1938, FWP, State Guide File, Barbour County, box A15, WPA Records, LC.

A myriad of factors significantly affected the health and longevity of the mill village population—occupational hazards, nutrition, heredity, and personal lifestyle. Moreover, Eufaula's overall environment and infrastructure were key determinants in this equation. For over five decades, beginning in the late 1880s, the small town of Eufaula was choked with coal dust and smoke from mills, factories, foundries, locomotives, and residential stoves and fireplaces. Therefore, the very air that residents breathed was not conducive to good health.

Also, as "a town within a town," in regard to health and sanitation issues, the mill village was dependent upon Old Eufaula's municipal governance and political suzerainty. Issues that literally were of life and death importance were the purview of the mayor, city council, and an ad hoc health and sanitation board. Although the direct link between sanitation and disease had been an established article of faith for physicians and scientists since well before the Civil War, by 1900, other than quarantines, rudimentary preventative measures against epidemics had not been formulated in Eufaula. Between 1900 and 1918, periodic outbreaks of smallpox, diphtheria, typhoid fever, measles, and influenza threatened the entire town, not just the "Factory District."[16]

Sanitary water and sewage services were, of course, inimical to maintaining healthy conditions in any city or town. Since the 1870s, Eufaula's city officials had struggled financially and politically in ensuring that citizens had access to fresh water and adequate sewer lines. Similarly, the Bluff City's transition to the modern electrical age was slow and cumbersome. Except

---

[16] *Montgomery Advertiser*, 6 June 1903, 9; 20 June 1903, 10; 5 January 1907, 7; 16 September 1908, 7; "Smallpox in Barbour," *Montgomery Advertiser*, 2 March 1910, 11; "Pupils Must Be Vaccinated," *Montgomery Advertiser*, 18 September 1910, 2; "Eufaula Is Facing Smallpox Epidemic," *Atlanta Constitution*, 14 January 1912, 8; "Eufaula Schools Close," *Montgomery Advertiser*, 13 February 1912, 3; "Smallpox Epidemic Keeps Schools Closed," *Atlanta Constitution*, 19 February 1912, 4; "A Bride of Four Months Dead," *Columbus Daily Enquirer*, 25 August 1901, 3; "News of Eufaula," *Montgomery Advertiser*, 16 April 1910, 3; "Entire Family Ill from Well Water," *Columbus Ledger*, 6 November 1913, 7; Dr. W. S. Britt to Editor, 27 June 1914, *Montgomery Advertiser*, 29 June 1914, 4; "James E. Fuller," obituary, *Columbus Daily Enquirer*, 21 November 1914, n.p.; "Eufaula Schools Are Dismissed on Account of Measles," *Montgomery Advertiser*, 8 December 1917, 2; "Two Children Die within One Week," *Montgomery Advertiser*, 8 January 1918, 5; "Measles Close Eufaula Schools," *Montgomery Advertiser*, 10 January 1918, 3.

during World War I, coal was cheap and plentiful. Converting the town's gas and lighting plant from coal and steam to electricity was expensive, primarily because of the requisite skilled labor, engineering expertise, and new equipment. Nevertheless, by around 1910, most of Old Eufaula's commercial and residential areas were connected to the city's electrical, water, and sewer lines. Delivering a full range of utilities and paving south of Broad Street presented a far greater challenge.[17]

Although Southside's second and third ward councilmen fought tenaciously for improved municipal services in the mill village, city officials' main priorities lay in Old Eufaula. To be fair, many Southsiders could not afford higher tax levies and consistently voted against proposed bond issues to fund expanded utilities and paving projects. Consequently, in the early 1920s, Southside's power, water, and sewer grids remained incomplete, with many residents relying upon gas or kerosene lighting, wells, cisterns, and privies. The first electrical streetlights in Comer Town were installed in 1927. Paving was also non-existent except for portions of South Eufaula and South Randolph Streets and Dale Road. With the establishment of the Barbour County Board of Health in 1922, the enforcement of standard sanitation regulations and mandatory immunizations dramatically reduced the dangers of deadly epidemics throughout Eufaula.[18]

Survival in Southside encompassed more than overcoming the rigors of an unhealthy environment, antiquated infrastructure, and a dangerous workplace. Just below the surface of daily life lay a complex undercurrent of social

---

[17] Flewellen, *Along Broad Street*, 140–41, 176–79, 195–99, 218–19, 249–52; "Eufaula, Ala.," *Macon Telegraph*, 17 February 1888, 3; 10 March 1888, 3; 23 March 1888, 3; 14 November 1888, 8; *Montgomery Advertiser*, 3 February 1910, 9; "Eufaula," 8 September 1910, 7; "Eufaula Light Plant Burns," *Montgomery Advertiser*, 10 February 1911, 10; "Eufaula in Total Darkness," 18 April 1911, 9; "Eufaula Gets Bond Money," *Montgomery Advertiser*, 30 September 1911, 2; "Great White Way at Eufaula Flashes Forth," *Montgomery Advertiser*, 21 June 1912, 7; "Eufaula Lighted Like Montgomery Is," *Montgomery Advertiser*, 10 July 1912, 4; "E[u]faula's Mayor Sounds Economy As a Keynote," *Montgomery Advertiser*, 18 April 1913, 3.

[18] Flewellen, *Along Broad Street*, 249–52; "Eufaula, Ala.," *Macon Telegraph*, 8 January 1905, 7; "Eufaula Planning for Street Paving," *Montgomery Advertiser*, 18 January 1921, 5; "Personals," and "Spooler Room," *Avondale Sun*, 4 November 1927, n.p.; Tom Alsobrook family life history, 13 October 1938, folder 18, FWPP, SHC, UNC; "Public Health," 1939, FWP, State Guide File, Barbour County, box A15, WPA Records, LC.

and psychological pressures that exacted a heavy toll upon Eufaula's mill villagers. In the late nineteenth and early twentieth centuries, Eufaula was still quite isolated, connected only by the railroad and the river to larger cities and towns in Alabama, Georgia, and Florida. At that time, vehicular travel on unimproved roads could best be described as an adventure. Since they were not welcome in the homes, society, businesses, and churches of Old Eufaula, Southsiders experienced a deeper degree of isolation. Many of these people were familiar with the loneliness of rural life in which their closest neighbors were several miles away. However, they now were victims of a far crueler isolation—within a populated town.[19]

Furthermore, the boredom and repetitive cycles of their work and daily existence grew increasingly oppressive. Perhaps most importantly, very few secrets existed in Southside—there was simply no personal privacy. Living in close quarters in which a next-door neighbor's snoring could be clearly heard can be emotionally suffocating. Marital infidelities, spousal abuses, alcohol and drug addictions, unwanted pregnancies, mental breakdowns, and personal medical histories were all subject to public discussion in Southside. Before World War I, when mill hand Curtis T. James suffered a "spell" and frantically ran around his yard for two hours, his neighbors watched and then openly gossiped about what type of malady had befallen him. In the late 1920s, Community House director Mary Lanier suffered multiple nervous breakdowns; the *Avondale Sun*, carried stories about each episode and details of her medical treatment.[20] Children were not exempt from public scrutiny. In May 1921, the *Southside News* printed this comment about Mr. and Mrs. J. W. Lindsay's young daughter: "We were interested in noting the improvement in Mary's eyes; while far from normal they are much better; she can see well enough to get around by herself."[21]

Although such remarks were not mean-spirited or intentionally intrusive, mill villagers carefully took note of them. Many Southsiders graciously accepted printed "personals" as evidence of the mill village's nurturing sup-

---

[19] Flewellen, *Along Broad Street*, 115–16, 186.

[20] Flynt, *Poor but Proud*, 99–100, 103; Hall et al., *Like a Family*, 172; "Aunt Lula" to "My Dear Niece [Oma Parish Alsobrook], 17 January 1927, in author's possession; "Personals," *Avondale Sun*, 23 October 1925, 10; 11 June 1926, 3; 25 June 1926, 8; "Community House," *Avondale Sun*, 30 October 1925, 10; 4 December 1925, 10; *Avondale Sun*, 8 January 1926, 7; 18 June 1926, 10; 2 July 1926, 8.

[21] "Here and There," *(Eufaula) Southside News*, 1/9 (May 1921): 2.

port system. But for those individuals who had grown more alienated and disillusioned, their personal privacy was very important and worth preserving—even if they had to leave Eufaula.

Mill families generally were a restless, nomadic band—frequently moving and seeking more attractive job opportunities, homes, and communities. They definitely ascribed to the "grass is greener" concept. During the early 1900s, when the Eufaula and Chewalla Cotton Mills encountered financial difficulties, a number of Southside operatives "floated" to other textile sites—Huntsville, Selma, and Columbus—and quickly found employment. The majority of these workers later returned to Eufaula, such as John Thomas Alsobrook and Thomas Mallie Parish who moved to Huntsville around 1903. They both were back at work in the Eufaula Cotton Mill when the new owner Donald Comer arrived in 1908. Through the early 1920s, Southsiders were on the move—to other mills, back to farms, and within the village itself.[22]

During the 1920s, a pattern emerged in which Southsiders frequently moved to new addresses inside the mill village. Apparently, houses did not remain vacant very long. In spring 1926, an *Avondale Sun* reporter described this process:

> There has been quite a lot of moving in the community lately. The Adams family have moved to Comer Town in the house the Boland family previously occupied. The Edwards family have moved into the house the Adams family formerly occupied on Davis Street. The Tharps have moved into one of the new houses in Morning Side. The Lockwoods have moved into their new house at the chicken farm. Mr. Bert Worbington and family will

---

[22] MacDonald, *Southern Mill Hills*, 147; Flynt, *Poor but Proud*, 96, 98; J. Craig Smith, "Southern Cotton Mills and the People Who Work in Them," address to Birmingham Kiwanis Club, 6 September 1932, *Avondale Sun*, 10 September 1932, 11; Frank Tannenbaum, "The South Buries Its Anglo-Saxons," *Century* 106 (June 1923): 206; "Plant at Eufaula Will Be Idle till September," *Columbus Ledger*, 24 June 1903, 6; "Here and There," *Southside News*, 1/9 (May 1921): 2–3; "Personals," *Avondale Sun*, 14 May 1926, 7; 4 February 1927, 8; 16 February 1929, 5; "Weave Room," 13 July 1928, n.d. John Thomas Alsobrook and Thomas Mallie Parish were my great-grandfathers. For an in-depth analysis of job opportunities in Huntsville's mills at that time, see Whitney Adrienne Snow, "Cotton Mill City: The Huntsville Textile Industry, 1880–1989," *Alabama Review* 63/14 (October 2010): 248–53.

occupy the Lockwood house.[23]

Given readers' familiarity with their Southside neighbors, the reporter obviously saw no need to print specific addresses. Almost a year later, residential relocations continued at a steady pace with similar results. Will and Emma Smith's family moved in with her mother, Mary Toler, on South Randolph Street. After the Reverend Junior James "moved to the country" from Washington Street, his home was quickly occupied by a family identified as "the Kennedys."[24] Donald Comer's popular home ownership loan program probably accelerated these chain-reaction moves in Southside, which continued apace into the late 1940s and early 1950s.[25]

During the years when so many Southsiders were transients, the two mission churches—originally established in the 1890s—played pivotal roles in maintaining the mill village's solidarity. Built within a block of each other on South Eufaula Street, the Washington Street Methodist and Second Baptist Churches became aggressive competitors during their early years. According to a witty contemporary aphorism, when the Washington Street choir sang, "Will there be any stars in my crown?" from down the street came the Second Baptists' full-throated refrain, "No, not one, No, not one." These two circuit churches were not founded by mere coincidence in 1893–1894. By that time, with the Eufaula and Chewalla Cotton Mills fully operational, new workers continued to stream into Barbour County. Old Eufaula's downtown Methodist and Baptist congregations adamantly opposed adding mill families and other Southsiders to their membership rolls. Therefore, the Eufaula Methodist and First Baptist Churches organized elaborate fund-raising campaigns to build two Southside chapels as "mission" projects. Despite his lengthy service as a Methodist layman, Donald Comer evinced no favoritism toward the Washington Street venture. He later contributed equal portions of Cowikee Mills' commissary profits to both churches.[26]

---

[23] "Personals" *Avondale Sun*, 14 May 1926, 7. The new Morningside neighborhood was located at the end of South Randolph Street.

[24] "Personals," *Avondale Sun*, 4 February 1927, 8.

[25] "Weave Room," *Avondale Sun*, 13 July 1928, n.p.; "Personals," *Avondale Sun*, 16 February 1929, 5; "Granddaddy DeVenny's Life," 2000 typescript, attached to, Jeanine Smith DeVenny email to the author, 16 February 2016.

[26] Smartt, *History of Eufaula*, 124–25; Purcell, "History of Eufaula First Methodist

Like other mill owners of his time, Comer undoubtedly was very comfortable with the Southside churches' basic gospel message extolling the virtues of sobriety, duty, and thrift while excoriating a litany of worldly pleasures. Preachers in a thousand mill villages across the South delivered similar messages to their flocks. As one sociologist noted in 1929, "[I]t was a gospel of work, of gratitude for present blessings, and of patience with economic and social maladjustment as temporal and outside the sphere of religious concerns."[27]

The Southside gospel also was an heir to the impassioned sermons of enslaved preachers before the Civil War who exhorted their small congregations to bear all earthly sorrows and burdens with patience and dignity in anticipation of future heavenly glories. Yet, as they gave full voice to the "Negro" spirituals in their hymnals, Southsiders remained blithely unaware of their historical kinship with African Americans.[28]

The Southside gospel essentially served as a social control mechanism that encouraged workers to lead orderly, productive, and sanctified lives. The gospel thus dovetailed perfectly with mill owners' opposition to anything perceived as disruptive to productivity—demon rum, unions, Pentecostal sects, generally known as "Holy Rollers," and wild-eyed traveling evangelists.[29]

During the 1920s, Eufaula's chapter of the Knights of the Ku Klux Klan periodically voiced its support for Southside gospel's advocacy for moral reform. In September 1924, robed Klansmen interrupted a revival service at Washington Street Methodist Church and presented the Reverend C. N.

Church," 14; Oma Alsobrook, "Brief History of Washington Street Methodist Church," 1; A. E. Barlar, "Washington Street Church," *Eufaula Tribune*, Historical and Progress Edition, 5 December 1940, 7; "Parkview Baptist Church Centennial," 2–4; Wendell Franklin Wentz email to the author, 21 February 2015; "Eufaula," *The WPA Guide to 1930s Alabama* (1941; repr. Tuscaloosa: University of Alabama Press, 2000) 341.

[27] Harriet L. Herring, *Welfare Work in Mill Villages: The Story of Extra-Mill Activities in North Carolina* (Chapel Hill: University of North Carolina Press, 1929) 99.

[28] By the late 1930s, at least four hymns categorized as "Negro" spirituals were popular with Methodists and Baptists: "Down by the River-Side," "I Know the Lord's Laid His Hands on Me," "Lord, I Want to Be a Christian," and "Swing Low, Sweet Chariot" (*Cokesbury Worship Hymnal* [1938; repr., Nashville, TN: Abington Press, 1966] 255–59).

[29] Hall et al., *Like a Family*, 124, 177–79; Herring, *Welfare Work in Mill Villages*, 100–101; Cash, *The Mind of the South*, 296–99.

Williams with a check for twenty-five dollars and a letter "complimenting him on the excellent service he is giving to the community."[30] The Klan had barged into a house of worship, but apparently this brazen act was not considered to be "disruptive," undoubtedly because the hooded Knights hailed from Southside and Old Eufaula.

The historical record lacks any specific details about the service the Reverend Williams rendered that earned the Klan's commendation. Like other Southside clergymen, he delivered sermons based on the Ten Commandments, the "rules of the church," and the "doctrine of the Bible," which specifically addressed the necessity of resisting all manner of secular temptations. His sermons in 1924 were sprinkled profusely with phrases that bespoke the Southside gospel: "the victory of self over sin," "the reward gained by right-living and sacrificing unto the Lord," the community's need, like the prophet Isaiah, for "a cleaning and a revelation," and being in the "right places...where Jesus can be found."[31] When John Thomas Alsobrook and six other new converts joined the Washington Street Methodist Church in September 1924, they were welcomed as those "who have aligned themselves with us for the repulsion of sin in our community."[32]

---

[30] "Religious," *Avondale Sun*, 12 September 1924, 4. The KKK had a strong presence in Barbour County dating back to the Reconstruction era. The so called "new" Klan, re-instituted in 1915, recruited members in the 1920s from both Old Eufaula and Southside. Eufaula's KKK chapter publicized its self-appointed role as an enforcer of the community's moral standards and downplayed any of its racist, anti-Semitic, anti-Catholic, and xenophobic policies. The Eufaula KKK actively campaigned in behalf of its members who were candidates for local offices, such as Barbour County superintendent of roads. F. B. Cullens to the editor, 12 October 1921, *Montgomery Advertiser*, 16 October 1921, 4; "Miss Annie Britt Standifer Chosen as Beauty Queen," *Avondale Sun*, 12 October 1925, 10; W. C. Standifer to Cecil L. Davis, 3 March 1927; Calvin C. Scheffer to Governor Bibb Graves, 23 March 1927, both in "KKK 1927," Governor Bibb Graves Administrative Files, box SG021164, Alabama Department of Archives and History (ADAH), Montgomery, AL; Ginny Dunaway Young emails to the author, 19 February, 9 May 2015.

[31] Quotes or paraphrases from Williams's sermons (in order) in *Avondale Sun*, "Mother's Day Observed," 16 May 1924, 10; "Religious," 24 October 1924, 8; "Church News," 26 September 1924, 8; 7 November 1924, 8.

[32] "Washington Street M. E. Church, South," *Avondale Sun* 19 September 1924, 8. It is unclear if these words were written by the Reverend Williams or a member of his congregation.

The rough-hewn, morose Alsobrook was an unlikely recruit for Washington Street's morality campaign. He and barber Amos Starnes could best be described as "reluctant" or "casual" Christians. They smoked, drank occasionally, and primarily attended worship services at their wives' insistence. When Starnes reached Eufaula at age twenty-four in 1913, after a decade of wandering from South Carolina to Texas as an itinerant laborer, Jim K. and Nora Hatfield assessed him as a ne'er-do-well drifter and a "rounder." They were horrified when he courted and married their seventeen-year-old daughter, Willie Mae, a year later.[33]

Willie Mae Starnes entered the mills as a child and worked for Donald Comer as a weaver for over thirty years. After her husband was rejected for military service because of flat feet during World War I, she encouraged him to attend barber school in Columbus, Georgia. Amos Starnes later purchased the Bluff City Inn's barber shop, in partnership with Coy "Slick" Etheridge. Carefully marshaling their meager financial resources, the Starneses sent both of their children to college during the Great Depression. Despite the Hatfields' dire predictions, the Starneses were married for almost sixty years. Their entire family worshiped together at Washington Street Methodist, but in contrast to his abiding wife's faith, the church never became a focal point in Amos Starnes's life.[34]

Starnes and John Thomas Alsobrook were two prime examples of Southsiders who attended church but did not respond enthusiastically to evangelical appeals from the pulpit. However, others took deeper bites of the Southside gospel's apple and subsequently became dedicated Methodist and Baptist lay leaders. Thomas Mallie Parish and Eddie Cox—friends and neighbors of Starnes and Alsobrook—devoted much of their adult lives to Washington Street Methodist as stewards and Sunday school teachers and superintendents. Cox also held the distinction of serving in similar leadership positions at Second Baptist between around 1915 and the late 1920s. Joseph D. Porter, D. F. "Doc" Barker, and Dan Jimmerson were three of the most influential laymen during Second Baptist's formative years. In the early

---

[33] Ginny Dunaway Young, "Ancestors of David Ernest Alsobrook," in author's possession.

[34] Ibid.; Amos Webster Starnes's World War I Draft Registration Card, 5 June 1917, Record Group 163, National Archives and Records Administration, Morrow, GA. All other draft registration cards herein cited are from this depository, hereafter referred to as NARA, Morrow, GA.

1920s, Barker donated the first pastorium for the church on Davis Street, in Comer Town and served as a deacon and Sunday school superintendent. Broad-shouldered and heavy-set, with a blacksmith's powerful hands and arms, he sported a thick brush mustache and dark, neatly trimmed hair. The proprietor of a lucrative livery stable and grocery on South Randolph Street, Barker in essence was the unelected "Mayor of Southside" during the 1920s and 1930s. Indomitable and fearless, his generosity toward anyone in need of food, shelter, firewood, or a job became legendary.[35]

The popularity of "Doc" Barker, Dan Jimmerson, and Joe Porter— Eufaula's last surviving Confederate veteran—attracted a number of families residing in Comer Town and along South Randolph and South Eufaula Streets to Second Baptist. However, a great deal of fluidity existed in the two Baptist and Methodist congregations' membership, exemplified by Eddie Cox's shifting affiliations and married couples of different denominations' valiant attempts to accommodate each other's faiths. In 1898, Thomas Mallie Parish, a Washington Street charter member, married Jessie Estelle Gillis, who was reared in a Baptist household near Glennville, Alabama. They decided to retain their separate church memberships. When Jessie Parish died at age sixty-eight in 1939, the Reverend C. O. English, the Second Baptist pastor, conducted her funeral, assisted by the Washington Street minister, J. O. Wilson. She was eulogized as "a member of the Baptist church, [who] always lent her influence to both churches in the community in any way possible...." Like her Methodist husband, she remained "unswerving and loyal at all times" to the church of her youth.[36] Jessie Parish's

[35] "Parkview Baptist Church Centennial," 3, 5–7; Alsobrook, "A Brief History of Washington Street Methodist Church," 1–2; "Anti-Can't" Bible Class, photograph with membership roster, *Southside News* 1/9 (May 1921): 4; "Washington Street Stewards and Pastor," photograph with membership roster, *Avondale Sun*, 6 March 1935, 6; *Southside News* 1/5 (10 January 1921): n.p., reprinted in *Avondale Sun*, 10 December 1945, 7; "Eddie Cox," *Avondale Sun*, 11 August 1941, 12; 27 February 1950, 2; June Barker Clenney email to the author, 4 August 2015, with biographical material about her grandfather, D. F. "Doc" Barker; "Men of Rival Stables Engage in A Shooting," *Montgomery Advertiser*, 24 January 1914, 10. In January 1914, Barker sustained a compound fracture to his leg after an argument with a rival mule trader in front of the court house escalated into a shooting "affray."

[36] "Mrs. Mallie Parrish [*sic*] Passed Last Week," *Avondale Sun*, 6 November 1939, 6 (quotes); "Deaths in the Valley, Mrs. Mallie Parish," *Columbus Daily Enquirer*, 22 Octo-

funeral service was held at her home rather than at Second Baptist or Washington Street—a common practice at that time.

Like the Parishes, other Southside couples of different faiths worked out their own attendance arrangements between the two churches. In autumn 1938, Tyson Smith, whose parents were Washington Street founding members, married Hallie Hartsfield, a devout Baptist. Although they kept their original memberships, Tyson and Hallie Smith also occasionally worshiped together at both churches. Tyson Smith later explained that they remained in separate churches because Washington Street and Second Baptist both needed their financial support.[37]

The lively, legendary competition between the two churches probably added further pressure to the Smiths, Parishes, and other couples in reaching decisions about their memberships and attendance. For recruitment campaigns, both churches were ideally located in the heart of Southside. Therefore, the distance between homes and the churches did not play a major role in Southsiders' religious affiliations. Of far greater importance were families' ancestral ties to the Baptist and Methodist faiths. Anomalies and exceptions existed within each family, but generally, for example, the Parishes, Dunaways, and Corbitts attended Washington Street Methodist, and the Barkers, DeVennys, and Wentzes chose Second Baptist. Barbour County's large Hatfield contingent, with its multiple branches, matriarchs, and patriarchs, joined both churches, with perhaps a greater number at Washington Street. These denominational affiliations of only seven Southside families are merely suggestive of patterns or trends in church membership that significantly shifted after several generations. Moreover, beginning in the 1920s, beloved, charismatic pastors such as Washington Street's Arthur Bennett Carlton and Second Baptist's William Thomas James personally recruited new Southside converts to their respective congregations.[38]

Each of Southside's churches featured an array of Sunday school classes, Bible study groups, and missionary and charitable circles. Second Baptist's Women's Missionary Union (WMU) emerged during the 1920s as one

---

ber 1939, 11; Young, "Ancestors of David Ernest Alsobrook," in author's possession.

[37] "Hartsfield-Smith Marriage," *Avondale Sun*, 10 October 1938, 10; Jeanine Smith DeVenny email to the author, 4 March 2014.

[38] Oma Alsobrook, "A Brief History of Washington Street Methodist Church," 1–2; "Parkview Baptist Church Centennial," 6.

of the church's most prominent organizations. Between 1920 and 1940, the WMU's tireless leaders included Drucie Porter Hughes, Florence Ginwright Wentz, Myrtle Poteat Barker, Nola Blanton DeVenny, and Callie Conner. At Washington Street after World War I, the "Anti-Can't" Bible Class produced several talented members who helped shape the church's future development—Arthur Eugene Barlar, Florida Dewar, J. R. "Bob" Hatfield, Mallie Parish, Myrtle Bell, Annie Slay, Albert Hatfield, and Lola Lewis. These Methodists and Baptists represented only a handful of the men and women who faithfully spent their lives in service to these circuit churches.[39]

Since many Southsiders originally came from rural communities, they incorporated many of their old traditions into the churches in Eufaula. "Dinner on the grounds," "all-night and all-day sings," extended wakes, or "sitting up" with the bereaved and the deceased, and "pound parties" for new preachers' families all became commonplace in Southside churches. Sundays in Southside were reserved for worship, rest, and visiting with families and friends on the churches' grounds or on front porches.[40]

Music was an essential element in Southside churches' worship services, revivals, and social activities. Many talented young musicians in the 1920s and 1930s—J. T. Dunaway, Cleveland Adams, Elbert "Red" Beasley, Lewis Simpkins, Fannie and Ruby Corbitt, and Earl and Frances Starnes—participated in Washington Street Methodist's elaborate musical programs. They perfected their skills on the piano and various other instruments and sang in the choir. Many of these youngsters also performed at the Second

---

[39] "Women's Missionary Society," photo, *Avondale Sun*, 1 February 1937, 6; "Second Baptist Church WMU," *Eufaula Tribune*, Historical and Progress Edition, 5 December 1940, n.p.; "Anti-Can't" Bible Class, photo with membership roster, *Southside News* 1/9 (May 1921): 4.

[40] Gilbert T. Rowe, "Cotton Mills of the South," *Charlotte Observer*, 2 August 1903, 7; Flynt, *Poor but Proud*, 98; Herring, *Welfare Work in Mill Villages*, 87; Hall et al., *Like a Family*, 20–21, 146, 152, 169; "New Methodist Pastor Pounded upon Arrival," *Avondale Sun*, 11 December 1925, 10; "Sacred Harp Singers Meet," *Columbus Daily Enquirer*, 26 October 1938, 8; Gertha Couric and Luther Clark, "All Day Singing," 29 June 1939, Federal Writers' Project, Life Histories/Stores (Ex. Slave Tales), Short Stories, Barbour County, box SG022774, WPA Files, ADAH; Wendell Franklin Wentz email to the author, 22 February 2016. "Pound Parties" originated with the Quakers, and the attendees furnished new arrivals in town with "pounds" of groceries for their pantries. By the late nineteenth century, such social events had spread from the Carolinas to East Alabama.

Baptist Church and in the downtown houses of worship.

But it was the old traditional hymns that most inspired Southsiders, and Baptists and Methodists alike sang many of the same old standards—"The Old Rugged Cross," "Blessed Assurance," "In the Garden," "I Love to Tell the Story," "Sweet Hour of Prayer," "Work, for the Night Is Coming," "Amazing Grace," "I'll Fly Away," and many others. Jeanine Smith DeVenny recalls in the 1950s sitting in a pew beside her father at Washington Street and "hearing his bass voice" as he sang "The Church in the Wildwood," and on another occasion when her brother Tyson's "sweet young voice fill[ed] the church" with the lovely verses of "In the Garden." Her "many memories from that sweet little church" include tall, willowy Ruby Corbitt Beverly playing the piano "with gusto" and diminutive Estelle Ward, who "was small in stature," but whose lilting soprano voice "could be heard...clear to the Baptist Church."[41]

From his front porch across the street, teenager Wendell Franklin Wentz listened to the Methodists' revival hymns: "It was warm on those nights, and the church windows were open, and I could hear every word being sung."[42] "Pentecostal Power," "This Is My Father's World," "Dwelling in Beulah Land," "My Savior's Love," and "I Know the Lord's Laid His Hands on Me," soon were added to his favorites list. Before leaving for Mercer University and preparation for the Baptist ministry, Wentz often attended revivals at Washington Street where he was impressed with the music and the sermons. When Wentz was eighteen years old, Will Smith, his Methodist neighbor, invited him to an "all-day singing and dinner on the grounds" at a country church. He never forgot that particular experience—the long, waist-high tables piled with "so much food," and the joyous fellowship and singing that lasted until dusk.[43]

Many Southsiders considered music, particularly the beautiful old hymns, to be their churches' finest gift to their people. Of course, the two churches furnished many other memorable gifts to Southsiders—spiritual guidance and consolation to families after shattering personal losses, food,

---

[41] June Barker Clenney email to the author, 20 February 2016; Jeanine Smith DeVenny, "Hymns from My Childhood," attached to email to author, 26 February 2016.

[42] Wendell Franklin Wentz, "Favorite Hymns of Childhood," attached to email to author, 22 February 2016.

[43] Ibid.; Wendell Franklin Wentz second email to the author, 22 February 2016.

clothing, and shelter to the destitute, and fellowship and organized social activities for everyone. Providing a social life for the mill village was especially important prior to the establishment of the Cowikee Community House in 1918. Both churches reinforced the village's inner life that was deeply rooted in family ties. Kinship had shaped the original migration of mill families to Eufaula in the late 1880s and early 1890s and remained a powerful unifying force in village society.[44]

Between around 1890 and 1945, through blood ancestries, marriages, and cherished friendships, virtually everyone in Southside was connected in some fashion. And in many cases, the bonds of friendship, like marriages, reached across generations. An examination of selected mill village families reveals the resiliency of these relationships. This analysis also provides evidence of a propensity among mill villagers for alcoholism, drug addiction, violence, and other negative traits stereotypically attributed to poor whites. Still, a richer, more nuanced narrative emerges of people who exhibited unusual strength and fortitude in the face of adversity and tragedy.

In fall 1953, one of Donald Comer's weavers wrote movingly about her personal impressions of the cotton mill experience and its people. She recorded one particularly salient point about the individual textile worker: "Each of them has a story all his own and…it gets into the mill and becomes part of an intimate and subdued drama…. It has always been there. Like a smooth-running river that flows on and on. But under the surface the currents flow. Sometimes swift and angry and bitter."[45]

And the mill families had their own stories as well. These family narratives seldom provide dramatic insight into historically significant events or roles of prominent leaders at the state or national levels. However, in their basic simplicity and grittiness, these stories speak directly to the universality of the human experience and spirit.

Almarine Parish and Epsie Matthews were born in the Wiregrass section of South Alabama in the early 1850s. After their marriage around 1873, the Parishes lived in Covington, Dallas, and Crenshaw counties, in the city of Montgomery, and by the early 1900s, on Dale Road in Eufaula. As with

---

[44] See Hall et al., *Like a Family*, 140, for an examination of this trend in other mill villages.

[45] Margaret Billingsley, "Listen to the Loom," *Avondale Sun*, 30 November 1953, 3. She was employed in the Eva Jane Weave Room in Sylacauga, AL.

other impoverished farm and mill families, the Parishes continually searched for better financial opportunities. They operated a boarding house in Montgomery and a grocery in Eufaula. The Parishes had ten children, two of whom died in infancy. In 1893, their sixteen-year-old daughter, Alma, known as "Allie," married John Frank Dunaway in Selma. Over the next two decades, they had five children, including the precocious musician, J. T. Dunaway, who was born in 1902.[46]

A number of Dunaways and Parishes were mill operatives in Eufaula and other towns at some point in their lives. John Frank Dunaway, who came to the Bluff City in the 1880s, served as a weaving foreman at the Chewalla Mill. He also was employed for several years at John P. Foy's Eufaula Oil and Fertilizer Company. Dunaway and his relatives all bore the brunt of the mills' harsh working conditions and the ostracism of living in Southside. Carrie Belle Parish, one of Almarine and Epsie's daughters, worked first as a child operative for Captain J. W. Tullis and then after 1909, for Donald Comer, ultimately serving about forty years as a weaver. She took great pride in her textile career, but she bitterly recalled that many Eufaulians outside the mill village considered Southsiders to be disreputable and untrustworthy.[47]

The Parishes, Dunaways, and other mill families were proud of their work, but tensions sometimes brewed on and off the job—leading to tragic consequences. Carrie's older brother, twenty-two-year-old Turner Parish, was employed at Chewalla Mill. On 12 July 1906, he fatally shot Courtney Harrison after an altercation in a brothel near Eufaula. The *Montgomery Advertiser* described Harrison, a local shoemaker's son, as "wild and reckless." As for his assailant, the paper reported that "little has been known of Parrish [*sic*]. He is a factory operative and enjoyed the reputation of being quiet and orderly."[48] A few months later, on 20 March 1907, while released from jail on bond for Harrison's murder, Parish attacked Chewalla Mill superintendent Dan Poole with a knife while in a drunken rage. Bleeding profusely from a gaping wound in his neck, Poole fired five rounds from his revolver at

---

[46] Young, "Descendants of Almarine Parish," in author's possession; Ginny Dunaway Young emails to the author, 27 July 2012, 7 May 2015, 2 February 2016.

[47] Ginny Dunaway Young emails to the author, 19 June 2013, 2 February 2016; Mrs. Lee Snipes [Carrie Belle Parish Snipes] life history, 13 October 1938, folder 10, FWPP, SHC, UNC.

[48] "Killing in Eufuala [*sic*]," *Montgomery Advertiser*, 13 July 1906, 2.

Parish, "killing him almost instantly." Poole, who recovered from his wound, was cleared of any charges three days later after authorities ruled that he killed Parish in self-defense.[49]

This was not the only fatality that the Parish and Dunaway families had to face in 1907. On 9 March 1907, shortly before Turner Parish's shooting death, John Frank Dunaway's younger brother, William, took his own life with an overdose of morphine. He had grown increasingly despondent over his indebtedness and was drinking heavily in the days leading up to his suicide. He left behind a widow and four young children. In a firm cursive hand, the Barbour County coroner entered the names of William C. Dunaway, age thirty-five, and Turner Parish, age twenty-three, on consecutive lines of his mortuary ledger for March 1907.[50] Then less than six months later, O. V. Parish, Almarine and Epsie Parish's three-year-old grandson, died after being severely burned. His grieving parents, Willie and Katie Parish, accompanied their child's small casket on the train to Montgomery for burial at Oakwood Cemetery. The inscription on the young boy's headstone read: "Sleep on sweet babe and take thy rest; God called thee because he thought it best."[51]

By fall 1907, the Parishes and Dunaways had exhausted their spiritual and emotional resources. Fortunately, the majority of the surviving family members, with only three exceptions, survived well into their sixties, and several lived much longer, such as Epsie Parish, who died at eighty-two in 1936. She survived her husband by twenty-five years. He perished in 1910 at age fifty-eight from arteriosclerosis, nephritis, and cirrhosis of the liver. Willie Parish, forty-one, was interred next to his son in 1924, and Cliff Parish's wife, Villie Hatfield Parish, died in 1941 when she was fifty.[52]

---

[49] "Tragedy in Eufaula," *Montgomery Advertiser*, 21 March 1907, 2 (quote); "Poole Is Released," *Montgomery Advertiser*, 22 March 1907, 2.

[50] "Register of Deaths," March 1907, Barbour County Coroner, copy from Ginny Dunaway Young Collection.

[51] "Boy Dies of Burns," *Montgomery Advertiser*, 12 September 1907, 9; "O. V. Parrish [*sic*] (1905–1907)—Find A Grave Memorial," #52673767, www.findagrave.com (accessed 29 February 2016); email Ginny Dunaway Young to the author, 29 February 2016.

[52] Young, "Descendants of Almarine Parish," in author's possession; Viola "Villie" Hatfield Parish (1890–1941) was the daughter of Jim K. And Nora Hatfield. She married Clifford "Cliff" Howard Parish around 1905. Their marriage thereby established a

Many other Southside families' experiences closely paralleled those of the Parishes and Dunaways. Since so many people were related, the mill village population essentially was a large extended family. To use a figure of speech that is appropriate for a cotton mill town, the connections between Southside families often resembled interwoven threads in a skein of yarn. And such became the case between the Parish-Dunaway and Alsobrook families.

Although it is not known precisely when these three families first crossed paths, John Frank Dunaway, Thomas Mallie Parish, and John Thomas Alsobrook probably met in Eufaula between around 1889 and 1893. During those years, when Dunaway worked for the Chewalla Mill and the Eufaula Oil and Fertilizer Company, Parish and Alsobrook were on the Eufaula Cotton Mill's payroll. Given the intimacy of life in a small town such as Eufaula, it seems almost inconceivable that these three young men were not acquainted. Then, in 1893, Dunaway and Parish became brothers-in-law. Meanwhile, around 1900, Almarine and Epsie Parish closed their boarding house in Montgomery and moved to Eufaula with several of their children.[53]

When the lives of Thomas Mallie Parish, John Frank Dunaway, and John Thomas Alsobrook intersected a decade earlier, these men were just beginning to strike out on their own. Alsobrook lived and worked with his mother, Henrietta, who also was employed in Captain J. W. Tullis's mill. In the early 1890s, J. T. Alsobrook was known familiarly in Eufaula as "Tom," an eligible bachelor in his twenties who dressed immaculately and was always well groomed. Just under six feet tall, lean but powerfully built, he carried himself ramrod-straight on the streets of Southside and Old Eufaula. With his deep-set eyes, angular facial features, wispy mustache, and wavy dark hair combed back from his broad forehead, Tom Alsobrook appeared to be in his late thirties or early forties.[54]

----

familial link between the Parishes via the Hatfields to the Starnes family (Amos and Willie Mae Hatfield Starnes). Amos and Willie Mae's daughter, Frances Starnes, married Thomas Neville Alsobrook, who was Cliff Parish's great-nephew.

[53] "Cowikee's Roll of Honor," *Avondale Sun*, 3 March 1934, 12; Young, "Ancestors of David Ernest Alsobrook" and "Descendents of Almarine Parish," in author's possession; Ginny Dunaway Young emails to the author, 27 July 2012, 19 June 2013, 7 May 2015, 2 February 2016, 29 February 2016.

[54] This physical description is based upon the only existing photograph of J. T. Al-

At some point in the mid-1890s, he met and fell in love with a petite, strikingly attractive young woman from Georgia, Minnie Lee Price, who was about seven years his junior. They married in 1896, when she was around eighteen and he was twenty-five. They had two sons, Thomas Neville, born in 1897, and Ernest Milton, in 1899. During the early years of the marriage, Henrietta Alsobrook lived with the family in a small rented house on East Washington Street.[55]

Around 1903, apparently seeking a better cotton mill job, Tom Alsobrook moved his family, including his mother, to Huntsville. Over the following four years, despite improving the family's financial situation, he suffered three devastating personal losses. On 8 December 1905, Minnie Lee Alsobrook died at age twenty-six. Her son Ernest later described that his last memories of his mother were her agonizing screams. Her bereft husband returned his beloved "Miss Minnie" to Eufaula for burial in the secluded northwest corner of Fairview Cemetery.[56]

After the death of his wife, Tom Alsobrook believed that he could withstand any of life's vicissitudes. During the following summer, however, he suffered another unfathomable loss. On 12 July 1906, the *Atlanta Constitution* reported: "Thomas [Neville] Alsobrook, an 8-year-old boy was killed today [11 July] by being run over by an apple wagon in West Huntsville. The boy's body was almost cut in two, and he died at the hospital without regaining consciousness. The driver of the wagon has not been found."[57]

Tom Alsobrook laid Neville to rest next to his wife in Fairview Cemetery. He desperately tried to lose himself in his work at the Huntsville Mill. After several months, probably to escape the painful memories associated with Huntsville, Alsobrook returned to Eufaula with his mother and eight-year-old son, Ernest. His former bosses and his friend, Thomas Mallie Par-

---

sobrook from that era (in the author's possession).

[55] 12th US Census, 1900, Schedule No. 1, Population, Barbour County, Alabama, NARA; Young, "Ancestors of David Ernest Alsobrook," in author's possession; Tom Alsobrook family life history, 13 October 1938, folder 18, FWPP, SHC, UNC; Alsobrook family photo, c. 1900–1902, in author's possession.

[56] "Funeral of Mrs. Alsobrooks [*sic*]," *Montgomery Advertiser*, 12 December 1905, 2; Young, "Ancestors of David Ernest Alsobrook," in author's possession. Minnie Alsobrook's cause of death is not known. Her son Ernest later told his wife about being summoned into the room to see his mother and she "went to screaming."

[57] "Cut in Two by Apple Wagon," *Atlanta Constitution*, 12 July 1906, 8.

ish, welcomed Alsobrook back to the Eufaula Cotton Mill. But in April 1907, Henrietta Alsobrook died, leaving him alone with Ernest.[58]

After his mother's death, Alsobrook and his son boarded with Calvin and Eula Stephens at 427 South Eufaula Street. Barber Amos W. Starnes, who knew Alsobrook during those years before World War I, later recalled seeing him so deeply distracted and introverted that he would pass acquaintances on the street without even acknowledging their presence. Starnes thought that Alsobrook was one of the most peculiar, eccentric men he ever had known. Still consumed with grief by the deaths of his wife, son, and mother, Alsobrook also was terribly lonely and realized that young Ernest, who began working in the mill around 1910, needed a mother's care. So in 1912, he married thirty-seven-year-old Annie Lou Freeman, whom he had met at the mill.[59]

At this juncture in his life, Tom Alsobrook's closest compatriot was Thomas Mallie Parish—"Mallie," as he was called by family members and friends. The gentle, affable Mallie Parish appeared to be diametrically different from the brooding, taciturn Tom Alsobrook. Prematurely balding, with a straying right eye, his arms and legs wracked with rheumatoid arthritis, Parish in his physical appearance sharply contrasted with the lean, ruggedly handsome Alsobrook.

However, these two men, both born in the early 1870s, shared the "brotherhood of the loom" in Eufaula and Huntsville, and their wives were Cowikee operatives. The Parishes' only child, Oma, like Alsobrook's surviving son, Ernest, was born in 1899. She had long, light-brown hair, hazel eyes, a small mole on her chin, and an olive complexion like her father's. Ernest Alsobrook closely resembled his late mother, "Miss Minnie"—deeply expressive eyes, thick hair, and a silky-smooth complexion. Whenever he was photographed, Ernest seldom smiled and habitually cocked his head at an angle. He and Oma Parish were quiet, well mannered, and sociable and

---

[58] Henrietta Alsobook obituary, *Montgomery Advertiser*, 28 April 1907, 13; Tom Alsobrook family history, 13 October 1938, folder 18, FWPP, SHC, UNC.

[59] 13th US Census, 1910, Schedule No. 1, Population, Barbour County, Alabama, NARA; Tom Alsobrook family life history, 13 October 1938, folder 18, FWPP, SHC, UNC; Oates, *Annual Report of the Factory Inspector of the State of Alabama...1912*, 80. My grandfather, Amos W. Starnes, mentioned J. T. Alsobrook's bizarre behavior to me several times during the 1960s. Whenever I misbehaved or exhibited petulant behavior as a teenager, Starnes addressed me as "Tom."

had acquired a wide circle of friends even as youngsters. They also shared a deep curiosity about the wider world beyond the confines of Southside.[60]

Oma Parish and Ernest Alsobrook became friends when they were around seven or eight years old. By their early teens, they were inseparable. Married in March 1918, when they were eighteen, they immediately started a family, with daughter Jessie Lee's birth in August 1918, followed in September 1920, by a son, Thomas Neville, named for his uncle who was killed in Huntsville. They called their son "my little man," or "Manzie," which in typical Southside fashion, eventually became the child's lifelong nickname, "Monzie." The young couple moved in with Mallie and Jessie Parish at 219 Washington Street. Ernest Alsobrook was hired in 1918 as an express messenger with the American Railway Express Company and was exempt from military service after the railroads were federalized during World War I.[61]

By autumn 1920, Ernest and Oma Alsobrook were happy and contented in Southside. But their lives soon took a precipitously downward turn. First, Ernest was diagnosed with bone cancer. In a desperate attempt to prevent the cancer from metastasizing, Dr. Walter S. Britt amputated the young man's right leg. Then, in late October 1920, a federal grand jury in Macon, Georgia, indicted Alsobrook and sixty-three other employees of the American Railway Express Company for criminal conspiracy in the theft of over a million dollars in freight shipments.[62]

---

[60] Young, "Ancestors of David Ernest Alsobrook"; photograph of Mallie, Jessie, and Oma Parish, c. 1909; misc. photographs of Ernest Alsobrook, c. 1910–1918, in author's possession; Tom Alsobrook family life history, 13 October 1938, folder 18, FWPP, SHC, UNC.

[61] Young, "Ancestors of David Ernest Alsobrook"; Ernest Milton Alsobrook's World War I Draft Registration Card, 12 September 1918, Record Group 163, NARA, Morrow, GA; E. M. Alsabrook [sic] union identification card, Brotherhood of Railway and Steamship Clerks, Freight Handlers, Express and Station Employees, 1920, in author's possession.

[62] Tom Alsobrook family life history, 13 October 1938, folder 18, SHC, UNC; death certificate, Ernest Milton Alsobrook, 19 December 1921, State of Alabama, Bureau of Vital Statistics, State Board of Health, Montgomery, AL; "Macon Grand Jury Indicts 64 Men For Alleged Thieving," *Augusta (GA) Chronicle*, 29 October 1920, 1; "Many Indictments in Court Charging Theft from Express Company," *Winston-Salem (NC) Journal*, 29 October 1920, 1; "Express Robberies in South Reach Big Sum," *Winston-Salem Journal*, 1 March 1921, 6; *United States of America v. E. M. Alsobrook, et al.*, #2268, 1920–1921, boxes 51–52, Record Group 21, Records of US District Court, Mid-

In March 1921, Alsobrook and four other express messengers confessed to stealing and selling expensive furs, silk shirts, rifles, pocketknives, children's clothing, hogs, chickens, fish, eggs, pecans, and hunting dogs.[63] On 16 March 1921, when Alsobrook testified, a reporter noted, "He came in on crutches and limped up to the stand. He was a young fellow around twenty."[64] Alsobrook stated that between September 1918 and April 1919, his route on board the Atlantic Coast Line Railroad ran from Eufaula to Ozark and from Albany, Georgia, to Madison, Florida. During one of those long runs, J. O. Hood, an express agent, recruited him as a member of the conspiracy. Under questioning from prosecutors, Alsobrook provided details about how the theft operation worked and the names of the messengers, agents, baggage masters, and conductors he had transacted business with along the rail line.[65]

On 9 April 1921, after deliberating for twenty-eight hours, the jury returned guilty verdicts for thirty-six of the defendants. Two weeks later, Judge Beverly D. Evans sentenced thirteen of the men to prison terms of one year and a day. The remaining defendants received fines ranging from $300 to $3,000. The five messengers who had pled guilty all received fines rather than prison sentences, including Alsobrook, who was ordered to pay $300. In his closing comments, Judge Evans surprisingly admonished the plaintiffs: "[T]he express company did not pay the messengers wages sufficient to give them an adequate living."[66]

Alsobrook paid his fine and returned to Eufaula. Eight months later, on 18 December 1921, he succumbed to cancer, a month after celebrating his twenty-second birthday. Like her father-in-law sixteen years earlier, twenty-two-year-old Oma Alsobrook became a single parent. She quickly

---

dle District of Georgia, Macon Division, NARA, Morrow, GA.

[63] "Indictments Made in Express Theft Case," *Greensboro (NC) Daily News*, 29 October 1920, 12 (itemized list of stolen goods); "Five of 64 Plead Guilty of Robbery," *Charlotte (NC) News*, 14 March 1921, 1; "Express Messengers Are Now Being Tried," *(Greenwood, SC) Index-Journal*, 15 March 1921, 1.

[64] "'All Right' Is Thieves' Mark Says Alsabrook [*sic*]," *Macon Telegraph*, 17 March 1921, 1.

[65] Ibid., 1, 8.

[66] "Convict 36 of Express Thefts," *Miami (FL) Herald*, 10 April 1921, 1, 4; "36 Found Guilty on Five Counts in Express Case," *Charlotte Observer*, 10 April 1921, 1; "Sentences Given in Express Cases," *Atlanta Constitution*, 1 May 1921, 5 (quote).

discarded Ernest's crutches and tattered one-legged trousers—painful reminders of the last traumatic year of their marriage. Although she realized that her husband had become a criminal to support his struggling family, Oma never spoke again of that time in their lives. Then, about six months later, on 15 June 1922, her four-year-old daughter, Jessie Lee, died from a bronchial infection. Florida Dewar, the child's Cowikee Community House kindergarten teacher, tenderly penned a condolence note: "With love and sympathy from those who are sorrowing, and in memory of one whose dear smile was always an inspiration to me."[67]

Not long after her daughter's death in 1922, Oma Alsobrook and her son, Monzie, began sharing a house with her parents at 423 South Eufaula Street. They remained at this address until after World War II. The young widow worked as a weaver alongside her father and other Parish relatives at the Cowikee Mill. In September 1926, a brief personal note appeared in the *Avondale Sun*'s "Weave Room" column: "Oma says she thinks she will keep the loom she has as one widow has had the luck to marry off of them."[68] But she remained unmarried for forty-three years, until her death in December 1969. Her grandson once boldly asked if she had ever considered remarrying. She patiently explained that she had rejected several suitors' proposals because she had only one true love in her life and could never care so deeply for anyone else.

She devoted much of her time to rearing Monzie and caring for her aging parents and father-in-law. Jessie Parish and Tom Alsobrook died in 1939, followed by Mallie Parish in 1945. She personally "adopted" Washington Street Methodist ministers and their families for many years. In addition to her busy church schedule, she chaperoned Cowikee Community House parties and excursions to Donald Comer's plantation home and to Camp Helen, Avondale's summer retreat on the Florida Gulf Coast. When her son was overseas in the US Navy during World War II, she hosted homesick servicemen who were visiting in Eufaula and often became their

---

[67] Death certificates, Ernest Milton Alsobrook, 18 December 1921; Jessie Lee Alsobrook, 15 June 1922, both from State of Alabama, Bureau of Vital Statistics, State Board of Health, Montgomery, AL; Florida Dewar to [Oma Parish Alsobrook], n.d., c. June 1922, in author's possession.

[68] 14th–16th US Census, 1920–1940, Schedule No. 1, Population, Barbour County, Alabama, NARA; "Weave Room," *Avondale Sun*, 10 September 1926, 4.

surrogate mother.[69]

One of her proudest moments was seeing her son graduate from Alabama Polytechnic Institute in Auburn in 1948—the first member of the Alsobrook family to earn a college degree. By the time of her retirement from Cowikee Mills in the early 1960s, she had observed the gradual erosion of the walls between Southside and Old Eufaula. Like so many other Cowikee and Avondale employees, she personally knew the man who expedited the walls' collapse after World War II—James McDonald Comer.

If Oma Alsobrook ever experienced any self-pity or bitterness about the course of her life, she kept such feelings to herself. On 21 January 1968, upon learning that her best friend's husband had died, she said, "Living in a small place like Eufaula, where almost everybody is related or is a close friend, can be both wonderful and heartbreaking, but I wouldn't want to ever live anywhere else."[70]

---

[69] Young, "Ancestors of David Ernest Alsobrook." Petty Officer 2/c James Luke, billeted at the US Naval Air Station, Glenview, IL, was one of the servicemen she hosted. *Avondale Sun*, 10 October 1945, 6; James Luke to Oma Alsobrook, 28 September, 5, 19 October, 7 November 1945, in author's possession.

[70] Remarks, Oma Parish Alsobrook to her grandson (the author), 21 January 1968.

Chapter 4

"Mr. Donald" and His Mill Workers

He was just sent to us by God.
—James "Doc" Hughes, 1938

In April 1941, Frances Starnes wrote to her future husband from Alabama College in Montevallo: "Mr. Donald Comer is making a speech here tomorrow and I'm going to try to see him and talk to him about helping me to find a job. You know he has a lot of pull in the State and that's what I'll need."[1] She was not simply name-dropping. Like hundreds of children of Avondale and Cowikee Mills employees, she personally knew James McDonald Comer, patriarch of his family's vast textile empire. Her mother worked for years in Eufaula's Cowikee Mill No. 1, alongside other relatives. "Mr. Donald" knew Frances Starnes from her participation in the Cowikee Community House kindergarten and band programs. She had performed in theatrical and musical productions in his presence, had received her kindergarten graduation diploma from his own hand, and had eaten homemade ice cream and scuppernongs at his plantation. Comer fondly remembered her as one of the Community House's "little darlings": "If Miss Florida Dewar, who used to be in charge of our kindergarten, ever loved any one little girl more than anyone else it was Frances."[2]

Exactly how Comer responded to Frances Starnes's plea for his assistance is not known, but by early June 1941, she was employed as a social worker with the Lamar County Department of Public Welfare in Vernon, Alabama. Cowikee Mills president and treasurer Comer Jennings also personally loaned her enough money to relocate to the small West Alabama town.[3] Frances Starnes's story, like those of so many other mill families,

---

[1] Frances Starnes to Thomas Alsobrook, n.d., c. 10 April 1941, in author's possession.

[2] "Donald Comer Writes," *Avondale Sun*, 14 March 1955, 4. See Comer's tributes to the Starneses, *Avondale Sun*, 19 April 1954, 5; 12 August 1957, 4. For more about Florida Dewar, see ch. 5.

[3] Frances Starnes to Thomas Alsobrook (2 letters), n.d., c. 3 June 1941; n.d., c. 20

lends credence to Comer's legendary status as the friendly, approachable in-
dustrialist who genuinely cared about his employees and their kin and
watched over them from "cradle to grave."

In 1938, weaver Carrie Parish Snipes, who had toiled in Eufaula's cotton mills since childhood, expressed her feelings about her job and "The
Boss":

> It used to be we were just factory folks or "lintheads." Now we are "Mill
> Operatives" and we hold our heads high. All work is honorable, you know,
> and we are proud of ours. We are proud to work for Mr. Donald Comer
> and there has never been a strike or any trouble in any of the mills. We
> would all fight for him, not against him.[4]

Carrie Snipes's compatriot at Cowikee Mill No. 1, boiler fireman Ben
T. Clements, shared her sentiments: "It's good to work for men like Mr.
Donald Comer and Mr. Comer Jennings. There ain't nothin' that they
wouldn't do for us and I'd almost die for them."[5] Loom fixer James "Doc"
Hughes added, "Mr. Donald Comer is responsible for all the good things
around here. Nobody knows what he has done for us."[6] Hughes, who had
accrued forty-five years in Eufaula's cotton mills, effusively praised Comer:

> Mr. Donald has improved everything.... I use[d] to work from six in the
> morning 'til six in the evening for thirty-five cents a day. Now from six in
> the morning 'til two in the afternoon, thirty-five cents an hour. Mr. Don-
> ald done [sic] that when he bought the Mill. There ain't never been no-
> body just like him. He was just sent to us by God, I believe. And how we
> all love him for what he has done for us.[7]

November 1941, in author's possession. This was not the first time she had asked for
assistance from the Comer family. Four years earlier, Hugh Comer wrote her a letter of
recommendation to Montevallo. Hugh M. Comer to Mary McCoy, 11 August 1937,
copy in France Starnes's scrapbook, c. 1937–1942, in author's possession.

[4] Mrs. Lee Snipes [Carrie Belle Parish Snipes] life history, 13 October 1938, folder
10, FWPP, SHC, UNC.

[5] B. T. Clements life history, 13 October 1938, ibid.

[6] Mr. and Mrs. James C. Hughes family life history, 20 October 1938, folder 11,
ibid.

[7] James C. Hughes family life history, follow-up interview by Gertha Couric, 23
November 1938, Federal Writers' Project, Life Histories/Stores (Ex-Slave Tales), Short
Stories, Barbour County, box SG022774, WPA Files, ADAH. A concerted effort was
made to pressure the original grammatical usages, syntax, and colloquial expressions of

These five employees all worked in the old Eufaula Cotton Mill prior to the Comer family's acquisition of the property in 1908 and its re-birth a year later as Cowikee Mill No. 1, or later as the "Big Mill." They did not need mill inspectors or social reformers to validate what they knew from their own experience. Their personal memories of working conditions in the mill over the past forty years easily led them to anoint Donald Comer as their messiah. Regardless of their positions in the mill caste system—from sweeper to foreman—Comer treated them all with respect and compassion. In return they remained loyal and devoted to him throughout their lives and passed on this legacy of mutual trust and respect to their children and grand-children.[8]

Comer's bond with his employees and their families was one characteristic of paternalism that existed in mill settlements across the South. Sociologists, economists, and other scholars who meticulously studied Southern cotton mills after World War I often focused on paternalism's evolution and its practitioners. In one prevalent interpretation that emerged from their research, twentieth-century cotton mill paternalism evolved from the philosophy that existed in the post-1865 South, particularly during the early 1880s. The men who led the "Cotton Mill Campaigns" and built the first modern mills in the South were local "figures of distinction" who inherited their mantles of leadership from antebellum planters. In the words of two Depression-era scholars, these new *patrons* "supplied the essential boon for a broken people—the opportunity to work. The reward they reaped was adoration.... It was fatherhood."[9]

Paternalism also became an obsession for the gifted journalist Wilber J. Cash, who grew up among cotton mill workers in the 1920s in Gaffney, South Carolina. No surviving evidence indicates that Donald Comer read Cash's classic, *The Mind of the South*, or that the two men ever met or corresponded. However, Comer could have served as a model for Cash's sharply drawn vignette of the paternalistic mill owner: "More, he knew their pedi-

---

the Life Histories cited herein. However, words in the transcripts that possibly reflect WPA interviewers' biases toward interviewers, such as "ter" ("to"), "for" ("for"), "wuz," ("was"), and "jist" ("just") were revised accordingly.

   [8] See Flynt, *Poor but Proud*, 105–106, 112.

   [9] Broadus Mitchell, *The Rise of the Cotton Mills in the South*, 130–37, 151–57, 162; Broadus Mitchell and George Sinclair Mitchell, *The Industrial Revolution in the South*, 147–48.

grees and their histories. More still, with that innocent love of personal detail native to Southerners, he kept himself posted as to their lives as they were lived under his wing; knew their little adventures and scandals and hopes and griefs and joys."[10]

Although Comer's encyclopedic memory allowed him to compile data about his mill workers, his personal communion with them ran much deeper. Whenever he visited the mills or penned his columns in the *Avondale Sun*, Comer continually reminded "his people" of their shared histories. He asserted that the Comers and the mill workers' families had abandoned the farm for the town for the same reason: "Seven cent and eight cent [per pound] cotton just wasn't good enough." He characterized the first cotton mills as risky ventures for the managers and workers alike, but "better than the country."[11] His narrative omitted an important fact: When his father, Braxton Bragg Comer, moved from his Barbour County plantation to Anniston in 1885, he was one of Alabama's wealthiest landowners.

Of course, "his people" knew that Donald Comer was a child of privilege, but they seemingly forgave this omission and listened attentively to his simple, direct, and personal message of kinship:

> Some of us have worked together now nearly 50 years…. We not only have worked together; we have played together; we have camped and sailed together; we have broken bread together. I know something of your home life. We have shared common joys and common sorrows. You have given me your loyalty. I have never abused your confidence—and I never will. I have never known people anywhere who…were kinder, more considerate, more thoughtful or better neighbors.[12]

Comer's detractors scorned his historical homilies as excessively sentimental, patronizing, and demagogic. These charges contained an element of truth. Nevertheless, "his people" divined something remarkably different in his ordinary language, that, in the words of Abraham Lincoln, touched the "mystic chords of memory" deep within their hearts and souls.

When one of his veteran mill superintendents, Elbert S. Dunn, died in 1953, Comer eulogized him as one of those "natural textile men" who knew

---

[10] Cash, *The Mind of the South*, 217.

[11] "Address by Donald Comer at Donald Comer Day Celebration," Sylacauga, AL, 30 April 1952, *Avondale Sun*, 5 May 1952, 3.

[12] Ibid.

everything about the industry "from the cotton bale to a yard of cloth." But in Comer's estimation, Dunn's greatest talents lay in his understanding of people and his ability to "sympathize with them in every problem connected with their work or homes." Dunn personally knew each of his employees and their families. He was more than a boss; he was a "good neighbor and a friend."[13] Comer could have been drafting his own obituary.

Donald Comer's paternalism embodied much that he learned from his parents about Christian stewardship and the obligatory leadership role, philanthropy, and sense of *noblesse oblige* that were expected from families of their social, economic, and political stature. His father, Braxton Bragg Comer (1848–1927) was a dynamic, yet sometimes intimidating, force in his life. As president of the Alabama Railroad Commission and later as governor, B. B. Comer was a powerful orator, political leader, and champion of progressive causes and sweeping reforms in education, railroad freight rate regulation, and conservation. He played a defining role in the development of his son's "world views," particularly regarding ethical and religious matters. While Donald Comer's strict Methodist upbringing shaped his support of Prohibition and similar moral reform issues, his religious beliefs were infused with a healthy dose of the "social gospel."[14] A close friend once observed, Comer "seek[s] out the sick, the troubled, the unfortunate. His big heart is not shriveled or bound by race, creed, color or worldly goods. All are God's children to him."[15]

Comer included African Americans among "God's children," but like the majority of the white Southerners of his generation, he considered blacks

---

[13] "Donald Comer Writes," and "Rites Are Held for E. S. Dunn at Mignon Church," both in *Avondale Sun*, 27 April 1953, 5, 1. Dunn (1887–1953) first met Comer in 1909 during the renovation of the Eufaula Cotton Mill. He subsequently served in supervisory positions throughout the Avondale Mills system. See "Avondale Personality...," *Avondale Sun*, 21 November 1949, 1, 8.

[14] David Alan Harris, "Braxton Bragg Comer, 1907–1911," in *Alabama Governors*, ed. Webb and Armbrester, 150–56; Michael Alan Breedlove, "Donald Comer: New Southerner, New Dealer" (PhD diss., The American University, 1990) 61–93. Hereafter cited as Breedlove, "Donald Comer" diss.; B. B. Comer to Donald Comer, 18 September 1925, folder 7.16.31, box 16, Donald Comer Papers, BPLA. Until his death in 1927, B. B. Comer continued to give his son detailed instructions about managing the mills and the family's Barbour County plantation.

[15] French H. Craddock, quoted in 1952 in Breedlove, "Donald Comer" diss., 194.

to be inferior to Caucasians. Surrounded by African-American domestics and tenant farmers during his formative years on his father's plantation, Comer was accustomed to the traditional "master-servant" relationship that generally characterized racial interactions in the rural post-1865 South. Many of these African Americans or their ancestors had been held in bondage by his family. Nevertheless, as he grew to manhood, he eschewed the overt race-baiting that was commonplace at that time and consistently condemned lynchings and other forms of racial violence.[16] His racial views perhaps were influenced by his Army service as an officer assigned to the 25th Infantry Regiment during the Philippine Insurrection in 1899–1902. The 25th was among four African-American regiments that served both in Cuba and the Philippines during the Spanish-American War.[17]

Even if Comer had become more racially conciliatory after his overseas service with African-American troops, he still relegated all of his black mill employees to unskilled positions—laborers, watchmen, janitors, cotton bale openers, sweepers, laundresses, and wagon and truck drivers. On occasion he selected one of the drivers to be his personal chauffeur. Although both races filled the job designated as "sweeper" or "sweeper hand," only African Americans swept the sidewalks and alleys outside the mills. Moreover, only white sweepers could aspire to higher-paying, skilled positions as weavers, spinners, loom fixers, and foremen. Comer thus never promoted African Americans beyond their "place" in his mills.[18]

Because of their status as second-class citizens, blacks found that Com-

---

[16] Ibid, 14, 344.

[17] "Donald Comer" by Michael A. Breedlove, *Encyclopedia of Alabama* (online) http://www.encyclopediaofalabama.org/face/Article.jsp?id=h-2616 (accessed on 24 July 2012). Hereafter cited as "Donald Comer," *EOA* online; Lieutenant James McDonald Comer, AGO Doc. File #78646, box 589, Record Group 94, Records of the Adjutant General's Office, National Archives and Records Administration, Washington, DC.

[18] "Faithful Worker Dies," watchman Sol Mitchell's obituary, *Avondale Sun*, 10 October 1924, 8; "Will Shade," Comer's chauffeur, *Avondale Sun*, 10 September 1951, 11; "Mill Inspection," *Avondale Sun*, 29 May 1944, 9, 12; "Donald Comer Writes" *Avondale Sun*, 16 January 1950, 5; "These are the colored employees from Plants One and Three, Eufaula," photograph with caption, *Avondale Sun*, 16 March 1953, 10; "A Clean Sweep," photograph of African-American sweepers, *Avondale Sun* 22 November 1954, 13; "Clarence White Passes," obituary for janitor and yardman, *Avondale Sun*, 22 October 1956,7; Breedlove, "Donald Comer," diss., 14, 344.

er offered them a different brand of the paternalism reserved for whites. It essentially was "Jim Crow paternalism"—not quite equal, and definitely separate. For example, Comer authorized segregated educational, social, and recreational activities, such as food canning classes, barbeques, band concerts, and excursions, for his African-American employees and their families. He also permitted some black workers to participate in his home ownership program and furnished lumber and other building materials for home improvements. He was cautious in dispensing such largess to African Americans lest he risk alienating his white employees.[19]

Although Comer was never particularly fond of terms like "paternalism" or "welfare programs," he recognized early in his corporate career the importance of providing his employees with a variety of activities beyond the work place. Like all bright, successful businessmen, Comer understood the direct correlation between happy, contented workers and productivity. His frequent personal contact, coupled with his paternalistic gifts and programs, further cemented "a bond of loyalty" and granted him greater control over their daily existence, yet Comer the enlightened humanitarian also wanted his employees to have better, healthier, and more fulfilling lives.[20] By 1918 he had begun to introduce various free "welfare programs" into Eufaula's mill settlement—a kindergarten, playground, bands, athletic teams, swimming pools, cooking and sewing classes, and reading clubs, all headquartered at the Cowikee Community House. After World War I, these programs became more well developed, especially after Comer personally recruited trained social workers and educators to live and work at the Community House.[21]

---

[19] "Homes of Two Thrifty Colored Families Connected with Cowikee Mills," photograph, *Avondale Sun*, 2 November 1935, 6; "Miss Dewar Congratulates Cowikee Employees on Owning Homes," Florida Dewar McMullen to Lawyer Dudley and Terry Davis, 7 November 1935, in *Avondale Sun*, 30 November 1935, 5; "A Fish Fry," *Avondale Sun*, 18 April 1936, 7; "Cowikee Mills Colored Employe[e]s Enjoy Fish Fry," *Avondale Sun*, 2 May 1936, 3.

[20] Breedlove, "Donald Comer" diss., 186–87; Hall et al., *Like a Family*, 91–92.

[21] J. Fred Sparks to *Birmingham News*, 25 February 1925, cited in Breedlove, "Donald Comer" diss., 185. These programs were not a Comer innovation; they were based closely upon similar activities in other Southern cotton mill communities. See, for example, Hall et al., *Like a Family*, 131–39; Herring, *Welfare Work in Mill Villages*, 135–44; Rhyne, *Southern Cotton Mill Workers*, 27–36.

By the early 1930s, Comer also had established a large poultry farm within Southside in Eufaula and had developed a Gulf Coast recreational site near Panama City, Florida, which he named "Camp Helen," in honor of his brother Fletcher's wife. Camp Helen eventually became the most popular vacation destination for Avondale and Cowikee Mills families. In the 1940s, Comer launched plans for the Cowikee Mill Farm, just south of Eufaula, near Terese. Overlooking the Chattahoochee River, the Mill Farm featured a cattle and horse ranch, a large swimming pool, fishing pond, and picnic facilities.[22]

The popularity of these facilities and programs encouraged Comer to do more to improve his employees' quality of life by introducing several experimental initiatives. For example, between 1918 and 1931, all Avondale and Cowikee workers were given group life insurance policies funded completely by the companies. With the onset of the Great Depression, the Metropolitan Life Insurance Company abruptly cancelled these policies. Comer interceded and offered optional life insurance protection borne primarily by the two companies, with ten cents per week deducted from employees' paychecks. The new insurance coverage would be provided without restrictions as to workers' current ages or health. Although the payroll deductions were still too expensive for many employees, about half of Eufaula's Cowikee workers immediately enrolled in the plan.[23]

In spring 1941, Comer also offered additional health care insurance to his employees. Although this coverage was advertised as optional, a widowed weaver in Cowikee Mill No. 1, complained, "Well Mr. [Comer] Jennings had all of us to take out Hospital Ins. Last week.... It will cost 20 [cents] a

---

[22] "Lone Oak Leghorn Farm," *Avondale Sun*, 11 March 1933, 5; Breedlove, "Donald Comer" diss., 212; C. C. Dailey, "A Brief Historical Sketch of Camp Helen," *Avondale Sun*, Camp Helen Edition, 26 August 1933, 1–2; Edmund Blair, "A Trip to Camp Helen," *Avondale Sun*, 8 September 1934, 7; Cash Stanley, Sr., "What's Doing in Barbour County," *Alabama Journal*, n.d., excerpt in *Avondale Sun*, 22 June 1953, 2.

[23] Donald Comer, "To the Employe[e]s of the Avondale and Cowikee Mills," *Avondale Sun*, 19 December 1931, 1; "Avondale and Cowikee Employe[e]s ensure with Metropolitan For $2,516,400.00," *Avondale Sun*, 13 February 1932, 1; "Important Rules Governing Avondale and Cowikee Group Insurance," *Avondale Sun*, 23 April 1932, 3; Oma Alsobrook's life and dismemberment insurance policy, 1939, Metropolitan Life Insurance Company, with attached form letter, Donald Comer to the Employe[e]s of Cowikee Mills, n.d., c. July 1939, in author's possession.

week."[24] With monthly payroll deductions totaling over a dollar, this additional amount further stretched her meager income. However, she noted that her co-workers quickly used their new medical benefits: "Willie Grace Kennedy was operated on Fri. for Appendicitus [sic]. They are keeping the Hospitals full since that Hospital Ins. came into effect."[25]

Beyond insurance coverage, beginning in the early 1920s, Comer pursued a variety of educational initiatives, including "Opportunity Schools" that targeted illiterate workers, "industrial training" for foremen, and college scholarships for employees' children. In funding these programs, Comer partnered with state and federal officials, college educators, and philanthropists. But, the lion's share of the money came from Avondale and Cowikee Mills.[26]

Granting college scholarships to promising young men in Eufaula and other towns allowed Comer to groom them for future leadership positions in his mills. Although the terms of the scholarships did not obligate recipients to work for the mills, many of these students later accepted jobs from Comer. He often had to wait several years to reap any of the benefits from his investments in these young men's careers, but the Opportunity Schools yielded results almost immediately. In spring 1930, a recent graduate of one of the schools, writing his "first letter," thanked Comer for the chance to attend the "moonlight school" after work: "I am determined to improve my condition and make of myself a more valuable citizen of our community and country."[27]

This letter assuredly delighted Comer. This "good citizenship" theme permeated his ideas about the value of education. As one whose views had been molded deeply by the progressive era's quest for "good government" based upon a literate, well-informed electorate, Comer passionately believed that education was meaningless unless it produced men who made positive

---

[24] Oma Alsobrook to Thomas Alsobrook, n.d., c. April—May 1941, in author's possession.

[25] Oma Alsobrook to Thomas Alsobrook, n.d., c. 14 May 1941, ibid.

[26] Breedlove, "Donald Comer" diss., 76–79, 202–209; "Donald Comer Commends Opportunity School Pupils and Thanks Them for Letters," *Avondale Sun*, 19 April 1930, 1; "Donald Comer Writes," *Avondale Sun*, 6 March 1944, 13.

[27] William Moon to Donald Comer, 7 April 1930, in "Mr. Donald Comer Receives Letters from Opportunity School Pupils," *Avondale Sun*, 19 April 1930, 6.

contributions to society.[28] His thoughts on this topic were not reserved for young men. He wrote in 1929, "[W]here we find a young lady who is really ambitious and willing and anxious for a further education...to make herself more valuable to society...we are more than anxious to do our part to help."[29]

Comer also formulated some very precise goals for mill workers' "industrial schooling." He wanted to train men for careers as mill foremen or for leadership positions in textile manufacturing and engineering. His summer foremen's training sessions and his college scholarship program fully buttressed this goal. However, he believed that instruction for his female employees should focus on the domestic arts, home making, and child-rearing.[30]

In the mid-1920s, under the energetic leadership of Athens College president Mary McCoy, the Southern School for Industrial Workers (SIS) became the embodiment of Comer's vision for educating women mill workers. Modeled upon two-week summer sessions at Bryn Mawr College, SIS accepted applications from "Southern mill and factory girls," ages sixteen through twenty-four, who exhibited "Moral Character above reproach, Good Health, and Ability to Read and Write." The curriculum for the inaugural 1926 SIS summer session featured English composition and letter-writing, English and American literature, history, citizenship, art, music, "Pageantry and Dramatics," physical education, and "Sunday School Methods [and] Bible study." The SIS instructional philosophy was summarized by several aphorisms, for example: "Industrial workers lose their *hand skills* and their *joy in work* if they do not feed their minds with *ideas*."[31]

---

[28] Comer and his father were in complete agreement on the purpose of education. See Robert Jemison to B. B. Comer, 11 May 1925, cited in Breedlove, "Donald Comer" diss., 185.

[29] Donald Comer quoted in ibid., 79. On Avondale scholarships for women, see Mary Moody McCoy to Donald Comer, 12 June 1929, "Athens College" folder 7.45.31, box 45, Donald Comer Papers, BPLA.

[30] Breedlove, "Donald Comer" diss., 200.

[31] Ibid.; "Announcement, Southern School for Industrial Workers, Athens College, Athens, Ala.," n.d., 1926; and Oma Alsobrook's SIS "Certificate of Merit," 5 July 1926, both in author's possession. By the 1930s, summer schools for female industrial workers dealt increasingly with current labor issues. See, for example, Louise Leonard McLaren, "Workers' Education in the South," *Vassar Quarterly* 20/2 (1 May 1935): 101–106.

Despite the obscure meaning and infelicitous syntax of this slogan, mill owners were not fearful that the SIS would produce radicalized workers, seething with incendiary ideas. With an emphasis on "moral instruction," "citizenship skills," and "Swedish swimming and gymnastics," the SIS program was designed to return mill workers to their homes and jobs, mentally and physically invigorated. At least that was the hope shared by SIS teachers and mill owners.

On 22 June 1926, two young Cowikee Mill weavers, Ida Clark and Oma Parish Alsobrook, arrived at Athens College with seventeen other SIS students. Seven of their classmates were from other Comer mills.[32] Oma Alsobrook did not quite fit the SIS application requirements. She was a twenty-six-year-old widow with a young son. When she departed from Eufaula for the long journey to North Alabama, she left five-year-old Thomas "Monzie" in her parents' care. This was her first extended trip away from Eufaula since she had accompanied her family to Huntsville in the early 1900s. Although she was somewhat apprehensive about leaving her child for two weeks, she was thrilled about the prospect of meeting other "mill girls."

Near the end of the SIS session, she thanked Comer Jennings for sending her to Athens. She described her busy days in classes and on excursions, adding, "I must not let you think we study all the time, because we really do not...; most of the afternoons are spent in resting and visiting with the other girls."[33] She promised to share everything she had learned with other Cowikee employees and expressed her hope that "every one of our girls will have the opportunity to go as I am sure it will be better every year.... I think [these were] two of the most enjoyable weeks I have ever spent."[34]

In her own polite, understated manner, Oma Alsobrook truthfully conveyed her feelings to Jennings; the SIS instruction was adequate, but for her the most pleasant aspect of the session was the time spent with classmates, enjoying a two-week respite from the grinding, daily drudgery of her loom. Over the remaining forty-three years of her life, she traveled extensively throughout the Southeast on Cowikee excursions, but she never forgot her

---

[32] Oma Alsobrook, "Our Trip to Athens," *Avondale Sun*, 16 July 1926, 10.

[33] Oma Alsobrook to Mr. [Comer] Jennings, 2 July 1926, "Eufaula Girl Wins Honor," *Avondale Sun*, 16 July 1926, 10.

[34] Oma Alsobrook, "Our Trip to Athens," ibid.

first "great adventure" in 1926, far from her home and job, as an "older mill girl."[35]

SIS and other summer training sessions won many accolades from Comer's employees. None of these education programs, however, achieved the popularity of his home ownership plan, first unveiled before the Great War. Comer disliked the drab, regimented appearance of mill villages in Birmingham and Pell City, where many of the houses were erected in almost identical architectural styles, usually in the same era. He understood that earlier mills, including Avondale, built company housing for their workers to furnish them with convenient access to their jobs and to the only available electrical power and sanitary water.[36] Preferring the designation, "mill settlement," over "mill village," which he felt held too many negative connotations associated with textile workers, Comer eagerly wanted to turn this page in the industry's history and eradicate company towns. He later recalled, "My associates and the people in Eufaula were among the first in their determination to break through this old tradition."[37]

Soon after acquiring the bankrupt Eufaula Cotton Mill in 1908, Comer discovered that his seventy-five "inherited" employees did not reside in a village plotted and built by the previous managers. His new mill workers lived in homes of diverse architectural design and history in Southside, primarily on both sides of South Eufaula, South Randolph, and Washington Streets. Cowikee Mills later owned some Southside rental property, a half-block west of South Eufaula Street, on Hunter, Davis, and Comer Streets—an area designated informally as Comer Town.[38]

Donald Comer's veteran mill employees were among the first to purchase homes under his new loan program. Although a lively Southside debate raged over which mill worker bought the first house with a Comer low interest loan, by 1920, Eddie Cox and James Wesley Gill both were proud home owners, at 441 and 431 South Eufaula Street, respectively. They prob-

---

[35] Two of her most memorable excursions were to Mammoth Cave, KY, in the early 1930s, and to Blue Ridge, NC, in 1941; misc. photographs and postcards, in author's possession.

[36] Donald Comer, "Cotton Textile Mfg. During Last Fifty Years," *Avondale Sun,* 16 June 1952, 6.

[37] "Donald Comer Writes," *Avondale Sun,* 20 June 1955, 5.

[38] Description of Southside mill neighborhoods is based on a survey of 12th–16th US census, 1900–1940, Population Schedules, Barbour County, AL, NARA.

ably bought these houses around 1915–1917. Cox and Gill spent most of their remaining years at these two addresses.[39]

Their Comer Town neighbors to the west, Bennie Morgan Clark, 110 Davis Street, and James "Doc" Hughes, 111 Hunter Street, also bought homes with a Comer loan and never moved again.[40] In 1929 John Thomas Alsobrook used a mill loan at 5 percent interest to buy his home at 400 South Randolph from A. L. Bland. Paying ten dollars a month, Alsobrook had retired his house note by 1937. He marveled at Comer's generosity as a mortgage lender: "In case anybody has to skip a few payments, that's all right with the Mill. Ain't nobody had their home taken away from them yet."[41]

Prior to this purchase, he had lived in a succession of rental and boarding houses in South Eufaula, Washington, and Hunter Streets. This was the first and only time in his life that he owned a home; he resided at 400 South Randolph Street until his death in 1939.[42]

As exemplified by these mill workers' experiences, Comer's home ownership plan helped end their previously transient existence as renters and boarders. He also nurtured his employees' pride in home ownership by allotting acreage adjoining their properties for vegetable gardens and by providing flowers and shrubs from the mill nurseries for beautification projects. He offered additional farm loans for his employees who wanted to purchase country homes. By the early 1950s, 2,592 Comer employees had bought homes since the loan program's inception, and over 85 percent of the mills' total work force were homeowners.[43] In assessing his plan's results, Comer

---

[39] *Southside News*, 10 January 1921, n.p., printed in *Avondale Sun*, 10 December 1945, 7; "Personalities," Eddie Cox, *Avondale Sun*, 27 February 1950, 2–3; "Cowikee Personality...," James Wesley Gill, *Avondale Sun*, 2 January 1950, 1, 3; 14th–16th US Census, 1920–1940, Schedule No. 1, Population, Barbour County, Alabama, NARA.

[40] "Morgan Clark," *Avondale Sun*, 27 April 1935, 1; Bennie Morgan Clark's World War I Draft Registration Card, 12 September 1918, Record Group 163, NARA, Morrow, GA; "Worked in Mill for 39 Years," James "Doc" Hughes, *Avondale Sun*, 18 July 1938, 2; 14th–16th US Census, 1920–1940, Schedule No. 1, Population, Barbour County, Alabama, NARA.

[41] "Personals," *Avondale Sun*, 16 February 1929, 5; Tom Alsobrook family life history, 13 October 1938, folder 18, FWPP, SHC.

[42] 13th–16th US Census, 1910–1940, Schedule No. 1, Population, Barbour County, Alabama, NARA; "Mr. Thomas Alsobrook," *Avondale Sun*, 17 July 1939, 16; "Mr. Thomas Alsobrooks [*sic*] Passes," *Avondale Sun*, 14 August 1939, 15.

[43] "Eufaula," *The WPA Guide to 1930s Alabama*, 341; "Donald Comer Member of

observed, "[T]he worker who owns his house and land and can raise food and ignore landlords will have a mighty bulwark" against economic hard times.[44]

In the midst of the worst financial crisis in American history in the early 1930s, Comer believed that he had done everything humanly possible to improve his employees' standard of living. Most remarkably, he had kept all of his mills open during the Depression's early days when plants were closing everywhere.

However, the first significant challenge to Comer's paternalistic "romance" with his employees arose in 1933–1934 when the General Textile Strike swept across the South from the Carolinas to Alabama. Comer had played a pivotal role in drafting the National Recovery Administration's Cotton Textile Code, which guaranteed a forty-hour week, virtually eradicated child labor, and increased wages in Southern mills. He still stubbornly ignored the code's basic deficiencies—it was designed primarily as a production regulatory device for textile management and failed to address union demands for collective bargaining rights, higher wages, and greater job security. He simply refused to accept the premise of unions having a voice about hours, wages, and working conditions in cotton mills.[45] He held firm to this belief throughout his textile career.

By mid-summer 1934, United Textile Workers of America (UTW) union organizers were on the march in North Alabama. In July, when mill hands walked off their jobs in Birmingham, Gadsden, and Huntsville, the only Comer employees who joined the strike were 700 at the central Avondale Mill in "The Magic City."[46] A UTW leader in Birmingham angrily harangued mill workers with his alternative view of Comer's paternalism:

[He]...has paid you starvation wages and most of you have been borned [sic] and raised here and think he is a God.... I know he has stretched you out, cut your wages, then [told] you he was not making anything. [And]

Committee to Study Home Ownership Plan," *Avondale Sun*, 9 September 1933, 10; Marjorie W. Young, ed., *Textile Leaders of the South* (Columbia, SC: R. L. Bryan Company, 1963) 230; Dwight C. Van Meter, "Donald Comer and His 7,000 Partners," *The Rotarian* 78/3 (March 1951): 24.

[44] Comer quoted in Van Meter, "Donald Comer and His 7,000 Partners," 23.

[45] Breedlove, "Donald Comer" diss., 281–85, 290–91.

[46] "Workers in Eight Avondale Mills Pledge Loyalty," *Birmingham Age-Herald*, 25 July 1934, 1.

the children would think he was a God and he could raise them up and work them to death before they were grown.[47]

Such verbal tirades infuriated and terrified Comer and his associates. They feared that the UTW campaign would disrupt their mill workers' productivity and eventually destabilize the entire Southern textile industry. Comer warned Avondale and Cowikee stockholders if his workers unionize, "I am ready to liquidate."[48]

Comer's threat was premature. On 24 July 1934, 5,500 employees at eight of the nine Comer mills pledged their fealty to him with signed petitions.[49] At his two Cowikee plants in Eufaula, 300 employees representing every mill family, signed a letter "expressing our 100 percent confidence in your leadership and our appreciation for the many kindnesses shown us ...and that you were always doing the best you could for us and trying all the time to do better—dealing always with us fair and square."[50]

In Eufaula in September 1934, a local citizens' committee led by American Legionnaires, formulated a defensive strategy in response to rumors of an approaching "flying squadron" of union organizers. Claiming that their actions were undertaken "without the knowledge" of mill owners, the committee ordered the sheriff, Pitt Williams, and the police chief, Harry McCullohs, to post armed guards at the Hoboken community to the north and on the McDowell Bridge spanning the Chattahoochee River eastward into Georgia. The guards were instructed to remain vigilant until "rumors of any invasion cease." After being rebuffed in their request for an Army machine gun squad from Camp Benning, the committee leaders re-asserted their intention to protect Cowikee Mills property and to ensure that no workers were "intimidated or molested."[51]

As rumors of an imminent assault spread throughout Barbour County, several prominent farmers joined the committee's ranks in a demonstration

---

[47] Ike Robinton quoted in Breedlove, "Donald Comer," diss., 288.

[48] Breedlove, "Donald Comer" diss., 289.

[49] "Avondale Mills Employe[e]s Express Their Loyalty," *Birmingham News*, 26 July 1934, 6.

[50] "Breach Widens between Labor, Strike Leaders," *Birmingham Age-Herald*, 26 July 1934, 1.

[51] "Eufaula Citizens Organize to Protect Property and Workers in Local Plants," *Eufaula Tribune*, 13 September 1934, n.p., printed in *Avondale Sun*, 22 September 1934, 2.

of solidarity. C. M. Gammage angrily asked, "Without these factory payrolls where will lots of us be able to sell our chickens, eggs, and garden truck?" He promised to stand with mill workers "to defend their jobs" against the "flying squadron": "If any outsider tries to come into this community, you just blow your whistles and ring your bells and we farmers will unhitch our mules and get up our axe and hoe handles and join the fight wherever we are needed."[52]

Despite this fiery rhetoric and the citizens' committee's feverish preparations, the "flying squadron" proved to be only an illusionary threat to Eufaula's mills. Colonel H. L. Upshaw, the *Eufaula Tribune's* venerable editor, reported, "[I]n the opinion of [Army] officers and others, the whole matter is mere rumor, and there will be no attempt to interfere with the workers here."[53] Cowikee Mills employees and the local citizenry had united in their opposition to the union and support for Donald Comer. About a week after the strike had ended, 3,000 Cowikee Mills workers and family members gathered at the Community House in Eufaula for a barbeque to honor Comer for his leadership during the crisis.[54]

Although the strike had run its course by fall 1934, Comer brooded over its impact for several months afterward. He remained especially sour about his Birmingham mill's participation in the strike. In 1935 he scaled back social and recreational programs in the Birmingham mill village and transferred Avondale's corporate headquarters to Sylacauga. Such rare public displays of Comer's retaliation for perceived disloyalty revealed that his paternalistic velvet glove was fortified with steel. He also privately felt betrayed by the federal government for not aggressively defending mill owners against the union's "outrageous" attack in 1934. He bitterly confided to an associate, "[O]ur New England friends are in partnership with Union Labor Leaders in this program" to destroy the Southern textile industry.[55]

In the wake of the strike, Comer evaluated his workers' benefits programs and began to consider supplemental plans. He was careful not to tinker with the overwhelmingly popular, successful programs such as home own-

---

[52] C. [M.] Gammage to editor, *Eufaula Tribune*, n.d., c. 13 September 1934, n.p., published as "Farmers Ready to Defend Mill Workers," *Avondale Sun*, 22 September 1934, 6.

[53] Upshaw quoted in *Eufaula Tribune*, 13 September 1934, n.p., printed in *Avondale Sun*, 22 September 1934, 2.

[54] "Cowikee Mills Honor Mr. Comer," *Avondale Sun*, 22 September 1934, 6.

[55] Breedlove, "Donald Comer" diss., 319 (quote from Comer letter), 329–37.

ership loans, college scholarships, Opportunity Schools, and life insurance. Yet, he realized that these attractive benefits alone were not enough to stave off the Depression's devastating economic impact on his employees' purchasing power. He also wanted to give his workers a tangible alternative to union membership. To garner employees' and stockholders' support for the program he envisioned, he had to devise a way to increase wages without bankrupting his two companies.

In 1936 Comer launched a workers' bonus plan in which $150,000 was divided among 5,400 hourly employees.[56] This initiative marked a rudimentary step toward his most ambitious proposal of all—a profit-sharing program known as the "Partnership with People." Comer introduced his new program in 1938 at the central Avondale Mill in Birmingham. After this trial run, he expanded the plan in 1941 into the other Avondale and Cowikee plants.[57] As the profit-sharing plan's cornerstone, Comer agreed to pay his employees a competitive or "going wage" based on hourly wages in other companies' mills that were located in the same area of the state. Mill stockholders received five percent off the top of annual profits. Comer management and their employees then took a fifty-fifty split of the remaining earnings.[58]

On 16 October 1941, Avondale and Cowikee stockholders formally approved the terms of Comer's profit-sharing plan. Despite the unpredictable future of the international textile market after the Japanese attack on Pearl Harbor and America's entry into World War II, Comer reassured his employees that the plan would remain in effect. His brother, Hugh Comer, cautioned that since the plan was "voluntary on the part of the Company" any details about the formulation and distribution of profit shares would

---

[56] Ibid., 226. Management's use of bonuses, stock ownership, profit-sharing plans, and other types of "industrial democracy" in dealing with labor originated in France and Germany in the nineteenth century and subsequently spread to the United States. See Herring, *Welfare Work in Mill Villages*, 372–75, 377–78.

[57] "A Statement by Donald Comer," *Avondale Sun*, 24 June 1946, 1; J. Craig Smith, "Employees are People," remarks at State Rotary Assembly, Tuscaloosa, AL, 26 June 1948, printed in *Avondale Sun*, 5 July 1948, 2; Van Meter, "Donald Comer and his 7,000 Partners," 23. An alternative name for "Partnership with People" was "The Avondale Way."

[58] "A True 50–50 Profit Sharing Plan," *Avondale Sun*, 21 July 1947, 12; Smith, "Employees are People," *Avondale Sun*, 5 July 1948, 2.

"remain entirely in the hands of Management without question."[59]

During World War II, Comer management used a small portion of their profit shares to upgrade plants and equipment. They earmarked a greater amount (about $1.2 million) as seed money for an "old age retirement fund" to supplement employees' Social Security benefits. Scheduled to take effect in July 1945, this extra retirement plan was funded entirely by management without any employees' payroll deductions.[60]

During the profit-sharing plan's first five years in operation, about $5 million was divided among stockholders, management, and employees. By 1952 the accumulated profit-sharing payout figure had reached $15 million (with $10 million to workers), and the retirement fund was valued at over $9 million.[61] Between 1941 and 1951, employees' profit shares boosted their take-home pay by approximately 12.5 percent. In some instances, as in March 1947, bonus checks constituted about 40 percent of employees' base pay.[62]

The most obvious motivational tool of the profit-sharing plan was that employees received bonuses monthly rather than annually. As one observer of corporate finance noted in 1947, when Comer workers opened their monthly pay envelopes, they immediately knew how the companies were faring and could ask themselves if they were doing everything to reduce costs

---

[59] Hugh M. Comer, "Communication from Management regarding Bonus Payment Plan for Avondale and Cowikee Mills," *Avondale Sun*, 26 January 1942, 1. Cowikee Mills president and treasurer L. Comer Jennings added that both companies would pay identical bonuses to employees.

[60] Donald Comer, "To the Employees of Avondale Mills," *Avondale Sun*, 8 July 1946, 1; "Avondale Retirement Units Last Year Worth $10.34 Each," *Avondale Sun*, 2 September 1946, 1; "Avondale Contributes $1,103,974.84 to Employees Retirement Plan," 19 August 1946, 1.

[61] Donald Comer, "To the Employees of Avondale Mills," *Avondale Sun*, 8 July 1946, 1; "Donald Comer Signs Retirement Plan Check for Over Million and Half Dollars," *Avondale Sun*, 7 July 1947, 3; "Large Payment Will Be Due Retirement Fund on December 31st," *Avondale Sun*, 8 December 1947, 1; "Retirement Plan Payment," *Avondale Sun*, 29 March 1948, 1; "Our Chairman Signs Big Check," *Avondale Sun*, 14 March 1949, 1; J. Craig Smith, "Donald Comer Day," ed., *Avondale Sun*, 21 April 1952, 2; J. Craig Smith, "Our Deferred Profit Sharing Plan Still Increasing Our Retirement Fund," ed., *Avondale Sun*, 30 June 1952, 2.

[62] Van Meter, "Donald Comer and his 7,000 Partners," 23; Young, *Textile Leaders of the South*, 230; "A True 50–50 Profit Sharing Plan," *Avondale Sun*, 21 July 1947, 12.

while "promoting full production." This recurring monthly process "naturally keeps the employee alert and spurred to produce to the best of his ability."[63]

Comer and the rest of his brain trust openly hoped that the profit-sharing plan's incentives would motivate their employees and lead to greater efficiency and productivity and ultimately to larger annual earnings. By the late 1940s, this correlation between incentives and productivity had become institutionalized within the companies' management philosophy. In July 1948, J. Craig Smith, Comer's nephew and one of his most influential advisors, candidly admitted that while they remained "hopeful" about the plan's future, "do not feel [it] has yet proved itself." Smith remained publicly confident that profit sharing eventually would produce a more independent, efficient, and energetic team of employees who required less direct supervision. Their foremen in turn would be relieved of many mundane supervisory duties and could concentrate on technical instruction.[64]

Smith's predictions evolved into standard talking points for the entire Comer management team, including "The Boss." Comer often praised profit sharing's merits with an analogy from nature:

> Employees under such a plan do not need supervision. Each one of them will go to his respective job without being told to stop or come or hurry.... [W]e have a lot to learn from bees. So far as I know, there are no foremen in a beehive. Every worker bee goes about her way and brings the honey back and puts it into a common pool. They all share and make some extra honey for the man who provides them the hive—a place to work.[65]

Comer appeared unconcerned that someone might brand him a utopian dreamer, or even worse, a socialist or communist—a particularly damning charge during the Cold War. He devoted an inordinate amount of his time countering criticisms of his profit-sharing plan as "bait" to keep his employ-

---

[63] "A True 50–50 Profit Sharing Plan," *Avondale Sun*, 21 July 1947, 12.

[64] Smith, "Employees Are People," *Avondale Sun*, 5 July 1948, 2; Young, *Textile Leaders of the South*, 236–37. Smith's cautionary tone echoed the views of many economists who believed that profit sharing did not translate well to the textile industry because of unpredictable fluctuations in the cotton market and an emphasis on machinery and mass production over the skilled craftsman's unique contributions. See Lewis Corey, "The New Capitalism," in *American Labor Dynamics: In the Light of Post-war Developments*, ed. J. B. S. Hardman (New York: Harcourt, Brace and Company, 1928) 59–60.

[65] Comer quoted in "A True 50–50 Profit Sharing Plan," *Avondale Sun*, 5 July 1948, 12.

ees out of unions. He told one journalist in 1949, "[W]hen you consider the millions it costs you must admit it becomes pretty expensive bait."[66] Union leaders cited the absence of strikes in Comer mills since the plan's full implementation in 1941 as irrefutable proof of their allegation. One highly respected Alabama historian argues that mill hands "were not fools. They knew the difference between an owner or manager who genuinely cared about them and one whose main interest was keeping them out of unions."[67]

Comer viewed his "Partnership with People" as the crowning achievement of his career. It combined, in one program, much of his underlying vision of paternalism and a business philosophy based on long-term rather than immediate financial gains. The plan featured financial and personal incentives for all of the participating partners. For his employees, the partnership not only increased their purchasing power but also nurtured a personal pride in their jobs and in the mills. In providing workers with a vested interest in the two companies, Comer distinguished himself as a corporate visionary who foresaw a time in the future when many businesses would adopt similar programs.

Any balanced evaluation of Comer's life and career must include analyses of his positive and negative attributes and their effects. He definitely was a very determined—often stubborn—man whose views and decisions were governed rigidly by his religious principles and personal moral code. Comer's obstinate side is best exemplified by his unwavering support for Prohibition and opposition to organized labor. His anti-union stance was fairly typical of his generation of industrialists. Ironically, his negativism toward unions prompted him to produce more tangible employees' benefits, such as the profit-sharing plan. His obsession with the liquor issue was perhaps more detrimental to his management decisions because he often simplistically blamed most of society's ills on "demon rum."[68]

Comer's obstinacy, however, was tempered by his more personable qualities. He was not an intellectual, but he displayed an insatiable curiosity

---

[66] Comer quoted in "The Plant That Runs on Happiness," *Look* (2 August 1949): 28.

[67] "A True 50–50 Profit Sharing Plan," *Avondale Sun*, 21 July 1947, 12; Flynt, *Poor but Proud*, 105.

[68] See, for example, Donald Comer, "Equally Honest People Divided over Best Solution of the Liquor Problem," *Avondale Sun*, 25 March 1932, 2; "Mr. Comer Defines Stand on Prohibition Question," *Avondale Sun*, 3 December 1932, 1–2.

about a diverse litany of subjects. He read widely and also carefully considered the guidance and counsel of others whose expertise he valued. While he remained intractable in his views on the evils of both liquor and unions, he was remarkably open-minded on many other issues, most notably, child labor reform. Comer initially agreed with his father that child labor demanded only minimal regulatory measures. Deeply influenced in the late 1920s by reports issued by state child labor inspectors Ruth Scandrett and Mrs. A. M. Tunstall and his two decades of experience as a mill owner, Comer reversed course on this issue. By 1934 he had become a leading proponent of federal legislation to abolish child labor in its entirety.[69]

Comer's thinking on the regulatory role of the federal government in economic matters underwent a similar transformation after World War I. During the 1920s, Comer became closely aligned with "business progressives" who championed economic development based upon efficiency and order in society and industry, with limited involvement by the government. After witnessing the Great Depression's unprecedented destructive force and its toll upon his own employees, Comer became an unabashed New Dealer and an advocate for a robust federal presence in regulating the economy and in establishing an assortment of employment and welfare initiatives.[70]

Comer's proven ability to modify his views on various issues and then chart a new course carried over into his personal management style. Although quietly confident in his managerial ability, the introverted, self-effacing Comer rarely touted his own accomplishments. He clearly was a perfectionist and a "workaholic," but he never demanded more of his employees than he did from himself. From the beginning of his career in 1907, Comer also recognized that he actually knew very little about the industry.

---

[69] Grantham, *Southern Progressivism*, 195; Flynt, *Poor but Proud*, 108–110; Irene M. Ashby-Macfayden, "The Fight Against Child Labor in Alabama," *American Federationist* 8 (May 1901): 150–57; Donald Comer, "Child Labor in the South," address at the University of Virginia, 8 July 1931, in *Avondale Sun*, 18 July 1931, 1–2; "Donald Comer Favors Child Labor Amendment in Address at University of Alabama," *Avondale Sun*, 29 June 1935, 8; "Donald Comer," *EOA* online.

[70] Grantham, *Southern Progressivism*, xvi—xviii; George B. Tindall, "Business Progressivism: Southern Politics in the Twenties," *South Atlantic Quarterly* 62 (Winter 1963): 92–106; Robert H. Wiebe, *Businessmen and Reform* (Chicago, IL: Quadrangle Paperbacks, 1962) and *The Search for Order, 1877–1920* (New York: Hill and Wang, 1967); Breedlove, "Donald Comer" diss., 11–13, 229–34, 254–55, 286.

Following his father's example, he recruited mill superintendents and fore-men with decades of experience. A man with a greater ego than Comer's would not have admitted that he lacked the technical knowledge that others possessed.

Neither ego nor hubris ruled Donald Comer. He was a creature of hab-it who assiduously resisted any deviation from the norm in his schedule or lifestyle. Like his father, Comer was both a non-smoker and teetotaler and exhibited little tolerance for anyone who was addicted to either. Comer, however, had his own addictions. When he was eighty years old, he still consumed at least six cups of coffee each day and regularly devoured sizable portions of his favorite foods: fried chicken, grits, and "lots of ham gravy."[71] One of his brothers once described him as "of slight, almost frail build, [and] slightly stooped from intense work and lack of attention to his physical well-being."[72] He also had suffered from asthma since childhood and experienced severe malarial attacks dating back to his Army service in the Philippines.[73]

Nevertheless, despite his periodic bouts of illness, he maintained a rig-orous travel schedule to ensure his attendance at all Avondale and Cowikee board meetings and annual mill inspections. For rest and recreation, he re-treated to his yacht, the *Gomal*, for leisurely days of sailing along the Florida coast, or to the seclusion of his home in Bonita Springs, Florida, or the Comer plantation in Barbour County. Although he preferred daily life in the country over his estate in Birmingham, Comer's frequent visits to the plan-tation were best described as "working vacations." He often rode on horse-back around his 30,000 acres, checking crops and conferring with black ten-ant farmers. He and his wife, Gertrude, also entertained their children and grandchildren, other Comer relatives, and busloads of "his people' from Eufaula, Union Springs, and Sylacauga. But the mills were never far from his mind. In autumn 1943, while under strict doctor's orders to convalesce at the plantation after a serious illness, he twice sneaked away to the Cowikee Mills office in Eufaula.[74]

In Donald Comer's well-ordered world, whenever he visited Cowikee

---

[71] "Life Begins at 80," *Avondale Sun*, 30 December 1957, 8.

[72] Breedlove, "Donald Comer" diss., 1.

[73] Ibid.

[74] Ibid., 8–9; "Donald Comer," *EOA* online; "Donald Comer Is Back Home in Barbour," *Avondale Sun*, 4 October 1943, 1; "Donald Comer's Letter," *Avondale Sun*, 1 November 1943, 12.

Mills No. 1 and No. 3, his typical routine featured casual chats with Carrie Snipes, Eddie Cox, James Wesley Gill, "Queen," the African-American sweeper, and other "Big Mill" veterans he had known since 1909, along with superintendent Brady Rogers, Hoke Williams, Sam Anderson, and the rest of the "Little Mill" hands. Comer then would drop by the Community House kindergarten and playground to see the children and perhaps spend some time at the poultry and mill farms. Whether Comer was in Eufaula for a mill inspection or a personal visit, after around 1940, he rarely deviated from this schedule. And he looked forward to the personal touches he always found in Eufaula—Ruby Beverly's decorative flower arrangements in the mill office and Hoke Williams's ceremonial presentation of his cherished, home-grown watermelons.[75]

In the final analysis, James McDonald Comer, whose life and career often were overshadowed by his father's reputation as Alabama's charismatic reform governor, perhaps deserves a more prominent niche in the state's history. Through his persistence and strength of will, Donald Comer led his mills through the trials and turmoil of the Great Depression and two world wars. During the Depression, his mill payrolls and infusions of capital into local businesses rescued Eufaula and other Alabama mill towns from complete fiscal collapse. Comer also provided something of much greater value to his employees than merely paternalistic gifts. He restored their personal dignity and instilled in them a deep, abiding pride in their labor. When he died in 1963 at age eighty-five, his mill families wept unashamedly. They had lost more than the man with whom they had entrusted their lives for over five decades. They would always remember him as "Mr. Donald" and "The Boss." But he also was their friend and neighbor. His legacy has stood the test of time and will endure, even for Eufaulians who were born long after Southside and the mills ceased to exist.

---

[75] See, for example, "Donald Comer Writes," *Avondale Sun*, 23 July 1945, 4; 12 November 1945, 4; 8 August 1946, 4; 10 August 1953, 4.

Chapter 5

Bands, Kindergarten, and Baseball:
The Creation and Evolution of Eufaula's
Cowikee Community House

It is ours...
—Avondale Sun, *18 April 1924*

Each of the Comer Mills had a community house that functioned as a head-quarters for organized social, educational, recreational activities, and as an oasis where exhausted workers gathered with their families and friends for relaxation and fellowship. By the time the Cowikee Community House (CCH) opened in Eufaula in 1918, Donald Comer's previous experience in providing welfare services for his employees served him well. He knew precisely which programs had the greatest potential for success and understood the importance of recruiting well-trained, professional staff.[1]

Comer apparently believed that community houses located in smaller, isolated towns such as Sylacauga and Eufaula potentially were more beneficial to mill families than in urban areas with greater access to welfare resources. In both of these towns, and later in Union Springs and Ozark, Comer personally selected community house directors and carefully monitored their performance. Despite his optimism about the Eufaula CCH's future, Comer did not foresee the unbridled enthusiasm with which his workers would embrace the modest wood-frame structure and its programs as their own. He also underestimated the dramatic impact that the CCH would have upon the entire town.[2]

---

[1] Breedlove, "Donald Comer" diss., 185, 191–92; Edward Akin, "Avondale's Welfare Programs for Youth: The Programs and the People Who Made Them Work," paper presented at the Organization of American Historians Meeting, 11 April 1980, 1, 3–5; "A Brief History of the Avondale Mills at Sylacauga," *Avondale Sun*, 8 October 1932, 6–7.

[2] Breedlove, "Donald Comer" diss., 8–9. Comer's views on the best locations for community houses reflected his own preference for the bucolic, rural lifestyle. As shown

The community house "movement" first became associated with the Southern textile industry in the Carolinas in the late nineteenth century and quickly spread to other states in the region. During an era before the advent of state and federal welfare programs, community houses' staff focused on the most elementary needs of mill workers and their families. Social workers, teachers, and nurses, employed by the mills, provided instruction in personal health and hygiene, childcare, nutrition and food preparation, sewing, and family finances. The community houses also sponsored a wide range of organized recreational and social activities. Bands, baseball teams, and playgrounds (with free kindergartens and nurseries) were the most popular amenities provided by the mills.[3]

Mill managers generally supported such community house programs based on a belief that "wholesome pastimes" produced happier, healthier, and more productive workers. Home visitations by social workers and nurses also accelerated the assimilation process for families from farms into the daily routine of the mill village. Thus, these welfare programs assisted workers in their transition from the unstructured pattern of farming to the fixed hours, discipline, and repetitive details indicative of industrial labor. Recreational programs also expedited this process by reinforcing the necessity of rules, regulations, and schedules.[4]

In Southern mill villages, World War I ushered in a new wave in the construction of community houses and the implementation of expanded welfare programs. Soon after the United States entered the war in 1917, mil-

---

in the previous chapter, although Comer owned a large estate in Birmingham and traveled frequently to Baltimore, New York City, and Boston, he spent his happiest moments at his family's plantation in Barbour County.

   [3] Herring, *Welfare Work in Mill Villages*, 106–107, 115, 128–29, 135–44; Rhyne, *Some Southern Cotton Mill Workers*, 27–30; Hall et al., *Like a Family*, 131, 134–35; US Department of Labor, Bureau of Labor Statistics, *Welfare Work for Employees in Industrial Establishments in the United States*, Bulletin No. 250 (Washington, DC: Government Printing Office, 1919) 74–77, 85, 89–90; *Examples of Welfare Work in the Cotton Industry: Conditions and Progress, New England and in the South* (New York: Woman's Department, The National Civic Federation, 1910) 1, 5–7, 12–15; Bernard M. Cone, "Some Phases of Welfare Work," *Southern Textile Bulletin* 3/18 (4 July 1912): 4; Lena Rivers Smythe, "Welfare Work Accomplishing Results," *Southern Textile Bulletin* 12/10 (2 November 1916): 1, 6–7.

   [4] Hall et al., *Like a Family*, 131–37; Herring, *Welfare Work in Mill Villages*, 106–107; Breedlove, "Donald Comer" diss., 187.

itary demands for cotton goods produced lucrative government contracts that led to unprecedented profits for the cotton industry and higher wages for mill workers. Since most able-bodied men were in military service, mills across the South experienced a severe labor shortage. To attract and keep workers, mill managers used their sizable profits in 1917–1918 to build new community houses and fund more diversified programs for their operatives.[5]

The patriotic fervor that swept the nation during the Great War also lent further impetus to the community house boom. In Eufaula, public attendance soared for "War Camp" events—Liberty Loan Bond rallies, parades, and community song fests, featuring orchestras and "Liberty Choruses."[6] These community gatherings contributed to a growing consensus throughout Eufaula for the establishment of a permanent home for future public events. With over 2,000 Barbour County men in uniform, virtually every Eufaula family had a personal stake in the war. Nevertheless, the invisible but seemingly impregnable wall between Southside and Old Eufaula remained intact. Families across the town "kept the home fires burning" during the war, but those "leisured women" from Old Eufaula assumed key leadership roles in organizing patriotic campaigns.[7]

For example, Caroline Copeland Clayton, the wife of attorney Lee J. Clayton, Sr., chaired the Woman's Liberty Loan Committee. She and her colleagues took the campaign beyond the confines of Eufaula into Clayton, Clio, Louisville, and Comer, the rural community near "Mr. Donald's" plantation. "Caro" Clayton's efforts paid dividends in Barbour County and Eufaula. During the Third Liberty Loan drive in spring 1918, Eufaula dou-

---

[5] Herring, *Welfare Work in Mill Villages*, 118–20, 128–29; "Glenola Cotton Mill Is Bought by Philadelphia Man," *Montgomery Advertiser*, 10 June 1918, 2; O. W. Douglas, "Industrial Recreation and Welfare," *Southern Textile Bulletin* 16/4 (26 September 1918): 1.

[6] Herring, *Welfare Work in Mill Villages*, 120; "White Addresses Barbour People on Liberty Loan," *Montgomery Advertiser*, 8 April 1918, 2; "Eufaula Woodmen Buy Loan Bonds," *Montgomery Advertiser*, 12 April 1918, 9; "Eufaula Observes National Song Week," *Montgomery Advertiser*, 19 February 1918, 8; Hastings H. Hart, *Social Problems of Alabama: A Study of the Social Institutions and Agencies of the State of Alabama as Related to Its War Activities* (Montgomery, AL: State of Alabama, 1918) 16, 18, 20.

[7] For an incisive examination of the roles of "leisured women" throughout the nation, see Lynn Dumenil, "American Women and the Great War," *Organization of American Historians Magazine of History* 17/1 (October 2002): 35–37.

bled its subscription quota and Comer residents purchased $2,150 in bonds. The Woman's Committee helped Barbour became one of the first counties in the state to "go over the top" in the bond campaign.[8]

These women also patronized other organizations that had specific missions and strong leadership. The Women's Patriotic Prayer League, for example, included Old Eufaula society matrons and wives of ministers and civic leaders, and rotated their meetings among Eufaula's different churches. In September 1918, they convened at Washington Street Methodist Church to honor two local soldiers—Porter Rankin Doughtie and Hinton Watson Holleman—who had been killed in France. The League's meeting at this small church in the heart of Southside delivered a stark reminder that the war's burdens fell equally upon all of Eufaula. While the program offered the usual patriotic poems, hymns, and prayers, four presentations dealt specifically with the Red Cross.[9]

At least two League members, Mrs. Clifford A. Locke and Mrs. Albert C. Moulthrop, also were active in the local Red Cross chapter which met at the Carnegie Library. Their meetings usually included a presentation by a speaker whose husband or son was serving in France, solicitations for donations, and recruitment of volunteers.[10] Red Cross fund-raising campaigns were very successful all over Barbour County. In April 1918, Mr. and Mrs. W. A. Ham hosted a joint Red Cross-Liberty Loan barbeque at "Woodlodge," their country home in Glennville. "An immense crowd" partook of the feast and donated several thousand dollars to the two causes. Two

---

[8] "Barbour County Climbing Fast," *Montgomery Advertiser*, 22 April 1918, 3; "Eufaula Doubled Quota in Third Loan Campaign," *Montgomery Advertiser*, 5 May 1918, 7; "Eufaula Woodmen Buy Loan Bonds," *Montgomery Advertiser*, 12 April 1918, 9. Other members of the Woman's Liberty Loan Committee included Mrs. Charles S. McDowell, Mrs. Clifford A. Locke, Mrs. Walter S. Britt, Mrs. E. H. Dantzler, Mrs. W. L. Wilde, and Miss Lottie Petry.

[9] "Eufaula," *Montgomery Advertiser*, 13 January 1918, 17; "Eufaula Society," *Columbus (GA) Daily Enquirer*, 21 September 1918, 8.

[10] "Eufaula," *Montgomery Advertiser*, 6 January 1918, 19; "Camp Pike Worker Holds Rally in City of Eufaula," *Montgomery Advertiser*, 24 July 1918, 5; The Alabama Council of Defense appointed Mrs. Moulthrop to chair the Barbour County woman's division of the "Four-Minute Speakers" Bureau. When men were unavailable, the women spoke on various patriotic topics.

months later, Cowikee Mill employees contributed $600 to the Red Cross.[11] The local chapter's recruitment efforts also bore fruit. In August 1917, Mrs. Clifford A. Locke's daughter, Marie, volunteered to serve as a Red Cross nurse.[12]

Many of the same women who were leaders in the Red Cross, the Patriotic Prayer League, and the Liberty Loan campaigns also patronized Old Eufaula's array of social clubs. The town's three oldest literary societies—the Perian, Lanier, and Symposium clubs—filled their itineraries with discussions of world events, music, poetry, games, door prizes, and soldiers' service projects. The women of the Lanier Club in January 1918 discussed the reconstruction of France, Chinese poets, and "other interesting topics of today." The society editor summarized the afternoon's work: "This club will send a large number of scrapbooks to soldiers and other patriotic work was discussed."[13]

Also in January 1918, the Symposium Club, hosted by Catherine Jelks Comer (the daughter of former Governor W. D. Jelks and his wife, Alice), devoted their "spend-the-day party" to "patriotic work." "[A]rmed with sewing bags," the members produced "cootie garments" for distribution to soldiers by the National League for Public Service. In autumn 1918, the club selected "war refugees" as the discussion topic for the next year's meetings.[14]

---

[11] "Barbour County Climbing Fast," *Montgomery Advertiser*, 22 April 1918, 3; "Glenola Cotton Mill Is Bought by Philadelphia Man," *Montgomery Advertiser*, 10 June 1918, 2.

[12] "Miss Marie Locke to Go to France As Red Cross Nurse," *Columbus (GA) Ledger*, 26 August 1917, 3; "Wife of Editor Dies at Eufaula," *Columbus Daily Enquirer*, 9 May 1929, 2. After the war, Marie Locke married Carl S. Strang, *Eufaula Tribune* editor. She died in 1929 at age thirty-eight.

[13] FWP, State Guide File, Barbour County, box A15, WPA Records, LC; *Montgomery Advertiser*, 13 January 1918, 17; misc. historical sketches of women's clubs, *Eufaula Tribune*, Historical and Progress Edition, 5 December 1940, n.p.

[14] "Eufaula," *Montgomery Advertiser*, 6 January 1918, 19; "Eufaula Society," *Columbus Daily Enquirer*, 21 September 1918, 8. Derived from the Great War's "trench vernacular," "cootie garments" were chemically treated underwear used as a preventative against lice and other vermin. British scientists at Oxford University devised the chemical process and shared it with the Canadian Red Cross, the French government, and the US surgeon general. "University Treats Soldiers' Garments for Vermin," *The Iowa Alumnus* 15/6 (March 1918): 168–69; G. C. Boroughs, "Rival Textiles and Substitutes," *The Clothing Designer & Manufacturer* 13/5 (August 1918): 245–46; Doran Cart (senior curator, Na-

The Symposium and Lanier clubs, along with other women's organizations, collectively "did their bit" on the Eufaula home front, and they contributed to the entire community's spirit of solidarity in the war effort. However, despite their earnest dedication, these prominent club women never
welcomed Southsiders into their ranks. Old Eufaula's women, like its men,
still saw Southside as the "Factory District," whose residents were entitled to
charity but not equality.[15]

Although the World War I era did not eradicate the barriers between
Southside and Old Eufaula, it helped create an environment that was conducive to establishing a community house. The expansion and diversification
of social services programs by the Red Cross, YMCA, YWCA, Salvation
Army, and similar groups had a dramatic effect upon small Southern communities like Eufaula. The war's demands on the civilian population placed
the South's systemic social problems and deficiencies under a microscope.
These revelations—widely reported in the national press—attracted a new
generation of social workers, including many women, to the South. Moreover, these developments on the home front reinvigorated social work in the
entire region, which, in the words of one practitioner, previously was "a
washed out, broken down, sour, dilapidated field."[16]

Twenty-six-year-old Red Cross nurse Marie Locke personally witnessed the positive results of social work in Eufaula and became a vocal advocate for a community house.[17] She found enthusiastic allies in Donald
Comer and Cowikee Mills superintendent Robert Dallas Jones. Construction began during winter 1917–1918, and the CCH opened its doors in early spring 1918.[18] One reporter casually noted, "An attractive looking 'community home' has been built just back of the Cowikee mill and a social

tional World War I Museum and Memorial, Kansas City, MO) email to author, 16 July
2015.
    [15] FWP, State Guide File, Barbour County, box A15, WPA Records, LC; misc.
historical sketches of women's clubs, *Eufaula Tribune*, Historical and Progress Edition, 5
December 1940, n.p.; "Charity Ball at Eufaula," *Atlanta Constitution*, 31 December 1911,
3; "To Remember Poor," *Montgomery Advertiser*, 22 December 1922, 5. Among the three
literary societies, only the Symposium Club later donated books to the CCH's library.
    [16] Grantham, *Southern Progressivism*, 390–97. Quote is found on pg. 393.
    [17] "Wife of Editor Dies at Eufaula," *Columbus Daily Enquirer*, 9 May 1929, 2.
    [18] "Eufaula," *Montgomery Advertiser*, 7 April 1918, 22.

service worker from Birmingham has charge."[19]

This "social service worker" was Ohioan Mary Ellen Fausnaugh, age thirty-nine, the first CCH director handpicked by Donald Comer. Her previous jobs were as a stenographer and bookkeeper in Findlay, Ohio; Montgomery; and Birmingham. In April 1913, while studying at the Scarritt Bible Training School in Kansas City, Missouri, she was ordained as a deaconess by the Woman's Missionary Council of the Methodist Church in Birmingham. After graduating from Scarritt in 1914, she spent the next four years in Memphis and Birmingham.[20]

Donald Comer undoubtedly was impressed with Miss Fausnaugh's academic credentials. The Scarritt curriculum, which prepared young women for careers as missionaries, social workers, nurses, and teachers, included rigorous instruction in the "English Bible, book by book," "Evidences of Christianity and Doctrines," "History of the Christian Church Missions," "Methods of Christian Work," and "Conduct of Religious Meetings." Students who were enrolled in "Nurse Training and Elementary Medicine" were required to attend eighteen medical lectures in addition to intensive laboratories. For specialists in "City Mission Work," classes were offered in "House to House Visiting," "Lessons in Domestic Economy," sewing, housekeeping, bookkeeping, and music. All of Scarritt's students were required to complete a course titled "Temperance Viewed from the Standpoint of Science and Morals."[21]

Regardless of their academic majors, Scarritt women also conducted specialized field assignments at local churches, schools, orphanages, and settlement houses. One Scarritt graduate who went on to a distinguished career in social work later paid tribute to her training:

[It] opened to us an interesting world where men and women were striving to adjust and fit back into normal life, the unprivileged, the handicapped, the delinquent, and the dependent. We were shown the problems of human society and given preventative measures to be used over and over again

---

[19] "Glenola Cotton Mill Is Bought by Philadelphia Man," *Montgomery Advertiser*, 10 June 1918, 2.

[20] "Officials of Woman's Council Make Reports," *Montgomery Advertiser*, 12 April 1913, 3; "Miss Fausnaugh Visits," *Avondale Sun*, 8 August 1924, 4; Ginny Dunaway Young email to author, with attached Fausnaugh biography, 26 February 2015.

[21] Maria Layng Gibson, *Memories of Scarritt*, ed. Sara Estella Haskin (Nashville, TN: Cokesbury Press, 1928) 46–47.

in the battle waged against poverty, disease, and ignorance—the great triumvirate.[22]

Despite this idealized view of the social worker's approach to society's ills, Scarritt graduates seemingly were well prepared for their future careers. Mary Ellen Fausnaugh appeared to fit Donald Comer's proscribed template for the perfect community house director—a mature woman of impeccable character and strong religious faith who was dedicated to a life of service to others. Unbeknownst to Comer, however, her career aspirations lay overseas in the foreign missions field. Consequently, she remained in Eufaula for only two years.

During her brief tenure as the CCH director, Miss Fausnaugh earned the respect and trust of Donald Comer and Robert Jones. As the CCH's first resident, she lived in a modest, second-floor apartment. Establishing a precedent for future directors, she quickly immersed herself in the daily routine of Southside. She taught at Washington Street Methodist Church's Sunday school and joined the Women's Patriotic Prayer League during World War I.[23]

In fall 1918, as Miss Fausnaugh's first year on the job ended, the Spanish Influenza engulfed Eufaula, hitting Southside especially hard. In December 1918, Dr. Walter S. Britt reported that "nearly everyone here has now had [the flu]."[24] Thanks to the vigilant efforts of Dr. Britt, other local physicians, Red Cross volunteers, health officials, and ministers, the flu's death toll was minimal. Out of 150 flu cases in October 1918, only one patient succumbed. Nevertheless, Eufaula's leaders exhibited an abundance of caution. The city council ordered the closure of the schools, churches, movie theaters, and "all public gathering places."[25] With much of the flu concentrated in Southside, the ban on "meetings of all sorts," including those previ-

---

[22] Ibid., 79–80.

[23] "Eufaula Society," *Columbus Daily Enquirer*, 21 September 1918, 8.

[24] *Montgomery Advertiser*, 8 December 1918, 3; Ginny Dunaway Young email to author, 19 July 2015. Sixteen-year-old J. T. Dunaway was the only member of his family of seven who escaped the flu in 1918. He nursed the other family members and never forgot the horror of that experience. For the rest of his life, he vividly recalled the 1918 flu epidemic in Eufaula and worried when the flu season arrived each year.

[25] *Montgomery Advertiser*, 18 October 1918, 5; 31 October 1918, 5; "Eufaula Public Places Closed," *Montgomery Advertiser*, 13 October 1918, 3.

ously scheduled at the CCH, extended into December 1918.[26] Public fears associated with the 1918 epidemic carried over into the next year and seriously hampered Miss Fausnaugh's plans and programs.

In 1920, she left Eufaula for a stenographer's position with the federal government in Washington, DC.[27] Four years later, Southsiders fondly remembered "Miss Mary" as "a woman of great ability and attainments" who opened the CCH and "laid the foundation for all the splendid accomplishments of the home."[28] She devoted the rest of her life to social work and public service at home and abroad.[29] During her two years as the CCH's first director, a rudimentary playground was developed, the first Boy Scout troop was established, and the Cowikee Mill Band was organized.

Eufaula had a rich tradition of bands and orchestras dating back to the late nineteenth century. Eufaula's Union Female College sponsored a variety of concerts to showcase the talents of students and faculty. Traveling musical troupes also performed in town. In 1897 the local militia company, the Eufaula Rifles, was reorganized as a unit of the Alabama State Troops. The company's troops and local civilians formed ad hoc bands for annual balls and other special occasions. In 1908, Professor S. V. DeTrinis, a clarinet virtuoso from Italy, organized the Second Regiment Band as an auxiliary to the Eufaula Rifles. This brass band was composed of about thirty men, only three of whom were trained musicians. They performed at state military drills and encampments, gubernatorial inaugural parades, Confederate commemorative events, and Chautauqua literary and musical festivals.[30] Af-

---

[26] "Flu Ban Goes on Again in Eufaula," *Montgomery Advertiser*, 29 November 1918, 13.

[27] Young, Fausnaugh biography; "Miss Fausnaugh Visits," *Avondale Sun*, 8 August 1924, 4.

[28] "Miss Fausnaugh Visits," *Avondale Sun*, 8 August 1924, 4.

[29] "Personals," *Avondale Sun*, 15 August 1924, 10; "Writes from China," *Avondale Sun*, 6 March 1925, 8; "Mary Fausnaugh Called by Death," *(Findlay, OH) Republican-Courier*, 6 November 1963, 4. In 1924 Miss Fausnaugh became the bursar at the Woman's Union Christian Medical College in Shanghai, China. By 1930 she had returned to the United States and subsequently held several jobs with the federal government, including a clerk's position at the Agriculture Department. She also served as a volunteer at the Margaret J. Bennett Home in Baltimore, MD, a settlement house for "homeless, needy, and deserving" women. She spent the last two years of her life as a resident of the Asbury Methodist Home in Gaithersburg, MD, and died at age eighty-four in October 1963.

[30] "Now Watch Them, The Eufaula Rifles...," *Birmingham Age-Herald*, 10 Sep-

ter Alabama National Guard units were federalized during the Mexican Border Crisis in 1916 and again during World War I, the Second Regiment Band ceased to exist.

In August 1918, seventeen men and boys of the new Cowikee Band assembled for the first time at the CCH. Donald Comer wrote a check for $2,000 to purchase their instruments. Before they played a single note, band members posed for photographs in their "uniforms": white cotton shirts and trousers, celluloid collars, black ties, and various styles of billed caps. Within a year, the mill purchased dark grey, military-style uniforms for the band. C. H. Lowe, cloth room overseer, was the first Cowikee band director, assisted by H. W. White, "an experienced cornet player" and overseer of the carding and spinning rooms. Their pupils ranged in age from about ten to fifty. Sixteen-year-old J. T. Dunaway, who earlier had been rejected as a tenor soloist in a school operetta because he was a Southsider, was among the musicians in the band. The other original band members were Rolly Anderson, Emmett Barefield, Walter Folsom, Jr., Albert Gill, Floyd Gill, Herman Jones, James Jones, Willie McGilvary, Roy Rogers, J. W. Primm, Marvin Tharp, Monroe Tharp, "Mr. Camp," "Mr. Quattlebaum," and "Mr. Perry." Perry later succeeded C. H. Lowe as the director.[31]

The first band initially faced difficulties in arranging regular practices that did not conflict with mill shifts. They began practicing three times a week, eventually expanding to five sessions. In summer 1919, after a year's training, the band camped at Blue Springs, a popular recreational site near Clio. Their Blue Springs performances were their first public events beyond the confines of Eufaula. In mid-July 1920, they played at a reunion of the

---

tember 1897, 3; "News of Eufaula," *Montgomery Advertiser*, 5 June 1910, 3; "Eufaula Will Turn Out," *Montgomery Advertiser*, 14 January 1911, 2; "Bid Soldiers "Good-Bye,'" *Montgomery Advertiser*, 4 July 1911, 6; "Second Regiment Band," *Montgomery Advertiser*, 7 July 1911, 4; "The Eufaula Rifles May Be Mustered Out," *Atlanta Constitution*, 28 March 1912, 4; "Brenau Cha[u]tauqua," *Montgomery Advertiser*, 21 May 1908, 3; "Eufaula Festivity," *Montgomery Advertiser*, 22 May 1908, 5; "Was Alumnae Day," *Montgomery Advertiser*, 26 May 1908, 9; "Eufaula's Big Show," *Montgomery Advertiser*, 30 May 1909, 22; "Eufaula Rifles at Encampment," *Columbus Ledger*, 20 July 1913, 3.

[31] "Cotton Mill Men Organize a Band," *Montgomery Advertiser*. 8 December 1918, 3; "First Cowikee Mill Band," photo with roster, *Avondale Sun*, 26 October 1936, 7; "Short History of Cowikee Mill Band," 21 September 1938, Federal Writers' Project #4454, folder 16, box SG022777, WPA Files, ADAH.

famed World War I Rainbow Division in Birmingham. Donald Comer personally funded the band's travel and other expenses and hosted a dinner in their honor at his Red Mountain estate. From these humble origins, the Cowikee Band later acquired a reputation as ranking among the best of the Comer Mills' musicians.[32]

Several of the Cowikee band members joined Barbour County's first Boy Scout troop, also headquartered at the CCH. At that time, the Scouting movement was still in its infancy in the United States. Arthur Eugene Barlar, a twenty-two-year-old retail hardware salesman and World War I Army veteran, had been interested in the Boy Scouts prior to his military service. After his discharge in December 1918, he organized Boy Scout Troop 10 and became its first Scoutmaster. Gene Barlar was a seasoned outdoorsman, but he was a novice within Scouting's complex universe of ranks and advancement and governing bureaucracy at the council, district, and national levels. When he established Troop 10, he could not even recite the Boy Scout oath and laws. He literally learned on the job, eagerly devouring information from the published Boy Scouts manuals of that era.

During the 1920s, under Barlar's tireless leadership, Troop 10 produced Barbour County's first Eagle Scouts and became one of the most active units in the Southeast Alabama Council. His Scouts blazed the trail after 1930 for the creation of three additional units—Troops 11 and 13, sponsored, respectively, by the Kiwanis and Rotary clubs, and Troop 64 in Eufaula's African-American community. Despite Gene Barlar's dedicated service as a Scouting pioneer in Eufaula, by 1940 his seminal role had faded into obscurity.[33]

---

[32] "Short History of the Cowikee Mill Band," 21 September 1938, FWP#4454, folder 16, box SG022777, WPA Files, ADAH; *Avondale Sun*, 2 August 1930, 6; "Rainbow Division Reunion," *Montgomery Advertiser*, 12 July 1920, 4. This event in 1920 was described as "by far the largest and most significant of the early reunions of the men who fought in France." The Cowikee Band's inclusion in the reunion festivities was a great honor because Barbour County had furnished a large number of doughboys to the 167th Infantry Regiment, often hailed as "the pride of the Division."

[33] "Boy Scouts, Troop #10," 28 September 1938, FWP#4454, folder 16, box SG022777, WPA Files, ADAH; "Boy Scouts," *Avondale Sun*, 12 February 1926, 3; 25 February 1927, 6; 3 May 1927, n.p.; 3 June 1927, n.p.; "Scouts Organize a Local Troop," *Avondale Sun*, 28 April 1934, 4; "Another Scout Troop Sponsored," *Columbus Daily Enquirer*, 14 August 1938, 4; "Charter Renewal Papers Received," *Dothan (AL) Eagle*, 1

With the founding of Troop 10 and the Cowikee Band, the initial building blocks for the CCH's programs were in place. Although both of these enterprises were relatively inexpensive and universally popular in Southside, Donald Comer realized that additional social services were needed for Cowikee families. Therefore, Mary Ellen Fausnaugh's successor would be asked to do a great deal more as the CCH director.

Florida Henrietta Dewar, the new CCH director, came to Eufaula from Sylacauga in 1920, soon after Miss Fausnaugh's departure. Florida Dewar was a strikingly attractive woman at age forty, with deeply luminescent eyes, gentle facial features, and thick, prematurely grey hair. Her contemporaries described her as a woman of intelligence, grace, confidence, and compassion. She also had a very impressive résumé as a social worker and educator.

After a brief teaching career in her native Florida, she enrolled at Scarritt Bible Training School and completed the two-year curriculum in twelve months. She graduated in 1911 and was ordained as a Methodist deaconess in 1913. Like her CCH predecessor, Scarritt, Methodism, and Donald Comer shaped Miss Dewar's career decisions. In return, she deeply influenced Comer's evolving philosophy of social services for his mill families. From 1911–1914, Miss Dewar supervised the welfare programs at Birmingham's central Avondale Mill and taught Sunday school classes at the First Methodist Church, where the Comer family had worshiped for many years. Over the next two years, she was the superintendent of San Francisco's Mary Elizabeth Inn, a Methodist residence for young, single business women. Returning to Alabama in 1917, she served for three years as director of the Mignon Mill Kindergarten in Sylacauga.[34]

November 1944, 1; *Handbook for Scoutmasters* (New York: Boy Scouts of America, 1913), A. E. Barlar's annotated volume, in author's possession; Rev. C. Walker Sessions, "Scouting in Eufaula," *Eufaula Tribune*, Historical and Progress Edition, 5 December 1940, n.p.; "The First Boy Scout Band in the South," photograph with roster, *Avondale Sun*, 11 March 1957, 8. Throughout the 1920s and 1930s, Troop 10 occasionally was designated as Troop 1.

[34] "A Brief History of the Avondale Mills at Sylacauga," *Avondale Sun*, 8 October 1932, 6; "Mrs. Florida Dewar McMull[e]n," obituary, *Avondale Sun*, 15 July 1940, 11; "Former Resident of Largo Passes," *The (St. Petersburg, FL) Independent*, 24 May 1940, 11; Ginny Dunaway Young email to author, 4 December 2014; Breedlove, "Donald Comer," diss., 193.

Even before Miss Dewar arrived in Eufaula, Donald Comer was confident that she would transform the CCH's current operations. Dewar did not
disappoint him. She saw immediately that more programs were needed for
younger children. She instituted a free kindergarten that became a godsend
for mill families in which parents were working different shifts. The kindergarten, like other CCH programs, was not restricted to mill workers and
other Southsiders; any Eufaula family could enroll their children. Miss
Dewar also founded the Cowboys Club for boys who were too young to join
Troop 10, the Girl Reserves, a precursor of the Girl Scouts, a sewing club,
and a children's band.[35]

Although Florida Dewar loved the sights and sounds of happy children
at play, each of her programs included educational components. As Donald
Comer observed, she "formed little groups of children and taught them thus
early to play at things that [carried] with them lessons that builded for the
future."[36] But Comer believed that her greatest contribution was "teach[ing]
the boys and girls of the community in which she lived and worked, to love
music, flowers and the beautiful things of life."[37] In spring 1925, she wrote
to one of her kindergartners, "If you can't plant a flower *every* time you think
of me, ...just do it once in a while. I think it would be such a sweet thing to
do, and then some day I'd come and go with you to look at those flowers."[38]

Florida Dewar adored her "little darlings" in the kindergarten and band
and spent many long hours with them. Organized in 1922, the children's
band, later known as the "little band," absorbed much of her time as CCH
director. In contrast to the mill's first all-male band, Miss Dewar recruited
boys and girls between the ages of eight and sixteen. In July 1922, after only
a few months of practice, her band performed at the CCH, on Broad Street
in Eufaula, and in Sylacauga. They next received an invitation to the inaugural ceremony in January 1923 for Governor William W. Brandon and their
fellow Eufaulian, Lieutenant Governor Charles S. McDowell. After their
performance, one reporter noted, "[I]t isn't just a good band; but one of the

---

[35] *Avondale Sun*, 8 May 1925, 2; Roy Rhodes, "The Cowboys Club," *Avondale Sun*,
2 December 1933, 9; "Mrs. Florida Dewar McMull[e]n," obituary, *Avondale Sun*, 15 July
1940, 11.

[36] Donald Comer, "Good Bye, Miss Dewar," *Avondale Sun*, 30 January 1925, 6.

[37] "Comer Talks to Church Laymen," *Avondale Sun*, 16 June 1941, 4.

[38] Florida Dewar to Master Thomas Alsobrook, 3 May 1925, postcard, in author's
possession.

very best.... Miss Florida Dewar...takes the greatest interest in her charges, whom she loves and who love her. Perhaps that is the big underlying principle in the band's success."[39]

Miss Dewar modestly credited Billy Hrabe, "director and instructor in harmony," for the band's rapid development. The forty-three-year-old Hrabe was the director of the boys' band at the Alabama Masonic Home in Montgomery. Born in rural Kansas, he studied classical music in New York and Boston. Prior to World War I, Hrabe traveled as a musician with circuses, vaudeville troupes, and minstrel shows. Most notably, he played the cornet in John Phillip Sousa's band. He later directed the first band at Montgomery's Sidney Lanier High School.[40] The Cowikee Little Band's young musicians were fortunate to have an instructor of Hrabe's caliber, if only for a year.

Exemplified by her recruitment of Billy Hrabe as an itinerant instructor, Miss Dewar continually sought opportunities to broaden her band members' training and experience. During summer 1923, she rewarded eight musicians who had earned academic honors with a week-long trip to Atlanta. On the day of their departure, they posed proudly with their luggage piled in front of the CCH. The highlight of the trip was a live radio performance—a landmark event for that era of primitive broadcasting technology.[41]

---

[39] *Avondale Sun*, 8 May 1925, 2; "Donald Comer Writes," *Avondale Sun*, 12 August 1957, 4; "Cowikee Mill Bands Go to Sylacauga," *Montgomery Advertiser*, 2 July 1922, 21; "Eufaula," *Montgomery Advertiser*, 30 July 1922, 16; "Cowikee Mill Band of Eufaula Gives Concerts Sunday," *Montgomery Advertiser*, n.d., c. 15 January 1923, reprinted in *Avondale Sun*, 25 January 1960, 12 (source for reporter's quote).

[40] "Formal Opening of New Park Is Staged," *Montgomery Advertiser*, 13 November 1922, 8; "Cowikee Mill Band of Eufaula Gives Concerts Sunday," *Montgomery Advertiser*, n.d., c. 15 January 1923, reprinted in *Avondale Sun*, 25 January 1960, 12; John Allen Hrabe, "William (Billy) Hrabe," biographical sketch, 2014; "Great Ceremonial Staged by Grotto," *Montgomery Advertiser*, 2 September 1921, 5; "John Phillip Sousa and Famous Band Will Play...," *Montgomery Advertiser*, 19 February 1922, 2; "Plans Are Complete for Big Celebration," *Montgomery Advertiser*, 19 June 1922, 2; "Director and Assistant Musicians of National Experience," *Montgomery Advertiser*, 27 August 1922, 3; "Attend Sousa Concert," *Avondale Sun*, 29 February 1924, 10; *Biloxi (MS) Daily Herald*, 2 June 1930, 5; "William Hrabe Dies," *Birmingham News*, 9 February 1938, 3; Hrabe obituary, *Biloxi Daily Herald*, 9 February 1938, 7.

[41] "Short History of Cowikee Mill Band," 21 September 1938, FWP #4454, fold-

Summer excursions for the band's honor students continued after 1923. In mid-July 1924, the latest honorees—Tyson Smith, Albert Driggers, and Cleveland Adams—spent two weeks in Washington, DC. These three young sons of Southside had risen from mill families in which by age fourteen or fifteen each child was expected to contribute financially by finding a steady job. Although each of these bright, ambitious boys traveled separate pathways in their future careers, they forever would be linked as childhood friends and would never forget their Southside roots, "Mr. Donald," and Miss Dewar.

Born in 1906, Tyson Smith was a year older than Driggers and Adams. Standing well over six feet tall, Smith had luxuriant blond hair and the stylishly handsome bearing of the "Arrow Shirt Man" of the era. His parents, Will and Emma Hatfield Smith, both were mill workers. Because of a childhood injury to his left arm, he lacked the athletic prowess of his three younger brothers, Earl, Fred, and Winston. But Tyson Smith was a star in the classroom at Eufaula High School. In 1926 the Symposium Club awarded him their coveted prize for the highest average in mathematics. He jealously guarded his study hours while working in the mill and playing the cornet in the band. With financial aid from Donald Comer, between 1926 and 1930, he studied chemical engineering and played in the band at Birmingham's Howard College. Comer also hired him as a part-time lifeguard and playground instructor at the central Avondale Mill Community House. Smith graduated in 1930 and returned to his hometown. He spent much of his career as an accountant in the mill business office and later became a vice-president of the company. In 1938, he married Hallie Hartsfield, the CCH director. After spending the first three years of their marriage living in the CCH, they bought a home on Country Club Road, where they remained for the rest of their lives.[42]

---

er16, box SG022777, WPA Files, ADAH; *Avondale Sun*, 2 August 1930, 6.

[42] "Short History of Cowikee Mill Band," 21 September 1938, FWP #4454, folder 16, box SG022777, WPA Files, ADAH; "Off for Capitol," *Avondale Sun*, 25 July 1924, 4; Tyson Smith, "A Trip to Washington," *Avondale Sun*, 8 August 1924, 10; "School News," *Avondale Sun*, 4 June 1926, 8; "Band News," *Avondale Sun*, 3 September 1926, 10; "Personals," *Avondale Sun*, 10 September 1926, 4; 31 August 1929, 10; "Hartsfield-Smith Marriage," *Avondale Sun*, 10 October 1938, 10; *Avondale Sun*, 11 April 1955, 8–9; Jeanine Smith DeVenny (Tyson Smith's niece) email to author, 4 March 2014; Oma Alsobrook to Thomas Alsobrook, n.d., c. May 1941, in author's possession; 13th–16th

Tyson Smith's classmate, Cleveland Adams, entered the mill in Eufaula when he was fifteen to help support his family. Never taller than five feet, six inches, Adams had to stand on a box in performing his earliest mill tasks. His sister Pauline later recalled that he began disrobing on his way home from school. He then would climb into his overalls, grab a baked sweet potato, and be off to the mill for the night shift. During his high school years, he played the trombone and several other instruments in the Cowikee Band, served as an assistant Scoutmaster in Troop 10, and was an active member of Washington Street Methodist Church.[43]

After graduating from Eufaula High School in 1928, Adams was awarded a Victor H. Hanson *Birmingham News* scholarship to study textile engineering at Alabama Polytechnic Institute (API) in Auburn. In sending Adams off to college, his Southside friends lamented, "We are very sorry to have him leave for he has filled a real need in the life of the community. We shall miss him and his influence is always for good."[44]

At Auburn, Adams earned numerous academic honors, played in the API band, founded the Auburn Textile Society, held three offices in the YMCA, pledged Sigma Pi social fraternity, and was president of the Websterian Literary Society. Throughout his college career, he spent each summer furthering his practical knowledge of the textile industry by working in various Comer mills.[45]

In 1932, after earning his Auburn degree and accumulating ten years of experience in the mills, Adams returned to Eufaula. In 1933 he married his hometown sweetheart, Fannie Corbitt. Over the next twelve years, they had four children. From 1933–1938, he was Cowikee Mill No. 1's assistant superintendent and then served over the next three years as the plant's manag-

---

US Census, 1910–1940, Schedule No. 1, Population, Barbour County, Alabama, NARA.

[43] Author's telephone conversation with Mary Adams Belk (Cleveland Adams's daughter), 24 May 2014; "Boy Scouts," *Avondale Sun*, 26 February 1926, 10; "Band News," *Avondale Sun*, 25 August 1928, n.p.; "Was[h]ington Street M. E. Church," *Avondale Sun*, 8 September 1928, n.p.; "Joseph Decalve Adams, Jr. (1885–1925) and Descendants," Adams family history. I am indebted to Mary Adams Belk for providing me with this family history.

[44] "Playgrounds," *Avondale Sun*. 7 September 1929, 10.

[45] "Eufaula Boy Honored," *Avondale Sun*, 21 May 1932, 10; "Cleveland Adams Made Splendid Record at Auburn," *Avondale Sun*, 12 September 1931, 5.

er.[46]

Adams also resumed his leadership role in Southside as Troop 10's Scoutmaster and as a member of the Washington Street Methodist Church's board of stewards.[47] During World War II, assigned to the Southern Regional Laboratory in New Orleans, he supervised experimental textile design projects for the federal government. In 1944 he accepted a supervisory position with the West Point-Pepperell Manufacturing Company in Georgia. In 1952, he was appointed dean of the Auburn School of Textile Engineering, a position he held for twenty-three years.[48]

Albert Driggers, the third honor student selected by Florida Dewar for the 1924 excursion, unlike Adams and Smith, pursued a career outside the textile industry. Nevertheless, of these three young men, Driggers remained throughout his life most closely aligned with Donald Comer's political views, particularly regarding organized labor. Because of his mill family's inability to support their four children, Driggers spent his childhood in his grandmother's care in the country. "I never saw or was in a school house until I was ten years old," he recalled many years later.[49]

After he began high school at age sixteen, his father pressured him to quit and work full-time at the mill. His mother and Florida Dewar interceded. With the additional support of Comer Jennings and grocer D. F. "Doc" Barker, Driggers clerked at a mercantile store, played clarinet in the Cowikee Band, lettered in four sports at Eufaula High School, and earned excellent grades. Like Cleveland Adams, he also served as a Troop 10 assistant

---

[46] "Corbitt-Adams Marriage on Saturday Afternoon," *Avondale Sun*, 11 February 1933, 5; "Who's Who with Cowikee," *Avondale Sun*, 12 February 1940, 16; Mary Adams Belk email to author, 1 August 2015.

[47] "Boy Scouts, Troop #10," 28 September 1938, FWP #4454, folder 16, box SG022777, WPA Files, ADAH; "Troop 1, Eufaula Scouts," photograph with roster, *Avondale Sun, 16 December 1933, 2;* "Washington Street Stewards and Pastor," photograph, *Avondale Sun*, 2 March 1935, 6.

[48] "Cleveland Adams Transferred to Research Lab," *Avondale Sun*, 8 September 1941, 10; *Avondale Sun*, 14 June 1943, 4; "Bits and Tidbits," *Avondale Sun*, 29 November 1943, 2; "Eufaulian Named Regent at Auburn," *Avondale Sun*, Supplement No. 1, n.d., c. January 1952, 7; Mary Adams Belk email to author, 1 August 2015; Adams family history.

[49] "James Casie Driggers," *Avondale Sun*, 23 April 1951, 3; "Albert Driggers," *Avondale Sun*, 17 November 1934, 6.

Scoutmaster. Although between 1923 and 1927 Driggers spent four summers as a mill hand, he never again considered quitting school.[50]

Shortly after his twentieth birthday in August 1927, Driggers briefly worked at the L&N Railroad shops in Birmingham and then studied electrical engineering for a semester at Georgia Tech. Donald Comer assisted Driggers in securing a scholarship at Birmingham Southern College in 1928 and hired him as a part-time recreational instructor at the Avondale Mill Community House. He and his old friend Tyson Smith roomed together at the Community House.[51]

Under the supervision of Kathryn Malone, the Avondale Community House director, Driggers diligently pursued his part-time duties. During summer 1929, Miss Malone and Comer placed the mill athletics program under the control of the Birmingham Parks and Recreation Board. Driggers coached all of the sports, including the boys' and men's baseball squads and the girls' basketball team. His teams became so dominant that the city later barred them from competition—Drigger's "lint heads" were winning too many championships.[52] He also organized the Avondale Community House's first Boy Scout troop and chaperoned children's retreats at Blount Springs and Camp Helen. Even after Driggers graduated from Birmingham Southern in 1933 and embarked upon his lengthy career as a teacher and principal in Jefferson County, he remained on the Avondale payroll as a recreation instructor until the mill closed almost forty years later.[53]

---

[50] "Albert Driggers," *Avondale Sun*, 17 November 1934, 6; Akin, "Avondale's Welfare Programs for Youth," 5; "Boy Scouts," *Avondale Sun*, 26 February 1926, 10; "Mr. A. E. Driggers," *Avondale Sun*, 3 June 1940, 16. Mary Lanier, who succeeded Florida Dewar in 1925 as CCH director, also ensured that Driggers would not have to quit school.

[51] "Band News," *Avondale Sun*, 19 August 1927, n.p.; "Playgrounds," *Avondale Sun*, 7 September 1929, 10; "Albert Driggers," *Avondale Sun*, 17 November 1934, 6; "Mr. A. E. Driggers," *Avondale Sun*, 3 June 1940, 16; "Donald Comer Writes," *Avondale Sun*, 20 June 1955, 5; Akin, "Avondale's Welfare Programs for Youth," 5; 15th US Census, 1930, Schedule No. 1, Population, Jefferson County, Alabama, NARA.

[52] "Eufaula Boy Wins Laurels in Birmingham," *Avondale Sun*, 31 August 1929, 10; Akin, "Avondale's Welfare Programs for Youth," 3–6. 11. Pennsylvanian Kathryn Malone by all accounts was Avondale's own version of Florida Dewar. Miss Malone mentored Driggers during his years in Birmingham. After her death in 1930, he inherited her home in the mill village.

[53] Akin, "Avondale's Welfare Programs for Youth," 5–6, 11; "Albert E. Driggers," *Avondale Sun*, 29 August 1949, 2; "Donald Comer Writes," *Avondale Sun*, 20 June 1955,

In retrospect, a kind of dime-novel aura surrounds the life stories of Driggers, Adams, and Smith—"spunky lads" who rose from hardscrabble backgrounds and triumphed over seemingly insurmountable obstacles. Perhaps most remarkable is that they launched their careers as newly minted college graduates just as the Great Depression eviscerated the nation's economy, yet each became very successful in his chosen profession. Their stories undoubtedly embellished Donald Comer's evolving image during the 1930s as a genteel paternalist who plucked poor boys from his mill villages and launched them on a road to more productive lives. Without Comer's encouragement and financial support, these young men might not have earned college degrees or survived the rigors of the Great Depression, which crushed the hopes and dreams of countless Americans. Driggers, Adams, Smith, and many of their Southside comrades had intelligence, ambition, grit, and leadership gifts that Florida Dewar recognized and nurtured at the CCH. Comer as "The Boss" received many public accolades for these success stories, but Florida Dewar was the beating heart and living soul of the CCH during its formative years.

Within the historical context of her era, Florida Dewar's views on education, child labor reform, race, and women's roles in society were decidedly progressive, and much more so than Comer's. Nevertheless, united by their religious beliefs, they shared a symbiotic relationship on many current issues. For example, Miss Dewar was an early champion of a mill workers' home ownership program and easily won Comer's support. However, her advocacy sometimes went further than he initially accepted. After two African-American mill hands had purchased homes, she wrote, "I believe in people of all races having enough money and 'thrift' to own their houses which they can make into homes. I congratulate you two men for having had your lot cast with a company that encourages home owning for their employe[e]s, black as well as white."[54]

Such racial views perhaps were too openly egalitarian even for a man as enlightened as Comer. While sometimes he only grudgingly and reluctantly agreed with Miss Dewar's viewpoints, Comer had great respect and admira-

---

5.

[54] "Miss Dewar Congratulates Cowikee Colored Employees on Owning Own Homes," Florida Dewar McMullen to Lawyer Dudley and Terry Davis, 7 November 1935, in *Avondale Sun*, 30 November 1935, 5.

tion for her. In January 1925, he candidly confessed to her, "I would be un-
true to myself if I failed to say how sustaining in my own life has been your
example.... I cannot believe that your life, devoted to the high ideals that it
is, can have been of greater influence here, there or yonder than it has been
with me."[55]

Comer also recognized that Miss Dewar's most enduring influence was
among the families of Southside, "where people lived who mostly worked
with their hands as well as with their hearts and heads."[56] She lived, worked,
worshiped, and socialized with Southsiders, sharing their food, gifts, joys,
and tragedies. One Southside resident observed, "[F]athers and mothers
learned to look to her for advice and comfort in their problems and trials.
Girls and boys in their teens valued the counsel that came from their older
Christian friend."[57]

Living in the CCH, in the shadow of the Cowikee Mill, Miss Dewar
grew accustomed to the familiar sounds of the shrill steam whistle that announced shift changes and the endless clattering of the looms. From her
front porch each day she saw the mill families trudging up the hill on South
Eufaula Street and returning home after their long hours at the looms were
done. She greeted the passing throngs of men, women, and children, whose
weary faces and garments were streaked with grime, sweat, and cotton lint.
She did not pity them; to her they were the salt of the earth: "I know the
talent that is on Southside," she wrote in spring 1925, continuing, "I know
the responsive chords and the big hearts of human kindness that art nestled
among those beautiful trees.... I have great faith in the future of Southside.
'The stock' is good."[58]

She genuinely liked these people. And she shared Donald Comer's vision of creating an environment that allowed "children and their elders to
enjoy every privilege that's open to anyone else in the country, whether it's
recreational, educational, cultural, or religious."[59] They were not satisfied
with simply providing mill families with social programs and playgrounds.

---

[55] Donald Comer, "Good Bye, Miss Dewar," *Avondale Sun*, 30 January 1925, 6.

[56] Ibid.

[57] *Avondale Sun*, 8 May 1925, 2.

[58] "Miss Dewar Writes," *Avondale Sun*, 10 April 1925, 7.

[59] Donald Comer quoted in 1960 in Edward Akin, "'Mr. Donald's Help': Donald
Comer, Avondale's Birmingham Operatives, and the United Textile Workers, 1933–34,"
5, paper presented at the Southern Historical Association Meeting, 1980.

Instead, they sought to create surroundings that were exquisitely landscaped and filled with flowers and trees and would appeal aesthetically to children and adults.[60]

The wooded ravine below the Central of Georgia Railroad tracks, between the mill and the CCH, immediately captured Miss Dewar's discerning eye. Abutting the playground, this untamed woodland would become her park. With Donald Comer's blessing, she hired William H. Kessler, a prominent Birmingham landscape architect, to design a comprehensive plan for the "Cowikee Community Park." By March 1921, Kessler's design had gone from the drawing board to preliminary construction.[61]

His plan called for removing the overgrown thicket in the ravine and planting flowering vines and shrubs. He projected that just below the railroad tracks, "a band pavilion will be erected in a music grove, where seats will be placed beneath the trees."[62] He also envisioned expanding the playground to the edge of a small lagoon, created by damming the creek that meandered through the site. Terraced, grass-covered rows of seats would be installed overlooking the band pavilion. Although Kessler's lagoon never was fully developed according to his design, probably because it would attract mosquitoes, his "Garden Theatre" became the centerpiece of the park.[63]

Superintendent Robert Jones assigned mill laborers to the project throughout the park's construction. As trees, shrubs, and flowers were planted, Miss Dewar added a crowning touch. Working closely with Jones and a local contractor, she supervised the installation of electrical wiring for play-

---

[60] For commentary on the relationship between playgrounds and parks, see, for example, Lena Rivers Smyth, "Welfare Work Accomplishing Results," *Southern Textile Bulletin* 12/10 (2 November 1916): 6; E. S. Draper, "Community Work in Southern Mill Villages," *Southern Textile Bulletin* 18/10 (8 May 1919): 31.

[61] "Eufaula Notes," *Montgomery Advertiser*, 27 March 1921, 7; William H. Kessler, "Cowikee Community Park," *Southside News* 1/9 (May 1921): 1–2; "The Year Brings Many Magic Changes in the Mountain Brook Home Development," *The Jemison Magazine* 2/1 (January 1930): 3–5. Kessler (1880–1966), a Nebraskan who was nicknamed the "L'Enfant of Birmingham," developed the grounds for many of the city's public buildings, churches, and residences in Forest Park, Redmont, Mountain Brook, and Central Park.

[62] Kessler, "Cowikee Community Park," 1.

[63] Ibid. 1–2; "Kindergarten Commencement Exercises and Pageant Enjoyed," *Montgomery Advertiser*, 20 June 1921, 5; "Formal Opening of New Park Is Staged," *Montgomery Advertiser*, 13 November 1922, 8.

ground and garden lighting fixtures.[64] Her decision had far-reaching results; future CCH events would not be limited to daylight hours. The park thus stood the test of time.

Several years after the park's dedication in 1922, a reporter observed:

> Few mills in the South are more interested in the welfare of its employe[e]s and beautiful Comer park has been fitted up for their comfort and recreation. Band concerts and athletic events add to the pleasure of park visitors. And the park is not confined to employe[e]s of the mill: everybody is welcomed and people from the entire town and from the surrounding country go there nightly.[65]

Although these words were written in 1929, four years after Miss Dewar's departure from Eufaula, she undoubtedly was pleased to learn of the park's popularity from her Southside friends. Most noteworthy is the fact that by the late 1920s, the CCH and the park were drawing visitors from throughout Eufaula and Barbour County. This trend increased during the Great Depression and World War II and signified the first discernible fissure in the wall between Southside and Old Eufaula.

Florida Dewar left many legacies. Her establishment of the park, the kindergarten, and the children's band laid the foundation for most of the CCH's future programs and missions. With the fielding of the first organized Cowikee Mill baseball team in spring 1922, the final major building block was laid in mill-sponsored programs. Donald Comer purchased the old fairgrounds site on South Randolph Street for his ball park, and Robert Jones oversaw construction of the grandstands and layout of the diamond. Operating under the regulations of the Eufaula Baseball Association, the team included mill hands and men recruited from the entire county.[66]

---

[64] *Montgomery Advertiser*, 20 June 1921, 5; *Avondale Sun*, 20 May 1933, 2.

[65] *Avondale Sun*, 22 June 1929, 7. Not surprisingly, by 1929, "Comer Park" had replaced the original name for the grounds.

[66] "Eufaula Team Will Play in New Park; Seeking Material," *Montgomery Advertiser*, 26 March 1922, 10; "Eufaula Ready for Opening of Season," *Montgomery Advertiser*, 11 June 1922, 6. Baseball had been popular in Barbour County since the late nineteenth century. Fierce rivalries developed among the teams from Eufaula, Clayton, and Dothan. The Eufaula Baseball Association was organized in 1911. See "Eufaula," *Columbus Daily Enquirer*, 25 June 1889, 1; "News of Eufaula," *Montgomery Advertiser*, 23 June 1910, 5; "Clayton Defeats Eufaula," *Montgomery Advertiser*, 23 July 1910, 9; "Eufaula to Have Baseball," *Montgomery Advertiser*, 21 March 1911, 11; "Eufaula Beats Dawson," *Mont-*

Between 1920 and 1925, the baseball team was the only significant CCH program that Florida Dewar did not personally administer. However, since it was organized during her tenure as CCH director, baseball also can be considered as part of her legacy. As an avid baseball enthusiast, Donald Comer proudly opened his new park in Eufaula in 1922 in the midst of much acclaim. If a public opinion poll had been taken in the 1920s on Comer's greatest gift to the community, baseball would have been ranked near the top. However, Comer offered a different opinion to Florida Dewar in 1925: "[I]t will be said that no greater blessing can come to any community than that a good, pure, true woman came and lived among them, and we consider our greatest service to Eufaula and ourselves was when you came to make your home with us."[67]

For Donald Comer, there never would be another CCH director of Miss Dewar's caliber, and his perception would prove to be an undue burden upon her successors. She definitely had set a high standard of excellence for those who followed.[68] Through her charismatic charm and persistence, Florida Dewar had planted the seeds of personal ownership for the CCH and its programs deep in the soil of Southside and in the hearts of mill families. One Southsider asserted in 1924 that it did not matter if the CCH had the "prettiest playground to be found anywhere." Of far greater importance was the ownership and inclusiveness of the playground: "What we do say is that it is ours; we have good times there; there is plenty of room for our playmates, our sweethearts, our mothers and fathers and babies—every one."[69]

Buoyed by glowing press accounts hailing his munificent funding for the mills' social programs, during winter 1925 Comer began searching for another Florida Dewar.[70] He eventually chose Mary Frances Lanier, a YWCA social worker in Oil City, Pennsylvania. Born in 1886 in Davidson

---

gomery Advertiser, 9 June 1911, 11.

[67] Donald Comer, "Good Bye, Miss Dewar," *Avondale Sun*, 30 January 1925, 6.

[68] Comer continued to sing Florida Dewar's praises for the rest of his life. See, for example, "Comer Talks to Church Laymen," *Avondale Sun*, 16 June 1941, 4; "Donald Comer Visits Cowikee Friends," *Avondale Sun*, 18 October 1943, 5; "Donald Comer Writes," *Avondale Sun*, 12 August 1957, 4. Florida Dewar died in 1940 at age sixty. See "Mrs. Florida Dewar McMull[e]n," *Avondale Sun*, 15 July 1940, 11.

[69] "Eufaula News," *Avondale Sun*, 18 April 1924, 7.

[70] See, for example, letter, J. Fred Sparks to *Birmingham News*, 25 February 1925, quoted in Breedlove, "Donald Comer," diss., 185.

County, Tennessee, Mary Lanier also had served as a Methodist missionary in Brazil.[71] Comer informed her that as long as she kept the band and kindergarten intact, he welcomed any new activities she wished to propose. But he was not quite ready to relinquish his control over the CCH's future. He curtly refused her request to hire a kindergarten assistant from among her colleagues in Pennsylvania. He insisted that she select someone in Eufaula.[72]

In early April 1925, Mary Lanier assumed her duties as the new CCH director. Since the CCH and playground had been closed for several months, dozens of excited children greeted here. They bombarded her with questions about her plans for the coming summer. One young boy exclaimed, "She'll sure have to run me off every night, 'cause I'm going to stay here all the time."[73]

Despite her warm public reception, Miss Lanier soon discovered that her predecessor was looking over her shoulder from afar. In an open letter under the guise of offering a "word of advice" to Southside parents, Florida Dewar urged them to "help Miss Lanier. I don't know her—never heard of her before; but I know she is a human being and as such her feelings are very similar to yours and mine."[74]

This awkward, lukewarm "endorsement" did not make Miss Lanier's tasks any easier. Nevertheless, she dutifully followed Donald Comer's initial directive. She hired Eleanor Dannelly, a Methodist minister's daughter, to assist with the kindergarten. She and Miss Lanier also taught at the Washington Street Methodist Church Sunday school.[75] Before leaving in June 1927, Miss Dannelly earned praise for "endear[ing] herself to the children and the entire community as few could do."[76] Subject to Donald Comer's approval, Miss Lanier hired several young women with outstanding teaching

---

[71] "Y.W.C.A. Sign Flung to the Breeze Today," *(Franklin, PA) News-Herald*, 4 September 1924, 10; "Girl Reserve Party," *News-Herald*, 12 December 1924, 15; "Quota Club," *News-Herald*, 10 January 1925, 15; "Miss Lanier Quits as Girl Reserve Secretary," *News-Herald*, 17 March 1925, 11; "Hi-Tri Club," *News-Herald*, 20 March 1925, 15; "Y.W.C.A. Board," *News-Herald*, 24 March 1925, 14; Ginny Dunaway Young emails to author, 7–8 March 2015.

[72] Breedlove, "Donald Comer," diss., 196–97.

[73] "Cowikee Community Park Opened Again," *Avondale Sun*, 17 April 1925, 9.

[74] "Miss Dewar Writes," *Avondale Sun*, 10 April 1925, 7.

[75] *Avondale Sun*, 17 July 1925, 10; 11 September 1925, 4; 9 October 1925, 10.

[76] "Miss Dannelly Departs," *Avondale Sun*, 10 June 1927, n.p.

credentials to assist with the band, kindergarten, and playground, including Edna Stroud and sisters Hallie and Nancy Hartsfield.[77]

By spring 1926, Miss Lanier also had added eighteen-year-old band-master Lewis Simpkins to the CCH payroll. Simpkins hailed from Pell City, Alabama, where he and his seven siblings grew up in the Avondale mill village. Although he had worked in the mill as a child, Simpkins came to Eufaula specifically to lead the band.[78] Still lacking his high school diploma, Simpkins appeared older than his years—he had dark, slicked-back hair, long arms heavily roped with muscles, and he peered at the world through thick glasses that magnified his eyes. Like many of his generation, he chain-smoked unfiltered cigarettes. Self-effacing, patient, and soft-spoken, Simpkins overnight became the favorite "new boy" in Southside. Other than playing in the mill band in Pell City, he had no previous musical training. However, he was a remarkably gifted teacher.[79] In 1929 one Southsider affirmed, "[W]e have learned to love him as a young man of sterling worth and character, who gives of his talent in music unreservedly and helps to make everything he takes a part in a success."[80]

The youthful, energetic Simpkins brought a new dimension to the mill music programs. The trumpet was his specialty, but he also played many other instruments, thus enhancing his instructional techniques. He reinvigorated the children's band as the "Junior Band." He also assembled a Sunday school orchestra that appeared at all of Eufaula's churches, one of the South's first Boy Scout bands, and the "Jazz Hounds," an ensemble of talented young musicians.[81] He expanded the repertoire of the mill's "Big

[77] *Avondale Sun*, 18 June 1926, 10; 10 June 1927, n.p.; 9 September 1927, n.p.; 23 September 1933, 8. Nina Dantzler, Jonnie Flynn, and Sammie Rayle were three other exceptional teachers Miss Lanier recruited and hired.

[78] *Avondale Sun*, 23 April 1926, 10; 14th and 15th US Census, 1920–1930, Schedule No. 1, Population, St. Clair County, Alabama, NARA.

[78] *Avondale Sun*, 23 April 1926, 10; 14th and 15th US Census, 1920–1930, Schedule No. 1, Population, St. Clair County, Alabama, NARA.

[79] "Washington Street M. E. Church," *Avondale Sun*, 27 January 1928, n.p. This description of Simpkins is based upon the author's recollections of meeting him in Eufaula in the early 1950s.

[80] *Avondale Sun*, 2 February 1929, 4.

[81] "Short History of Cowikee Mill Band," 21 September 1938, FWP #4454, folder 16, box SG022777, WPA Files, ADAH; *Avondale Sun*, 8 July 1927, n.p.; "Band News,"

Band" beyond patriotic marching tunes with a mixture of classical and popular music, spirituals, jazz, polkas, and the blues, often accompanied by vocalists. After a concert in spring 1920, a local music aficionado favorably compared the Big Band to any he had heard in person or on the radio.[82]

Like other mill bandmasters, Simpkins performed other duties at the CCH. He joined Cleveland Adams and Albert Driggers as an assistant Scoutmaster with Troop 10 and enthusiastically participated in local and regional camps. After Adams returned to Auburn in 1929, Simpkins supervised the Boys Carpenter's Club and chaperoned various parties and excursions.

In December 1929, Simpkins resigned as the mill band leader and accepted a position at the Gulfport Military Academy in Mississippi. He awarded scholarships there for two of his prized Cowikee Band pupils, Johnnie Bush and James Dunaway. In 1930 Simpkins married Beatrice Clark, whom he had taught to play the saxophone in the Cowikee Band several years earlier. The young couple returned to Eufaula in 1931 when Simpkins again briefly served as the mill band director. About three years later, he embarked upon a succession of jobs that took him to Pell City, Alexander City, and finally to Sylacauga, where he spent the rest of his career as director of the high school band.[83] During Simpkins's seven years in Eufaula, he built an organizational structure for the CCH's bands that endured for over four decades.

Lewis Simpkins's band leadership was one of Mary Lanier's success stories, along with her recruitment of several very talented kindergarten and

---

Avondale Sun, 13 July 1929, 7; "The First Boy Scout Band in the South," photograph with roster, c. 1928–1929, *Avondale Sun*, 11 March 1957, 8–9.

[82] "Praise for Band," *Avondale Sun*, 6 April 1929, 6. See also, "Cowikee Band Heard Sunday," *Avondale Sun*, 20 May 1933, 9, for additional accolades bestowed upon the mill's musicians.

[83] "Short History of Cowikee Mill Band," 21 September 1938, FWP #4454, folder 16, box SG022777, WPA Files, ADAH; "Community House Doing Fine Work with Young Folks," *Eufaula Daily Citizen*, n.d., reprinted in *Avondale Sun*, 7 September 1929, 10; "Eufaula Carpenters," *Avondale Sun*, 21 September 1929, 10; "Enjoy Summer Activities," *Avondale Sun*, 16 November 1929, 5; "Accepts Position with Mississippi Band," *Eufaula Daily Citizen*, n.d., reprinted in *Avondale Sun*, 7 December 1929, 9; "Band Notes," *Avondale Sun*, 14 June 1930, 6; 12 September 1931, 8; "Boy Scout Leaders," *Avondale Sun*, 16 March 1953, 1.

playground teachers. Seriously dedicated to her profession, she regularly attended state and regional social work conferences.[84] She also conducted her requisite responsibilities as the CCH hostess during annual mill inspections and visits by Donald Comer and other dignitaries.[85]

However, she never allowed her ceremonial duties to interfere with the needs of "her children" and their parents in Southside. For example, she diversified the programs of the Girls' Club to attract mothers working in the mill, such as weavers Oma Parish Alsobrook and Willie Mae Starnes. The club supplemented its social activities and excursions with discussions of books and current events that appealed to women of all ages.[86]

Miss Lanier also continually attempted to include the entire community in the life of the CCH. In January 1926, she invited Eufaula's churches to schedule their social events in the band hall. She later organized all of the Southside families into two teams, captained by children and adults, for a spirited competition in baseball, tennis, croquet, horseshoes, boxing, swimming, and dominoes.[87] Her efforts achieved impressive results. During summer 1926, with the CCH and its grounds open in the evenings, a reporter noted that "people in large numbers are availing themselves of the pleasures that the place has to offer."[88] In late June, over 200 visitors were at the CCH on a single Friday night, many of them either in the pool or on the playground.[89]

Unfortunately, the director's job took a heavy personal toll on Mary Lanier. She suffered two nervous breakdowns, forcing her to undergo extended "rest cures" at the Britt Infirmary.[90] Her condition worsened, and in

---

[84] "Personals," *Avondale Sun*, 17 July 1925, 10; *Avondale Sun*, 5 August 1927, n.p.; "Girls' Club," *Avondale Sun*, 15 March 1930, 3.

[85] See, for example, "Cowikee Mills Present Pleasing Picture to Visitors," *Avondale Sun*, 6 April 1929, 1.

[86] "Girls' Club," *Avondale Sun*, 15 March 1930, 3; 17 May 1930, 3; "Club Books Closed," *Avondale Sun*, 13 February 1932, 12; "Girls' Club Enjoys Florida Trip," *Avondale Sun*, 20 June 1931, 10.

[87] "Community House," *Avondale Sun*, 29 June 1929, 10; "Blues Win Contest," *Avondale Sun*, 13 July 1929, 7.

[88] "Community House," *Avondale Sun*, 2 July 1926, 8.

[89] Ibid.

[90] "Personals," *Avondale Sun*, 23 October 1925, 10; 11 June 1926, 3; 25 June 1926, 8; "Community House," *Avondale Sun*, 30 October 1925, 10; 4 December 1925, 10;

May 1930, she announced her retirement. "Her children" responded emotionally to the news. Her beloved Girls' Club officers wrote, "Words cannot express our regret and sorrow due to losing Miss Lanier." Several months later, they renamed their club after her.[91] The CCH's musicians praised her as "one of the best friends the band has had.... We thank you and may God bless you for what you have meant to us and for what you have done."[92] The Boy Scout band was "discontinued until further notice," and Troop 10's boys recognized her as "one of our chief backers" who always was "ready to help us and to do something for us."[93] Comer Jennings asked, "What are we going to do without Miss Mary? ...It's hard to lose such a friend...[who] has given unselfishly of her time, her energy, and her ability. It was her purpose to make our lives bigger, brighter, happier, nobler—and she has succeeded."[94]

Donald Comer, who seldom withheld praise for his employees, remained strangely silent when Mary Lanier left Eufaula. She had done everything that he asked her to do, but in Comer's estimation no CCH director would ever eclipse Florida Dewar. Nevertheless, Miss Lanier had trained Edna Stroud and Hallie Hartsfield well, and together they perpetuated the CCH's missions in the years that followed.

After these two young women married, respectively, Claude Davis, and Tyson Smith, they were known as "Miss Edna" and "Miss Hallie" to future generations of Southsiders. Native Georgian Hallie Smith studied education and social work at the University of Georgia, Sophie Newcomb College, and Alabama College at Montevallo. After teaching in Cuthbert and Valdosta, Georgia, by the end of the summer 1930, she was employed as a social worker at the CCH. At that time Tennessean Edna Davis was the kindergarten teacher. She later supervised the playground and the swimming pools. In fall 1935, Helen Mitchell Taylor joined her as an assistant kindergarten teacher.[95]

Avondale Sun, 8 January 1926, 7; 2 July 1926, 8.

[91] "Girls' Club," *Avondale Sun*, 17 May 1930, 3 (quote); "Club Books Closed," *Avondale Sun*, 13 February 1932, 12.

[92] "Band News," *Avondale Sun*, 31 May 1930, 7.

[93] "Scout News," *Avondale Sun*, 31 May 1930, 7.

[94] Comer Jennings, "Goodbye, Miss Lanier," *Avondale Sun*, 24 May 1930, 1.

[95] "Stroud-Davis Wedding Tuesday," *Avondale Sun*, 23 September 1933, 8; "Hartsfield-Smith Marriage," *Avondale Sun*, 10 October 1938, 10; 15th US Census, 1930,

By the mid-1930s, Hallie Smith had been promoted to the CCH director position. In 1938, a Works Programs Administration (WPA) writer described "Miss Hallie" as "beloved by all. They go to her with their joys and sorrows and she is always ready to help. She is most efficient and has an understanding heart."[96] However, her niece found the tall, "austere" Hallie Smith at the kindergarten "somewhat intimidating" and only learned several years later that she was very fun-loving and thoughtful. In 1943 Donald Comer surprisingly elevated her to the stature of Florida Dewar, urging that Hallie Smith has "long been the presiding genius over the Community House."[97]

Wendell Franklin Wentz, who attended the CCH kindergarten during World War II, vividly recalled that Hallie Smith often delivered books for him at his family's meat market on South Eufaula Street. He was very impressed with how much personal attention she gave to him and his friends.[98] Another kindergartner of that era remembered how Edna Davis and Jewel Wilson Jones watched over the playground and swimming pools "with so much patience, yet at the same time seem[ed] to enjoy being with us. They were indeed two very special friends."[99]

All of these women—Hallie Smith, Edna Davis, Helen Mitchell Taylor, and scores of volunteers—shared a love for "their children." In the words

---

Schedule No. 1, Population, Barbour County, Alabama, NARA; Tiffany Woo, "Former Mill Was Also a Community," *Eufaula Tribune*, 8 April 2009, A-11; Jeanine Smith DeVenny, "My Thoughts on the Cowikee Community House in Eufaula," 2015, DeVenny email (with attachment) to author, 27 July 2015; "Personals," *Avondale Sun*, 7 September 1935, 5; "Donald Comer Visits Cowikee Friends," *Avondale Sun*, 18 October 1943, 5; Bill Davis (Edna Stroud Davis's son) email to the author, 13 October 2015; Chauncey Sparks "To Whom It May Concern," letter of recommendation for Helen Mitchell, (6 February 1932) Hallie Taylor Dalon Collection; "Mitchell-Taylor Union Announced," *Columbus Daily Enquirer*, 2 September 1938, 7. Edna Davis was educated at Martin College in Pulaski, TN. Helen Mitchell Taylor graduated from the Troy State Teachers College.

[96] "Recreation Center/Community House," 21 September 1938, FWP #4454, folder 16, box SG 022777, WPA Files, ADAH.

[97] DeVenny, "My Thoughts on the Community House;" "Donald Comer Visits Cowikee Friends;" *Avondale Sun*, 18 October 1943, 5.

[98] Author's telephone conversation with Wendell Franklin Wentz, 13 July 2015.

[99] DeVenny, "My Thoughts on the Community House." See also, "Jewel Wilson," *Avondale Sun*, 13 February 1950, 10.

of one of these children, Jeanine Smith DeVenny, the CCH in the early 1950s was a second home—a safe place for both learning and play:

There were so many things to do at The Club—best swings ever, seesaws, ping pong tables, a maypole-like contraption with six or eight long chains that had bars attached to hold on to as we ran around and around until we were flying through the air, a big noisy barrel that rotated on a pipe, soft-ball field, library, tennis court. Later we had a television before we had one at home where we watched "I Love Lucy" on Monday nights. Growing up on the South side of Eufaula was a wonderful privilege I didn't fully recognize and appreciate until I was older. Imagine being allowed to go to such a fun place three times a week, morning and night during the school year. We were allowed to walk home alone at night with no fear of predators.... What a childhood![100]

Without her reference to television, Jeanine Smith DeVenny's description of the CCH could easily be set in earlier decades. Her memories of that special place closely resemble those of Southsiders who grew up a generation earlier. The years spanning the Great Depression and World War II were very important in the evolution of the CCH. From the 1930s on, the CCH became increasingly more like a home than a recreation center. When newlyweds Hallie and Tyson Smith moved into the CCH in 1938, their presence significantly altered the dynamic of the previous twenty years when the only residents were unmarried social workers and teachers. After the Smiths vacated the premises in 1941, Helen and Foster Taylor lived in the CCH with their young daughters for about three years, followed by Cowikee band director Elbert "Red" Beasley and his wife Ruby, a kindergarten teacher.[101]

Red Beasley represented a direct link to the early days of the CCH. He was a member of the first children's band in the early 1920s and as a young man became a cotton sampler and buyer for Cowikee Mills. The gregarious, ruddy-complexioned Beasley was another one of those young Southsiders who became indispensable to the community and the mill. Whatever task at the CCH needed to be performed, he was always available. He drove mill trucks and buses to Camps Rotary and Helen, the Comer plantation, and to

---

[100] DeVenny, "My Thoughts on the Cowikee Community House"; "Donald Comer Visits Cowikee Friends," *Avondale Sun*, 18 October 1943, 5.

[101] Wendell Franklin Wentz email to author, 23 April 2014; Oma Alsobrook to Thomas Alsobrook, 7 February 1941; Thomas Alsobrook to Oma Alsobrook, 20 April 1944, in author's possession.

far-flung destinations in Georgia and Florida. When the vehicles broke down on the road, Beasley repaired them. If the kindergarten children needed a driver or a chaperone, he did the job. If Troop 10 lacked an assistant Scoutmaster or "Mr. Donald" wanted a photographer for a mill event, Beasley readily volunteered.[102]

Despite his good-natured willingness to do any extraneous job, Beasley's primary interest was the mill band. Like Lewis Simpkins, he had no formal music education, yet Beasley had learned a great deal from Simpkins, Florida Dewar, and Billy Hrabe. In March 1934, after Simpkins left Eufaula, a band member inquired, "We wonder what 'Red' Beasley is going to decide to be: a trumpet player, clarinet player, or the band master himself."[103]

The answer came that fall when Beasley became the band director. He quietly picked up Simpkins's baton and demonstrated that he, like his predecessor, was an excellent music teacher. Over the next decade, several of his band members earned college music scholarships, including Humphry Foy, James McKenzie, Robert Flewellen, and Frances Starnes. In fall 1938, Julian Edwards, who had mastered the saxophone, violin, and piano under Beasley's tutelage, enrolled in the Chicago Conservatory of Music.[104]

While Beasley devoted long hours to perfecting his craft as a band leader, he also was interested in upgrading adult recreational opportunities. Around 1929–1930, he became a founding member of the Ryko Club, a popular young men's social organization. During winter 1937, he launched his most ambitious project, the Men's Recreation Club. Located in a renovated house adjacent to the band hall, this new club was equipped with read-

---

[102] "Eufaula Kindergartners Visit Cane Mill," *Avondale Sun*, 1 December 1934, 13; "Scouts Organize a Local Troop," *Avondale Sun*, 28 April 1934, 4; "Girls' Club Enjoys Florida Trip," *Avondale Sun*, 20 June 1931, 10; *Avondale Sun*, 5 July 1948, photographs by Beasley, 11.

[103] "Senior Band," *Avondale Sun*, 31 March 1934, 9.

[104] "Avondale Mills Concert Band at Eufaula," *Avondale Sun*, 20 October 1934, 15; "Senior Band," *Avondale Sun*, 17 November 1934, 10; "Cowikee Sunday School Orchestra," *Avondale Sun*, 16 February 1935, 3; "Sunday School Orchestra," *Avondale Sun*, 4 April 1936, 2; "Eufaula Music Lovers Club to Sponsor Week," *Columbus Daily Enquirer*, 1 May 1938, 19; "Attend Alabama Music Festival," *Avondale Sun*, 22 May 1939, 7; "Short History of Cowikee Mill Band," 21 September 1938, FWP #4454, folder 16, box SG022777, WPA Files, ADAH.

ing and game rooms, two billiard tables, a radio, cold drink stand, twelve showers, and a locker room. Spacious grounds outside were available for basketball and tennis courts. The mill provided for a caretaker to ensure that the club would be open for men working on different shifts. Some evidence suggests that the CCH's nickname, "The Club," originated with this facility.[105]

The new club's first board of directors included mill workers, managers, and other Southsiders: Oscar Hatfield, Claude Lundy, Cliff Atherton, Donise Ward, Cleveland Adams, Tyson Smith, and Jesse Hatfield. The membership's ranks revealed a similar diversity. Most importantly, the club's doors also were open to men throughout the town and visitors passing through Eufaula.[106]

Red Beasley's new venture was especially appealing to veteran mill hands like James "Doc" Hughes, age sixty-one. In autumn 1938, Hughes asserted: "I like to read, and when my wife ain't home in the afternoon and I don't have to work in the garden, I go over to the Men's Club, where I usually take a shower and then sit around and read or gab with my friends."[107] Even the deeply introverted, sixty-seven-year-old John Thomas Alsobrook "ease[d] over" to the club from South Randolph Street to read in the evenings: "I never got but five years schooling, but it comes in mighty handy when I want to sit and rest and find out what's happening in other places."[108] When elderly employees such as Alsobrook and Hughes were spending their leisure hours reading at the CCH, Donald Comer realized that his ambitious social welfare plans for "his people" had come to fruition. He also knew that much of the credit for his successful workers' programs belonged to Hallie and Tyson Smith, Edna Davis, Cleveland Adams, and Red Beasley, who had been associated with the CCH since the 1920s.

During the Depression years, the CCH often joined hands with the Alabama Department of Public Welfare and the WPA in caring for needy families. The sharing of personnel and other resources often blurred the bu-

---

[105] "Ryko Club," *Avondale Sun*, 19 January 1935, 7; "Visitors View New Club House," *Avondale Sun*, 1 February 1937, 5; "Men's Recreation Club," 10 October 1938; FWP #4454, folder 16, box SG022777, WPA Files, ADAH.

[106] "Men's Recreation Club News," *Avondale Sun*, 15 February 1937, 12.

[107] James C. Hughes family life history, 20 October 1938, folder 11, FWPP, SHC, UNC.

[108] Tom Alsobrook family life history, 13 October 1938, folder 18, ibid.

reaucratic lines of authority between the CCH and government agencies. One of the most effective of these partnerships was the Home Aid Project, headquartered at the CCH but supervised by Fannie Corbitt Adams, a WPA employee and wife of Cleveland Adams. Fannie Adams, assisted by CCH teacher Helen Mitchell Taylor and sixteen white and eight African-American volunteers, visited low-income Barbour County families and taught basic domestic skills such as cooking, nutrition, housekeeping, and child care.[109] Fannie Adams and her aides furnished the families with large quantities of potatoes, peanuts, cheese, and other foods along with recipes to make these supplies last longer. She suspected that these starving families immediately consumed all of the food that she had given to them.[110]

Food shortages were not a problem for most mill families during the Great Depression. Southsiders, many of whom were raised on farms, grew vegetables in gardens near their homes. They also took advantage of canning classes at the mill to preserve fruits and vegetables. The mill's Lone Oak Leghorn Farm, located at the southern terminus of Comer Street in Southside, sold baby chicks, laying hens, turkeys, quail, eggs, and poultry meat. By the late 1930s, the WPA reported that "there is not hardly a family in the entire mill district that does not raise its own chickens and eggs."[111] The chicken farm, along with two other "off-campus" facilities, Camp Helen and the Cowikee Mill Farm, were enthusiastically patronized by Southsiders and contributed to the impressive compilation of services provided by Donald Comer.

Near the end of the Great Depression, a lengthy WPA report summarized the impact of CCH programs upon Southside and its residents:

---

[109] "WPA Projects Plan House," *Columbus Daily Enquirer*, 19 May 1940, 2; "Home Aid Project," 10 October 1938, FWP #4454, folder 16, box SG022777, WPA Files, ADAH; Dr. P. P. Salter life history, interviewed by Gertha Couric, 26 April 1939, Federal Writers' Project, Life Histories/Stories, Barbour County, box SG0022773, WPA Files, ADAH.

[110] Mary Adams Belk email to author, 23 July 2015.

[111] "Colored Women Canners," *Avondale Sun*, 22 October 1932, 5; "Home Canning Plan," "Lone Oak Leghorn Farm," 10 October 1938, FWP #4454, folder 16, box SG022777, WPA Files, ADAH; "Chicken Farm Makes Good Showing," *Avondale Sun*, 30 July 1926, 7; "Lone Oak Leghorn Farm," *Avondale Sun*, 11 March 1933, 5. Quote is from WPA records cited above.

The great welfare work that the Comer Mills have carried on for so many years has made an enlightened and progressive citizenship. Every conceivable good had been given the families who are in the organization. The Community House has been a great center for the life of the community with its beautiful and well equipped grounds and play grounds, swimming pool, club work, study courses, social programs, and other activities. There is a fine kindergarten and a well trained band and orchestra. The personnel of the Community House is of the highest and lov[e]liest type, those whose every effort is for the help, health, and happiness of the young and old. There has been the greatest personal interest in the employees on the part of the employers, that has developed a fine sense of loyalty, understanding, and c[o]ntentment.[112]

These comments could easily be construed as merely paternalistic propaganda. Despite the rather hyperbolic assertion that the mills' social welfare programs produced "an enlightened and progressive citizenship," this document is an accurate compilation of the CCH's diverse activities. Still, this report does not address the CCH's impact beyond Southside. Since these popular programs were not restricted to mill families, they drew participants from throughout Eufaula, thereby sounding the earliest death knell for the town's old class distinctions. Nevertheless, only the unprecedented effects of the Great Depression and World War II would completely destroy the barriers between Southside and Old Eufaula and erase much of the social ostracism and discrimination suffered by several generations of mill workers' families.

---

[112] FWP, State Guide File, Barbour County, box A15, WPA Records, LC. Although this report was unsigned, Gertha Couric, the principal WPA writer in Barbour County, probably was the author.

Chapter 6

The Walls Come Down:
The Great Depression and World War II

I wish there would be war again.
– Unidentified textile operative, c. 1930

The erosion of the invisible barriers between the two Eufaulas was well un-
derway in the late 1920s as Cowikee Community House programs attracted
increasing numbers of participants from beyond the confines of the mill village, but this process was very gradual, marked by only incremental progress.
Between 1930 and 1945, the Great Depression and World War II generated
revolutionary social, economic, political, and cultural changes in the United
States. This era of unprecedented sacrifice, struggle, and triumph also had a
dramatic impact upon the small town of Eufaula. Through this transformation of the town and its people, the old walls of separatism faded into
oblivion.

In the early 1930s, many Americans believed that the stock market
crash in October 1929 had caused the Great Depression. Wall Street's demise more precisely was a symptom of the nation's sick economy and a grim
omen of the impending financial catastrophe. Between 1819 and 1914, the
United States had weathered cyclical financial "panics," or depressions, every
twenty years or so. But, according to one historian, the Great Depression of
the 1930s "smashed into the nation with such fury, that men groped for su-
perlatives to express its impact and meaning." Literary critic Edmund Wilson called it an earthquake. New York politician Alfred E. Smith compared
the disaster to war; financier Bernard Baruch claimed it was worse. An unemployed textile operative declared, "I wish there would be war again," im-
plying that the munitions industry would revive the dead economy. When
asked if he knew of any historical epoch comparable to the Great Depression, British economist John Maynard Keynes gloomily replied, "Yes. It was
the Dark Ages and it lasted 400 years." One of Keynes's colleagues in the
United States, John Kenneth Galbraith, wrote in 1954, "A case can readily
be made that, with the single exception of the Civil War, no event of the

past hundred years so deeply impressed itself upon the thoughts, attitudes and voting behavior of the American people."[1]

Understandably so, Galbraith, Keynes, and other contemporary economists heavily emphasized a direct causal relationship between the stock market crash and the Depression. Yet, in reality, the global economic forces that ultimately led to this disaster had been growing inexorably for a decade. In the late 1920s, systemic structural imbalances in international trade created slumping prices for many agricultural products and raw materials. Vast amounts of capital were siphoned from the United States as loans to European and South American countries. Germany, for example, borrowed American dollars to fund its World War I reparations payments to Great Britain, France, and Belgium. Simultaneously, as the United States' cash reserves were depleted by these loans, key domestic industries—automotive, construction, steel, and textiles—produced a surplus of goods that outstripped consumers' demands and purchasing power. Workers' real earnings had not kept pace with industrial output. Textile workers could not afford the cotton goods they produced. Unfettered installment buying became habitual among consumers. The largest portion of corporate profits were invested in stock transactions and dividend payments to companies' shareholders rather than in employees' salaries and new equipment. In short, the nation's economic structure was teetering precariously in the 1920s; a devastating collapse was almost inevitable.[2]

Immediately after World War I, the rural South and Midwest experienced a foretaste of the Depression as farmers' incomes and assets plummeted and thousands of country banks failed. In the South, cotton prices were the most visible barometer of hard times. In 1919–1920, the price per pound

---

[1] Vincent P. DeSantis, "The Great and Devastating Depression," *Notre Dame Magazine* (Winter 1987–1998): 25.

[2] Ibid., 25–26; Perrett, *America in the Twenties*, 338–39, 384; Flewellen, *Along Broad Street*, 295; Robert S. McElvaine, *The Great Depression: America, 1929–1941* (New York: New York Times Book Co., Inc., 1984) 17, 39–41; Eric Rauchway, *The Great Depression and the New Deal: A Very Short Introduction* (New York: Oxford University Press, 2008) 12–13, 15, 19–20; T. H. Watkins, *The Hungry Years: A Narrative History of the Great Depression in America* (New York: Henry Holt and Company, 1999) 40–41, 46–51; David M. Kennedy, *Freedom from Fear: The American People in Depression and War, 1929–1945* (New York: Oxford University Press, 1999) 17, 21–22, 35–39; Robert Sobel, *The Great Bull Market: Wall Street in the 1920s* (New York: Norton, 1968) 147.

for cotton dropped from thirty-five to sixteen cents. Between 1924 and 1930, this figure eventually bottomed out at eight to ten cents. The precipitous decline in cotton prices primarily was triggered by an overproduction of the crop by Southern planters and a shrinking global demand for finished cloth.[3]

This "mini-depression" in the 1920s cast a long shadow over Alabama's textile industry. Even the ebullient, optimistic Donald Comer apparently was unprepared for such wild fluctuations in the cotton market. In fall 1924, he penned a revealing, pessimistic assessment of the current situation:

> I found the little mills at Eufaula and Union Springs running just as well as they can...except we cannot make a nickel to save our lives. We have had a nice little loss to take care of there this year. We are about two months long of cotton and will probably stick to that plan for the balance of the season unless there is a change in the parity between cotton and cotton goods. We still have practically no business and what little there is...at prices that makes nobody happy.[4]

Fifteen years after launching his first Cowikee Mill in Eufaula, Comer could have capitulated to these financial losses and retired to his plantation as a gentleman farmer. But, he was a stubborn man and refused to accept defeat. He also probably feared his father's wrath if the Cowikee venture failed. Moreover, "Mr. Donald" had invested his time, energy, and the family's capital in Eufaula for the long haul. In March 1925, Comer reassured one struggling local businessman, "Cowikee Mills cast their lot with Eufaula back in 1909 and we are going to continue to paddle in the same boat with you."[5] By the mid-1920s, Old Eufaula had grown heavily dependent upon the mill's payrolls and the Comer family's financial generosity.

During the 1920s and 1930s, whenever the Bluff City's commercial interests faltered, Comer weighed in with his vast financial and political resources. He remained fearless and tenacious in his loyalty to Eufaula—even in facing the most powerful corporate entities at that time. When the city's

---

[3] DeSantis, "The Great and Devastating Depression," 26; Perrett, *America in the Twenties*, 329; Cash, *The Mind of the South*, 279–80, 369; Kennedy, *Freedom from Fear*, 17.

[4] Donald Comer to E. T. Comer, 3 October 1924, folder 7.14A.14, box 14-A, Donald Comer Papers, BPLA.

[5] Donald Comer to H. H. Conn[e]r, 9 March 1925, folder 7.17.1, box 17, ibid.

ice plant managers complained in 1925 that the Alabama and Georgia Power Companies were charging exorbitant rates, Comer boldly threatened to return his mills to steam-driven machinery.[6]

After the Depression hit Alabama with its full force in 1930–1931, Comer toiled relentlessly in behalf of the state's economic survival and recovery. Serving as a member of the Alabama Relief Administration, he assumed the thankless task of allocating state and federal funds for thousands of destitute citizens. He proposed several creative relief programs that targeted both urban and rural areas. In typical Comer fashion, he focused on the kinship of families and friends and their tradition of aiding each other during hard times. In July 1931, he reminded Governor B. M. Miller that scores of Alabama's urban dwellers had moved "rather recently from the country" and still had family members and friends "back on the farm." He assured the governor that with the technical assistance of the Alabama Cooperative Assistance Service at Auburn, farmers would embrace a food production and sharing program. "[A]ll that is needed to help us through this winter is just enough stuff to eat…to take care of the farmer and his family and then a little bit more to take care of his city cousin."[7] In floating his suggestions for new programs, Comer deftly and often resorted to political flattery.

In December 1935, he commended President Franklin D. Roosevelt on the progress of his Resettlement Administration in relocating destitute farm families to new homes. He then urged the president to institute a plan to "erect simple school houses in the Black Belt" that would serve a dual purpose as recreation centers, providing farm families with "a warm place, decently lighted, and with a radio."[8]

Although the state adopted a version of Comer's food-sharing proposal, it is not known how Roosevelt responded to his rural school plan. Nevertheless, both of these wealthy patricians shared a deep empathy for the plight of impoverished farmers, whether they lived in Warm Springs, Georgia, or Barbour County, Alabama. Regardless of his energetic efforts in be-

---

[6] Ibid.

[7] Donald Comer to Governor B. M. Miller, 21 July 1931, "Unemployment," folder 20, box SG019952, Governor B. M. Miller Administrative Files, ADAH.

[8] Donald Comer to President Franklin D. Roosevelt, 12 December 1935, quoted in Breedlove, "Donald Comer" diss., 253.

half of the entire state during the Depression, Comer remained attentive to the dire economic situation in Barbour County. In September 1932, he provided a $5,000 loan at no interest to pay Barbour County teachers' salaries for four months of the school term.[9]

But Comer faced a far greater challenge than bankrolling county schools. By the mid-1930s, textile mills were closing throughout the South. He wrestled with a difficult conundrum—close some of his Avondale and Cowikee Mills, fire or lay off employees, or reduce their hours. He finally chose the last option. In July 1935, he placed operatives at Cowikee Mill No. 1 on weekly shifts of thirty hours. Similar work schedules were implemented in other Comer mills, but they all remained fully operational during the 1930s. Since the National Recovery Administration's Textile Codes in 1935 had already frozen workers' wages at twelve dollars for a forty-hour week, Comer's dictum was not viewed by his employees as draconian or greedy—merely as a measure to keep the mills open. Although some of Comer's operatives returned to tenant farming during "short time" periods in the mills, the majority remained on the job. Steady employment—despite periodic reductions in hours—coupled with Comer's generous welfare benefits obviously appealed to workers with few viable options during the Depression.[10]

Although Comer temporarily diminished his employees' earnings, he provided them with an opportunity to work and avoid seeking state or federal relief. Mill operatives almost universally preferred being employed, even on "short time," because of the social stigma of "going on the dole." In contrast to Eufaula, in October 1934, 75 percent of the relief recipients in Girard and Phenix City, Alabama, were former operatives who were laid off from textile mills in adjacent Columbus, Georgia. Ravaged by the General Textile Strike of 1934 and rapidly decreasing demands for cotton products, these mills were running only single weekly shifts, which forced numerous layoffs.[11]

---

[9] Breedlove, "Donald Comer," diss., 219–20.

[10] *Avondale Sun*, 27 July 1935, 6; "Ozark Cowikee Community Faces Prosperous New Year," *Dothan Eagle*, 29 December 1936, 5; author's telephone conversation with Fred McWaters, 20 August 2015; Nancy Nolan life history, 20 October 1938, folder 13, FWPP, SHC, UNC.

[11] Memorandum, M. J. Miller to Aubrey Williams, 15 October 1934, Alabama-Field Reports, 1933–36, box 56, Harry Hopkins Papers, Franklin D. Roosevelt Presiden-

In Eufaula, Cowikee payrolls sustained mill families until the Depression ended. This infusion of capital into the local cash-starved economy also kept 150 to 200 Old Eufaula retail merchants afloat during the 1930s. The mills' presence also strengthened other local commercial activity—H. H. Conner's Cotton Oil and Fertilizer Company, the Dean and Moore Cotton Warehouses, Dan B. McKenzie's Eufaula Brick Company, Charles Ellis Ragan's Eufaula Ice and Coal Company, and two lumber yards owned by Ben Turner Slade and A. B. Garrison.[12] In the late 1930s, a Works Progress Administration writer claimed that "more than any one person," Donald Comer was responsible "for the industrial improvement of Eufaula" during the Depression.[13]

Despite such glowing accolades, even a man of Comer's inestimable talents and energy was incapable of single-handedly guaranteeing the Bluff City's economic survival. Between 1929 and 1933, all three of Eufaula's banks closed. By 1933, with a bonded indebtedness above $300,000, the town could no longer meet its basic fiscal obligations, including teachers' salaries and insurance premium payments. The water and sewage systems, streets, and architectural infrastructure also were dilapidated.[14]

Like a great tsunami, the Depression washed over the town and all of its residents, regardless of their social or economic status. After the state's meager unemployment relief funds dried up during summer 1933, the resources of local charitable organizations, such as the Christ Child Circle, were stretched beyond the breaking point. During the first six months of 1933, the town's Social Service Exchange provided food, clothing, medicine, and other basic necessities of life to 1,548 destitute Eufaulians. A small sample of the Exchange's expenditures bespoke of the Depression's human toll: "$1.05 for garden seed, 50¢ for two gowns, 65¢ for a fishing line to help a man make a living, 25¢ for a book of needles for a poor man, 35¢ for a table

---

tial Library and Museum, Hyde Park, NY (hereafter cited as FDR Library); "Mrs. P. C." to President Franklin D. Roosevelt, 4 September 1934, in Robert S. McElvaine, ed., *Down and Out in the Great Depression: Letters from the Forgotten Man* (Chapel Hill: University of North Carolina Press, 1983) 167–68.

[12] "Industry, Finances, Commerce, and Labor," FWP, State Guide File, Barbour County, box A15, WPA Records, LC.

[13] "History—Donald Comer," ibid.

[14] Flewellen, *Along Broad Street*, 299–313; Tom Rodgers, "October 1929 brought area economic misery," *Eufaula Tribune*, 31 October 2007, A7.

for a poor woman, 70¢ for cloth, and $1.00 for funeral expenses."[15]

Although the Depression's immediate effects were most readily visible among the poorest Eufaulians, the disaster eventually touched everyone. Pecans, hams, chickens, and vegetables were routinely accepted by Eufaula's physicians, dentists, and attorneys as payment for their professional services. A penniless artist showed up at the Bluff City Inn's barber shop and offered Amos Starnes an oil painting of a bucolic hunting scene in exchange for shaves and haircuts during his stay in Eufaula. Starnes had no need for any artwork, but he was touched by the sincere young man's plight and agreed to the barter.[16]

While Eufaula obviously had its own poverty victims to deal with, a steady stream of other needy people drifted through the town. Although the Central of Georgia line was bankrupt and in receivership by the early 1930s, this disruption in train schedules apparently did not seriously deter hobos from riding the rails. Throughout the Depression era, they visited Eufaula in numbers reminiscent of "Coxey's Army" during the Panic of 1893. Using their traditional system of identifying "friendly houses" with secret markings, hobos appeared at back doors all over town, seeking food and temporary jobs. But hobos in Eufaula found that they had competition. Gaunt, hollow-eyed refugees from Barbour County farms wandered aimlessly throughout Southside and Old Eufaula, begging for work and food. Displaced tenant farmers such as Mr. and Mrs. R. H. Singleton and their five children were typical of this group of desperate, dispossessed people. Their landlord in Clayton took everything they owned and forced them off his property. Mrs. Singleton appealed directly to First Lady Lou Hoover for relief: "[W]e are all nearly with out food and clothes...and have never knowed [sic] what it was to be hungry no[r] to be with out something to wear."[17] During the first three years of the Depression, the White House was inundated with such letters, primarily seeking food and second-hand clothing.[18] The Singletons

---

[15] Flynt, *Poor but Proud*, 285; Flewellen, *Along Broad Street*, 313 (quote).

[16] It is likely that this itinerant artist reminded Starnes of his own desperate financial straits when he arrived in Eufaula twenty years earlier. This "relic" of the Great Depression remained in possession of the Starnes family for more than forty years.

[17] Mrs. R. H. Singleton to Lou Henry Hoover, 4 May 1930, Lou Henry Hoover Papers, White House General Files, Requests for Assistance, Hoover Presidential Library, West Branch, IA.

[18] See J. H. Brown to Lou Henry Hoover, 28 November 1930; Estell Hall to Lou

were one family among many in Barbour County that the Depression had crushed. By 1933, as the crisis deepened, it was painfully clear that problems of this magnitude required immediate action and a deployment of resources on a massive scale. Neither Barbour County nor the state government could deliver these services.

In a dramatic scenario replayed across the nation, Eufaulians frantically looked to a newly elected president and his "New Deal" for salvation. During the first "One Hundred Days" of Franklin D. Roosevelt's administration, a sweeping series of emergency executive orders and congressional measures offered a financial life line to Eufaula. However, with banks failing across the nation, several governors pursued emergency measures before FDR was sworn in as president. On 1 March 1933, just prior to FDR's inauguration and call for a national banking holiday, Governor B. M. Miller ordered all Alabama banks to close for ten days. Only those banks that were certified by federal examiners to be solvent would be allowed to re-open. The Eufaula Bank and Trust Company was one of those financial institutions in Alabama that opened its doors. Amazingly, deposits overwhelmingly outdistanced withdrawals, and runs on banks quickly dissipated. Although FDR's national banking holiday was a last-ditch effort to bolster public confidence in the financial system, the Federal Deposit Insurance Corporation (FDIC) soon would provide actual guarantees for accounts.[19]

The FDIC was one of several new federal "alphabet" initiatives and agencies that delivered a semblance of economic stability to Eufaula and Barbour County in the 1930s. Other agencies included the Public Works Administration (PWA), Civil Works Administration (CWA), Works Progress Administration (WPA), and the Civilian Conservation Corps (CCC). A combination of PWA, CWA, and WPA funds was used to repair Eufaula's Carnegie Public Library, the waterworks, sewers, and streets, and

---

Henry Hoover, 7 February 1931; Anna Harris to Lou Henry Hoover, 31 March 1930; Maude Livingston to Lou Henry Hoover, 7 July 1930; Martha Long to Lou Henry Hoover, 8, 16 May 1930; Dora Burton to Lou Henry Hoover, 16 December 1930; Audrey Tarpley to Lou Henry Hoover, 3 September 1931; all in ibid; McElvaine, *The Great Depression*, 175.

[19] Moore, *History of Alabama*, 798; McElvaine, *The Great Depression*, 139–42, 163, 335. Flewellen, *Along Broad Street*, 312–13; Kennedy, *Freedom from Fear*, 131–37, 285, 366; "Finances, Commercial and Labor," FWP, State Guide File, Barbour County, box A15, WPA Records, LC.

for new construction projects, such as the high school gymnasium, which was built in 1935. Perhaps the most ambitious WPA initiative was the Home Aid Project. In partnership with the Alabama Department of Public Welfare and the Cowikee Community House, Home Aid instructors taught nutrition, child care, and other basic domestic skills in the residences of low-income white and African-American families in Barbour County. The WPA funded several other projects on a smaller scale that also provided employment for Eufaulians and proved to be of long-term significance. For example, near the end of the Depression, Gertha Couric, a former restaurant hostess in Eufaula, Birmingham, and Dothan, was hired as the lead researcher, writer, and interviewer for Barbour County's portion of the WPA State Guide Series, and "Slave Narratives," and "Life Histories."[20]

While the WPA and these other new federal agencies furnished jobs, and capital for Barbour County, one of the most popular New Deal programs was the CCC. FDR's personal creation, the CCC recruited young men between the ages of eighteen and twenty-five from relief rolls in cities and towns and assigned them to conservation projects in forests and other wilderness areas of the country. With Army officers as supervisors, CCC enrollees were fed, clothed, and housed by the government. Their pay was thirty dollars per month; twenty-five of which was mailed home to their families—a residual CCC benefit designed to stimulate local economies. CCC recruits built state and national parks and completed a variety of reforestation and land reclamation projects. The rigorous outdoor regimen, nutritious food, medical care, and military discipline also prepared hundreds of young men for service during World War II.[21]

---

[20] Flewellen, *Along Broad Street*, 314–17; Tom Rodgers, "Depression tested county residents," *Eufaula Tribune*, 7 November 2007, A7; "Home Aid Project," 10 October 1938, FWP #4454, folder 16, box SG022777, WPA Files, ADAH; Dr. P. P. Salter life history, 26 April 1939, interviewed by Gertha Couric, Federal Writers' Project, Life Histories/Stories, Barbour County, box SG022773, Gertha Couric life history; 25 January 1939, interviewed by Woodrow Hand, life Histories/Stories/General Research Articles, Barbour County, box SG022775, WPA Files, ADAH.

[21] William Warren Rogers, Robert David Ward, Leah Rawls Atkins, and Wayne Flynt, *Alabama: The History of a Deep South State* (Tuscaloosa: University of Alabama Press, 1994) 491–92; Adam Cohen, *Nothing to Fear: FDR's Inner Circle and The Hundred Days That Created Modern America* (New York: Penguin Books, 2009) 208–12, 214–19, 224–27; Kennedy, *Freedom from Fear*, 144; Watkins, *The Hungry Years*, 159–69; 267–68.

The Bluff City benefitted economically from two CCC camps—one about thirty miles east, across the Chattahoochee River at Cotton Hill, in Quitman County, Georgia; the second in Robertson's Mill, six miles southwest of Clayton. This latter camp was manned by about 220 African Americans who battled soil erosion alongside the county highway leading from Clayton to Louisville and Midway.[22] A like number of white recruits at the Cotton Hill camp labored on reforestation and soil conservation projects in Quitman County. Traveling by trucks to their work sites, both of these CCC contingents patronized Eufaula's retail stores. In June 1934, after the Cotton Hill camp's recruits relocated to Gainesville, Alabama, a local reporter praised their "splendid work during the past eleven months in the forests, etc.," adding, "They have also afforded good trade in Eufaula.... These boys are from different parts of Georgia and North Alabama, although they seem as if they should belong to Eufaula."[23] Although they performed essentially the same tasks, similar journalistic laurels apparently were not bestowed upon the young African Americans when they decamped from Robertson's Mill.[24]

Moreover, the CCC's terracing and other soil erosion preventative measures that were completed along a stretch of rural roads in Barbour County were much more visible to Eufaulians than reforestation projects in Quitman County, Georgia. Both groups of young men spent their hard-earned dollars in Eufaula. Since blacks were barred from Bluff City restaurants, the white CCC enrollees probably put a slightly larger amount of money into the local retail trade. Nevertheless, because of their status as second-class citizens, the African-American CCC workers were not publicly credited for their efforts in behalf of soil conservation or contributions to Eufaula's sagging economy during the Depression.

As shown by this episode, the New Deal did not usher in dramatic social changes in Eufaula, particularly in regard to well-entrenched racial atti-

---

[22] Flewellen, *Along Broad Street*, 316; "Conservation and Reclamation," CCC Company No. 1432, Robertson's Mill, FWP, State Guide File, Barbour County, box A15, WPA Records, LC.

[23] "C. C. C. Camp Moved," *Avondale Sun*, 2 June 1934, 10.

[24] Rogers et al., *Alabama*, 492. Of eighty-three African-American CCC camps in the South, Alabama had eleven, more than any other state in the region. Unlike other Southern directors of state relief, Alabama's Thad Holt appointed large numbers of black men to the CCC.

tudes. In Alabama and elsewhere in the South, many whites openly resented competing with African Americans for government jobs. Critics of the New Deal also continuously labeled PWA, CWA, WPA, and CCC projects as merely glorified "leaf-raking" or "make-work" for the lazy and undeserving.[25]

In fall 1935, Reverend J. E. Hobson, pastor of Eufaula's First Presbyterian Church, warned FDR about "experiments which the administration is trying out. The people here will gladly welcome a swift return to the old constitutional, conservative type of democracy. I am a democrat of the deepest dye, but we cannot afford to depart from the faith of your fathers." After conducting "a thorough investigation," he had found that "the New Deal does not appeal to the better, more conservative class of business men and the impression seems to be that any kind of Federal interference or compulsory control of private affairs will soon disrupt the South."[26] Hobson's comments echoed a widespread fear in the South that New Deal reform measures were overly inclusive of African Americans and poor whites.[27]

Hobson's lecture to FDR aside, in the case of Eufaula at-large, New Deal programs yielded positive results, most notably, the PWA and CWA renovation and construction projects. Contractors, carpenters, brick masons, and unskilled laborers were now working steadily for the first time in over three years. Although these jobs were only temporary, they bolstered the local economy and provided hope and self-respect to these workers and to the entire community—during a time when such positive feelings were in short supply.

On a smaller scale, Gertha Couric's experience with the WPA sharply illustrates the New Deal's impact upon individual Eufaulians. A widowed descendant of one of Old Eufaula's "pioneer families," Couric operated a popular tearoom in downtown Eufaula until the Depression forced her to sell it. After she pursued a succession of restaurant hostess jobs, around 1937, the WPA gave her a new opportunity as a researcher and writer. Couric's "Slave Narratives" and "Life Histories," however, exposed her own social and racial biases, she preserved an empathetic view of the lives of Afri-

---

[25] Feldman, *The Irony of the Solid South*, 91; McElvaine, ed., *Down & Out in the Great Depression*, 94; Cohen, *Nothing to Fear*, 273, 312.

[26] J. E. Hobson to President Franklin D. Roosevelt, 26 September 1935, FDR's Papers as President, President's Personal File (PPF), box 21A, Clergy Letters, FDR Library.

[27] Feldman, *The Irony of the Solid South*, 89, 92–93, 107, 110–13, 130–35.

can Americans, farmers, and Southsiders. Most importantly, she allowed her interviewees to speak in their own vernacular, a hallmark of the WPA Federal Writers' programs. While these interviews should be read with some cautious skepticism, they are still important primary historical sources.[28]

In contrast to Gertha Couric, who was not well prepared for her WPA position, Fannie Corbitt Adams and her assistant, Helen Mitchell Taylor, had excellent academic credentials and extensive teaching experience. Their training proved to be invaluable in administering the WPA Home Aid project. Of all of the WPA programs in Eufaula, it probably had the greatest practical impact upon the largest number of people.[29]

None of these New Deal projects completely resuscitated Eufaula's economy—in April 1939, Barbour County still had 1184 unemployed citizens. The Depression finally ended after the United States prepared for war in 1940–1941 and ultimately became the "Arsenal of Democracy" with its vast defense industry.[30] Eufaula survived the Depression, but without the Cowikee Mills' payrolls and New Deal programs, that task would have been much more problematic and prolonged.

The Great Depression left a deep imprint upon Eufaula and those who lived through the trauma of that era. This experience haunted both Southsiders and Old Eufaulians for the rest of their lives. Their children and grandchildren in turn inherited these memories of the most horrific economic catastrophe in American history. Southsiders clearly were better prepared than Old Eufaulians for the deprivations, anxieties, and challenges of the Great Depression. In the perceptive words of historian Wayne Flynt,

---

[28] Gertha Couric, life history, 25 January 1939, Life Histories/Short Stories/General Research Articles, box SG022775, WPA Files, ADAH; Bunn, *Civil War Eufaula*, 77–79; Ginny Dunaway Young email to the author, 22 April 2016.

[29] "WPA Projects Plan House," *Columbus Daily Enquirer*, 19 May 1940, 2; Mary Adams Belk email to the author, 23 July 2015; Chauncey Sparks, "To Whom It May Concern," letter of recommendation for Helen Mitchell, 16 February 1932, Hallie Taylor Dalon Collection; "Mitchell-Taylor Union Announced," *Columbus Daily Enquirer*, 2 September 1938, 7.

[30] "Finance, Commerce, and Labor," FWP, State Guide File, Barbour County, box A15, WPA Records, LC; Rogers et al., *Alabama*, 510; McElvaine, *The Great Depression*, 320–21, 331; Rauchway, *The Great Depression and the New Deal*, 126–27; Kennedy, *Freedom from Fear*, 363; Frederick Lewis Allen, *The Big Change: America Transforms Itself*, 1900–1950 (New York: Harper and Brothers, 1952) 152, 155.

poor Alabamians saw the Depression as merely "another episode in lives filled with trouble, not as a sudden reversal of fortune."[31]

Southsiders, who had known periodic hard times since the 1890s, had acquired some finely developed survival skills. Many had ancestral roots in the rural South; they were capable of growing their own food and were well acquainted with saving and sharing food and other essentials during lean times. Over forty years of living together as a community in the mill village had taught them how to be productive, frugal, resilient, and self-reliant. But, for wealthier middle-and upper-class Old Eufaulians, who had seldom lacked any creature comforts, the Great Depression was an electrifying jolt to their systems. By 1933, they found that food, clothing, shelter, and a paycheck were no longer guaranteed, regardless of their elite ancestry or pedigree in Eufaula's social register. This realization produced additional fissures in the barriers between the two Eufaulas. Thus the Great Depression stripped away all of the privileges of social class and sense of entitlement among Old Eufaulians. With the exception of African Americans, everyone in town now found their lives defined not by family lineage or residence, but simply by how well they managed to survive and keep body and soul together.

By the mid-1930s, Eufaula's public schools also played a similar democratizing, leveling role. Unlike many textile towns, Eufaula never had separate public schools for mill children. From the first grade through high school, Southsiders and Old Eufaulians attended the same classes. Since the early twentieth century, Eufaula's public schools had been known for their academic excellence. A number of outstanding educators who had taught in the Bluff City for at least twenty years were still active in the 1930s, including Bessie Hayles, Mignon Pitts, Ethel Blackmon, and Annie Miles Ballowe. These dedicated women and many of their colleagues were highly respected, loved, and feared by their students. Eufaula's teachers as a rule set high academic standards, demanded their students' best efforts, and rejected the idea of "social promotions." Thomas "Monzie" Alsobrook, for example, failed two elementary grades and did not graduate from Eufaula High School until 1940 at age nineteen. Although he was a talented football player, his gridiron heroics did not translate into a free ride in the classroom. Nevertheless, despite being an indifferent student, his academic background

---

[31] Flynt, *Poor but Proud*, 281.

in Eufaula prepared him well for later success in college.[32]

Annie Miles Ballowe—one of Eufaula's most brilliant teachers— exerted an extraordinary influence upon students who struggled in the classroom, such as Monzie Alsobrook. She readily admitted an affinity for the "under dog, not just the brilliant student…. The backward student was always welcomed at my home, and night after night, a group of these pupils brought their books, and…I would endeavor to make plain their problems."[33]

Perhaps one reason that she championed the "under dog" was that her own life's journey had been difficult. Orphaned as a child in Monroe, Louisiana, she lived with her grandmother in Cuthbert, Georgia. She graduated from high school at age fifteen. Three years later, she earned an A. B. degree at Athens State Normal School. In 1899, she came to Eufaula to teach at the Union Female College. She married Robert A. Ballowe in 1900. After his death in 1914, Annie Ballowe was left with six of her own children and four stepdaughters. Ballowe embarked on her Eufaula public school career with ten children to raise on a salary of forty-five dollars per month. She taught English and mathematics for about thirty-six years and finally retired in the late 1940s. Through her encouragement and scholarship fund-raising efforts, she assisted more students in attending college than any other person in Eufaula during her lifetime.[34]

Cleveland Adams, Tyson Smith, Albert Driggers, Fannie Corbitt, Frances Starnes, and Earl Starnes were just a few of Ballowe's Southside students who left Eufaula for productive college careers. Under Ballowe's tutelage, Earl Starnes was allowed to skip two years in high school, graduating when he was only fifteen in 1931. He subsequently earned his degree in electrical engineering at Auburn Polytechnic Institute in 1935 and pursued a

---

[32] "Eufaula Educators Busy," *Montgomery Advertiser*, 6 September 1910, 8; "Eufaula Teachers Elected," *Montgomery Advertiser*, 19 May 1911, 14; "New Principal Named for Eufaula High School," *Montgomery Advertiser*, 2 September 1917, 5; "Eufaula School Opens Sept. 7th," *Montgomery Advertiser*, 21 August 1921, 12; Eufaula High School Diploma, Thomas Neville Alsobrook, 28 May 1940, in author's possession.

[33] Annie Miles Ballowe life history, 15 February 1937, interviewed by Gertha Couric, Life Histories/Short Stories/General Research Articles, box SG022775, WPA Files, ADAH.

[34] Ibid. Flewellen, *Along Broad Street*, 422. Annie Miles Ballowe died in 1967 at age eighty-seven.

lengthy career at Avondale and Russell Mills.[35]

Regardless of the influence of the remarkably egalitarian Annie Ballowe, some Eufaula teachers grudgingly continued to belittle and ridicule Southside students from the 1930s well into the early 1960s. These remaining recalcitrant teachers directed their animus toward Southside's poorest children—those who lived at the end of South Randolph Street in Morningside.[36] By the 1930s, many of Eufaula's educators realized that Southside was producing a sizable number of talented scholars, musicians, and athletes. Even music instructor Agnes Wilkinson—who had once rejected young J. T. Dunaway as a tenor in an operetta before World War I—welcomed Southsiders as participants in her programs.[37]

The most obvious changes in relations between the two Eufaulas originated from within the students themselves. The twenty-eight members of the Eufaula High School Class of 1937 were freshmen when the Great Depression had become deeply entrenched. Of these students, who graduated in spring 1937, only five were Southsiders. The rest lived north of Broad Street or in rural northern Barbour County. Since early childhood, however, they had been together in school and at the Cowikee Community House. Their friendships transcended the old walls that divided the town. Southsider Frances Starnes lived at 508 South Eufaula Street. Her two best friends were Lillie Mitchell and Alice Comer—daughters of Old Eufaula families. These three young women shared a love of music and academics and remained close friends for many years after they graduated in 1937.[38]

During the 1930s, the growing popularity of high school football also chipped away at the remaining barriers of social exclusion in Eufaula. The

---

[35] Young, "Ancestors of David Ernest Alsobrook," in author's possession. Frances Joy Starnes (1919–2008) was my mother; Earl William Starnes (1915–2002) was her brother and my uncle. Their parents were Willie Mae and Amos Starnes.

[36] Wendell Franklin Wentz email to the author, 24 February 2016.

[37] "Closing Exercises of Eufaula Schools," *Montgomery Advertiser*, 25 November 1921, 10; "Eufaula Schools Have Unique Entertainment," 27 November 1921, 8; "Twenty-Four Graduate at Eufaula Schools," *Montgomery Advertiser*, 27 March 1922, 7; "Eufaula Event Is Successful," *Columbus Daily Enquirer*, 26 February 1938, 4.

[38] Misc. clippings, 1937; Lillie [Mitchell] to Frances Starnes, 3 May 1938, telegram; Alice [Comer] to Frances [Starnes], n.d., c. 7 November 1939, all in Frances Starnes Scrapbook, c. 1937–1942, in author's possession; 15th and 16th US Census, 1930–1940, Schedule No. 1, Population, Barbour County, Alabama, NARA.

Bluff City fielded its first high school football team in fall 1921. Three seasons later, twenty-three-year-old Thurman Jennings Campbell, a recent University of Alabama graduate, was hired as Eufaula High School's head football coach and principal. Powerfully built, with chiseled facial features, the handsome young coach built a strong foundation for the Eufaula football program. Over the next thirteen years, Campbell amassed an impressive record of 56-33-6, including unbeaten teams in 1934 and 1935. He also coached boxing and hosted Alabama Golden Gloves tournaments in Eufaula.[39]

In 1934, Otha Burnett Carter, age twenty-seven, a native of Gordo, Alabama, was hired as T. J. Campbell's assistant coach. O. B. Carter most recently had coached and taught in Louisville, Alabama, in rural Barbour County. Small of stature, the bespectacled Carter was a perfectionist and a fierce competitor. He proved to be an ideal coaching partner for Campbell. Together they produced the two undefeated teams that were built around Southside boys. Their teams practiced and played with spirit, grit, and aggressiveness and won consistently, including a fair share of games against traditional rivals Union Springs and Dothan. Several Eufaula High School players from Southside earned All-State honors, including, Will "Bubba" Snipes, Glenn Hatfield, Marvin Hatfield, and Hilton "Hezzie" Nolan. By the late 1930s, Old Eufaula's football boosters cared much more about players' talents than their genealogies. During the 1936 gridiron campaign, Carter and Campbell introduced the first nighttime football games in

---

[39] "Eufaula Items," *Columbus Daily Enquirer*, 17 December 1929, 5; "Miss Wilma Ross Weds Thurman Campbell," *Tuscaloosa News*, 28 August 1931, 6; "Tigers of Eufaula Win Football Cup," *Columbus Daily Enquirer*, 5 March 1934, 5; "Tourney Planned," *Columbus Daily Enquirer*, 18 January 1937, 8; "Eufaula Board Name Teachers," *Columbus Daily Enquirer*, 21 May 1937, 4; *Avondale Sun*, 3 January 1955, 3; "Thurman J. Campbell," obituary, *Huntsville (AL) Times*, 21 January 1986, 4; 13th and 14th US Census, 1910, 1920, Schedule No. 1, Population, Clay County, Alabama, NARA; 15th and 16th US Census, 1930, 1940, Schedule No. 1, Population, Barbour County, Alabama, NARA; Alabama High School Football History Society (AHSFHA), "T. J. Campbell," http://ljwvbly.ahsfhs.org/Teams2/coachestop1.asp?Coach=T.J.Campbell&Team=Eufaula (accessed 3 April 2016). A native of Clay County, AL, Campbell left Eufaula in spring 1937. He worked as a wholesale representative for several years in Talladega and served as superintendent of the Attalla City Schools for twenty-three years. He died in 1986 at age eighty-four.

Eufaula, thus allowing more mill families to see their sons in action.[40]

After Campbell retired in 1937 as head coach, Carter succeeded him. In addition to his head coaching duties, Carter also taught high school science, English, and history. He systematically replaced smaller schools on Eufaula's football schedule—Clio, Blue Springs, Ariton, and Brundidge—with larger ones well known for their athletic prowess—Selma, Auburn, Opelika, and Phenix City. During his five years as head coach, Carter amassed a respectable record of 22-19-4. In 1941 he launched a distinguished thirty-seven-year career as principal and superintendent of schools in Eufaula.[41]

But as a coach, Carter's greatest talent was an exceptional ability to mold the lives of young men, particularly Southsiders. When their playing eligibility had expired after graduation, he carefully followed their lives and careers. He assisted many of his players in seeking junior college and collegiate football scholarships, such as Ty Irby, John "Handsome" Lockwood, and Monzie Alsobrook. After learning that Alsobrook was miserably homesick at Perkinston Junior College in Mississippi, Carter wrote these comforting words to him in September 1940:

> Well, I have been hearing some good things about you. I know you can play ball and I'm expecting you to. Things may seem hard and bad at times, but remember things that are worth while don't come easy. If you make good like you have started out doing you can almost pick your school next year.... You can take it and I'm really counting on you. I have had a number of people to tell me that they knew you would make good.... [W]rite

---

[40] "Otha Burnett Carter," http://trees.ancestrylibrary.com/tree/71462450/person/30238100216 (accessed 16 March 2015); "Educator O. B. Carter dead at 86," *Eufaula Tribune*, 23 October 1994, 17; 15th US Census, 1930, Schedule No. 1, Population, Barbour County, Alabama, NARA; "Seven Battles On Local Grid," *Avondale Sun*, 28 September 1936, 13.

[41] "Educator O. B. Carter dead at 86," *Eufaula Tribune*, 23 October 1994, 1, 7: "New school is dedicated to Carter," *Eufaula Tribune*, 29 August 1978, 1; "It is fitting school is dedicated to Mr. Carter," editorial, *Eufaula Tribune*, 29 August 1978; "O. B. Carter," AHSFHA, http://ljwvbly.ahsfhs.org/Teams2/coachestop1.asp?Coach=O.B. Carter&Team=Eufaula (accessed 3 April 21016). Carter often disparaged Eufaula High School's "E&O Schedule," which meandered like the Eufaula and Ozark Railroad line through small towns in Barbour, Pike, and Dale counties.

me all about yourself.[42]

Since Alsobrook's own father died almost twenty years earlier, Carter's paternal support and guidance were invaluable to him, and he finished the year at Perkinston. But, sadly, for Alsobrook and thousands of other young Americans, "next year" would not be devoted to academics and football. Instead, they would be donning khaki instead of football uniforms and preparing for combat.

If high school football and the Great Depression created sizable breaches in the walls between Southside and Old Eufaula, World War II completed their demolition. Like the rest of America, Eufaulians first received the shocking news about the Japanese attack on Pearl Harbor via the radio. To avoid panic among the civilian population, the government tried to minimize the actual extent of the damage the Pacific Fleet had suffered. Several months elapsed before an accurate tabulation of the losses emerged—347 aircraft destroyed or severely crippled, eighteen warships sunk or inoperable (including eight battleships) and 2,403 Americans dead and 1,178 wounded. The Navy personnel losses alone were greater than the combined totals for the Spanish-American War and the World War I.[43]

Even before FDR's "Day of Infamy" address and the official congressional declaration of war, by the evening of 7 December 1941, all Americans understood what their country now faced—a global conflict of unprecedented proportions. The stakes for the nation's survival and ultimate triumph over the forces of fascism had never been higher. And that victory would demand a unified effort from all Americans, including Southsiders and Old Eufaulians. After Pearl Harbor, Southsiders' lives would no longer be defined solely within the context of the mills and the village. With their shared feelings of loss, betrayal, and anger, residents of the two Eufaulas now stood together against a common foe. On 8 December 1941, Frances Starnes briefly summed up her raw emotions:

> It is so hard to realize the seriousness of all of this. I still can't believe that we have actually declared war—I know that it will perhaps be a long time before the damn[ed] yellow Japs get over here, but think of all the lives already lost at Honolula [*sic*], and of all the lives that will be lost before it is

---

[42] O. B. Carter to Thomas Alsobrook, 3 September 1940, in author's possession.
[43] William L. O'Neill, *A Democracy at War: America's Fight at Home and Abroad in World War II* (New York: The Free Press, 1993) 6; Kennedy, *Freedom from Fear*, 522.

over.[44]

In the midst of their outrage over the attack, Eufaulians concentrated their thoughts and prayers on the local servicemen who reportedly were stationed at Pearl Harbor: Luther Braswell, Wallace Williams, John Stewart, Thomas H. Moorer, Reuben Ard Carr, and two sets of brothers—Bill and Arthur Gibson Gill, and Joe and Walter Britt Stevens. All of these young men survived the attack. Tom Moorer was one of the few Navy aviators who managed to launch his airplane and pursue the Japanese dive-bombers. Ard Carr was awarded a Silver Star for heroism under fire at Hickam Field in organizing a defensive perimeter with machine guns. He and his comrades remained at their red-hot weapons until they were relieved the next morning.[45]

Shortly afterward, Carr wrote a detailed account of the attack to his parents in Eufaula. He also included his own defiant prediction about the future:

> I personally think the damned Japs have bit off more than they can chew. We are giving them hell in the Philippines and I don't believe that they will ever be able to hit us here in the islands as they did on December 7. It is my belief that they committed national suicide by attacking us and they will damned soon realize it.[46]

Young Ard Carr did not survive the war. In May 1943, less than two years after Pearl Harbor, his bomber was shot down in a mission over Europe. The entire crew was lost. Before the war ended, about forty-five other young men from Barbour County died overseas. They hailed from Old Eufaula, Southside, and from rural corners of the county. Their addresses and social pedigrees no longer mattered. They all were simply honored as

---

[44] Frances Starnes to Thomas Alsobrook, 8 December 1941, in author's possession.

[45] "Eufaula Soldiers Saw Real Pearl Harbor," "Lest We Forget," *Eufaula Tribune*, 10 November 2002, 7; "Personals," *Avondale Sun*, 15 December 1941, 12; "Eufaula Boys in Service," *Avondale Sun*, 22 December 1941, 5; "Ard" [Carr] to "Mom, Dad, and Gaston," n.d. c. 10 December 1941, in "Boys in Service Write Home Folks," *Avondale Sun*, 26 January 1942, 10; "Carr Honored at Hickam Field," *Avondale Sun*, 13 July 1942, 1, 13; Flewellen, *Along Broad Street*, 339.

[46] "Ard" [Carr] to "Mom, Dad, and Gaston," n.d., c. 10 December 1941, in "Boys in Service Write Home Folks," *Avondale Sun*, 26 January 1942, 10.

warriors who died in the defense of their country.[47]

Barbour County suffered only about fifteen fewer casualties during World War I. But that conflict lasted only two years, and the mobilization of manpower was not as comprehensive as in 1941–1945. These two facts suggest why the two Eufaulas did not disappear by 1919. During World War II, every able-bodied male in Barbour County between the ages of about eighteen and forty-five either volunteered for military service or was drafted. By 1944–1945, married men, farmers, and defense workers were subject to the draft. By the end of the war, deferments were extremely rare, exemplified by those authorized for scientists engaged in the Manhattan Project and related research on the development of a nuclear weapon.[48]

With the implementation of the first military draft since the Great War in fall 1940, many Eufaula boys volunteered for service before being inducted into the Army. By that time, many Eufaulians felt that since war seemed inevitable, and it probably would be fought primarily at sea, their service of choice was the Navy. In February 1941, Oma Alsobrook wrote to her son Monzie: "I hear Lee Smith has joined the navy. There seems to be a chase among the younger ones to join the navy. I think John Stewart is going as soon as he is 17. Guess you knew Bill Nol[i]n was in the Submarines now."[49] Monzie, who celebrated his twentieth birthday six months earlier in September 1940, replied that he expected to be drafted soon. She immediately responded, "Don't mention Uncle Sam ever getting you. I don't want to think you or I are any better than others who are going but lets [sic] not cross the bridge until we get to it. It don't [sic] sound good."[50]

But that bridge already had been crossed many months before with the first draft registrations and mobilization of Army Reserve and National Guard units across the nation. In November 1940, Robert D. McKenzie, age thirty, a newly minted graduate of the Army Officers Training School in

---

[47] "Service Record Book of Men and Women of Eufaula, Alabama and Community," V. F. W. Post No. 5850, n.d., unpub. typescript, Eufaula Carnegie Library, Eufaula, AL, 10; "Barbour County War Dead, World War II," Appendix E, Flewellen, *Along Broad Street*, 499; "Barbour County War Dead," "Lest We Forget," *Eufaula Tribune*, 10 November 2002, 31.

[48] Flewellen, *Along Broad Street*, 333, 336–37; O'Neill, *A Democracy at War*, 392–93; Kennedy, *Freedom from Fear*, 632–35, 661–68, 709–11.

[49] Oma Alsobrook to Thomas Alsobrook, 7 February 1941, in author's possession.

[50] Oma Alsobrook to Thomas Alsobrook, n.d., c. 15 February 1941, ibid.

Virginia, personally recruited men from Barbour and Bullock counties, the Wiregrass, and West Georgia for Eufaula's reorganized National Guard unit—officially designated as Battery D, 104th Coast Artillery (Antiaircraft), Separate Battalion. Battery D eventually reached its full complement of four officers and about 150 enlisted men.[51]

The recently activated National Guard units lacked uniforms, weapons, supplies, rations, and armories. Above all else, their greatest deficiency was inexperience as soldiers. During the first three months of its existence, Battery D was not an exception. These troops obviously were just embarking upon their training to prepare them for combat. A few days before Battery D left for basic training at Camp Stewart in Hinesville, Georgia, Oma Alsobrook observed Eufaula's "citizen soldiers":

> [T]he Nat guards are in camp here until next week. They have headquarters at the knitting mill and are eating at Mrs. [Sig] Bloom's. Bubber [Will Snipes] & Toby [Olin C. Gordon] stay at home every night but drill all day. [T]hey really look tuckered out when they come home. Carrie [Snipes] has been sick all the week. I believe she is grieving over Bubber going off.... I know Cletus [Hartzog] is a soretail, he tried to get out of the Nat guards but failed. They made Chas. Hatfield a Sarg—what do you think about that? [His] long drawers is eating Bubber up. [T]hey are in two pieces. [H]e comes home at night & gets out of them quick.[52]

Oma Alsobrook, who personally witnessed these scenes at her Aunt Carrie Snipes's home on West Barbour Street, fully understood that although their young men were not professional soldiers, they would have to protect the nation. Despite their chaotic state of unpreparedness, Battery D's troops personified World War II's random, democratic mobilization process. Their ranks were drawn from both sides of town, with perhaps a slightly larger proportion of Southsiders. They included the sons of mill operatives like Will "Bubba" Snipes and Old Eufaulians such as William J. Comer,

---

[51] Flewellen, *Along Broad Street*, 332–33; John B. Wilson, *Maneuver and Firepower: The Evolution of Divisions and Separate Brigades*, Army Lineage Series (Washington, DC: Center of Military History, United States Army, 1998) 152–72: Kirsten E. Fischer, "Project preserves history of Eufaula's Battery D," "Lest We Forget," *Eufaula Tribune*, 10 November 2002, 14; "Service Book of Men and Women of Eufaula, Alabama and Community," 78; O'Neill, *A Democracy at War*, 87–89, 280.

[52] Oma Alsobrook to Thomas Alsobrook, n.d., c. 10 February 1941, in author's possession.

whose grandfather was Governor William D. Jelks and great-uncle was Governor B. B. Comer.[53] Somehow, over the next year, the Army had to forge this disparate group of young men into a disciplined fighting component. As they said final goodbyes and prepared for embarkation to Camp Stewart, Battery D was still a rag-tag gang of civilians.

On 17 February 1941, the Crystal Club on Orange Street hosted an evening of dancing and musical entertainment to honor Battery D. The popular orchestra leader Ambrose C. Hortman served as master of ceremonies for the floor show that preceded the dancing. After Richard Rutland, Jr., blew "Assembly" on his bugle, Sara Walker sang "I Hear a Rhapsody" and "We Three," followed by tap-dancing and acrobatics performed by Joy Wynne and Annie Will Standifer. An ensemble of "five colored men"—Joe Jones, Floyd Shorter, Buck Rousseau, Thornton King, and Ike Hudson— then led the guests in a medley of patriotic tunes, including "America" and "God Bless America." The soldiers concluded the show with their own performances. Ed Beverly, Jr., and Noah Lee Smith sang "Does Your Heart Beat for Me?" Pianist J. C. McCarthy played "Beer Barrel Polka," and Joe Stricklin, from Union Springs, tap-danced and presented a "tongue twisting humorous" reading. As everyone danced into the wee morning hours, the only reminder that the Battery D boys were now in the Army was the "Officers Only" second floor of the Crystal Club.[54] This joyous evening would be Battery D's last civilian diversion for more than three years.

The weather was cool and cloudy on 18 February 1941. All vehicles along Broad Street from Randolph to Forsyth Streets were cleared by the police. Around seven o'clock that evening, three sharp blasts from the town's fire siren announced the start of the evening's festivities. Led by the Cowikee Band and American Legionnaires, the Battery D troops marched from the knitting mill to the depot. Covering less than one city block, this would be perhaps the shortest march in Battery D's history. Captain Robert McKenzie and lieutenants Ralph Garrison, Malcolm Reeves, and Herschel Conner assembled their men into a tight square formation at the depot. Fireworks lit up the night sky as hundreds of Eufaulians gathered around the

---

[53] "Soldiering at Camp Stewart," *Avondale Sun*, 30 June 1941, 12; "Battery D Roster," "Lest We Forget," *Eufaula Tribune*, 10 November 2002, 14; Flewellen, *Along Broad Street*, 497–98 (Appendix D).

[54] "Dance Held at Crystal Club," *Avondale Sun*, 24 February 1941, 12.

troops at the depot. After the band played the National Anthem and a prayer by the Reverend C. Walker Sessions (First Presbyterian Church's pastor), remarks were delivered by Colonel H. L. Upshaw, editor of the *Eufaula Tribune*; city attorney Lee J. Clayton; and several other local dignitaries. Judge Clayton gestured towards the troops and said, "Out there are the grandsons of men who carved their names in imperishable fame at Chickamauga and other Southern battlefields; out there are the grandsons of a War-time Governor and distinguished Southern leaders."[55] Captain McKenzie laughingly remembered Clayton's lengthy speech more than sixty years later—"The train was going to leave and was blowing its whistle, but he wouldn't quit!" Finally the conductor warned, "I just wanted to let you know I'm going with the train; y'all can come if you want to!"[56] By eight o'clock that evening, the men of Battery D were loaded on the train and were on their way.

Oma Alsobrook accompanied Carrie Snipes to the depot that night. Although they both knew all of the Eufaula boys in Battery D, they primarily were there to send off her aunt's son, "Bubba," and son-in-law, Toby Gordon. "Lots of boys would have liked to back down when the time came I think," Oma later remarked. "There was a great many tears shed that night."[57] During the "great demonstration of love at the train," she also saw two young women almost come to blows over James N. Hall, and one soldier who was yelling frantically from the train's window, "'Goodby Susie.' I know he was cutting up for no one came as Susie."[58] Hilton "Hezzie" Nolan, a member of the Eufaula High School Class of 1941, also was in the crowd that night. Two weeks later, he wrote to a friend, "Boy, you ought to see the pool room after this National Guard stuff. It got everything from 'Dinah' [Daniel] Halstead on up. Now, if you wanted to see some 'hot stuff' in uni-

---

[55] Flewellen, *Along Broad Street*, 334; "Elaborate Program for Departure of Battery D," *Avondale Sun*, 24 February 1941, 12; "Fire Siren to Signal Departure of Local Battery," *Eufaula Tribune*, 18 February 1941, 1. "Throngs Cheer Battery as It Leaves For Camp Stewart; Parade, Speeches, Fireworks," *Eufaula Tribune*, 19 February 1941, 1 (Judge Clayton quote).

[56] Kristin E. Fischer, "Project preserves history of Eufaula's Battery D," "Lest We Forget," *Eufaula Tribune*, 10 November 2002, 14.

[57] Oma Alsobrook to Thomas Alsobrook, n.d., c. February—March 1941, in author's possession.

[58] Ibid.

form you should have been here. Some of them haven't been sober since they joined."[59]

Battery D trained at Camp Stewart and later at Fort Bragg, North Carolina. Some of the men were transferred to other Army units, including Captain McKenzie, who served in the Panama Canal Zone and Okinawa. The largest contingent of Battery D soldiers was dispatched to New Guinea. By that time, they had evolved into a rather "salty" bunch of young men. In October 1942, Charles Hatfield described them "as brown as a native and tough as a pine knot. Eufaula will have a job keeping us in check when we get back."[60] Battery D's average overseas tours of duty were about thirty-six months, and some of the troops served even longer. Miraculously, none of these soldiers perished in combat.[61]

Simultaneously, as the Battery D boys were being honed to a razor-sharp edge as fighting troops, other young men and women, who had never traveled very far from Eufaula, were shipping out for basic training and boot camp in far-flung Army, Marine, Navy, and Coast Guard posts. For the first time in their young lives, they visited locales that they had only heard about or seen in movies and news reels. Earl Starnes, stationed at the Army Signal Corps school at Fort Monmouth, New Jersey, used his leave time to take in "the bright lights" of New York City and hear live Big Band performances directed by Bennie Goodman and Glenn Miller.[62]

Sailor Bill Nolin, who graduated from Eufaula High School in 1940, was impressed with Rockefeller Center and Times Square but later observed, "Give me the good old town of Eufaula way down in Dixie. New York is too

---

[59] Hilton "Hezzie" Nolan to "Scotch" [Thomas Alsobrook], 27 February 1941, in author's possession.

[60] Sgt. Charles Hatfield to [Hallie] Smith, n.d., c. October 1942, in "With Our Boys in Service," *Avondale Sun*, 2 November 1942, 10.

[61] "Seven Members of Battery D Enroute Home from Pacific," *Avondale Sun*, 3 April 1944, 13; *Avondale Sun*, 10 July 1944, 10; 14 May 1945, 10; 23 July 1945, 3; "Mackenzie [*sic*] Celebrates 104th Birthday with Friends," *Eufaula Tribune*, 16 November 2014, 6A. McKenzie died in Eufaula at age 104 in January 2015.

[62] "Personal," *Avondale Sun*, 6 October 1941, 5; Frances Starnes to Thomas Alsobrook, n.d., c. January—February 1942, in author's possession; "Avondale's Manpower Contribution to National Defense," *Avondale Sun*, 1 December 1941, 16; Earl Starnes to Hugh Comer, n.d., c. 15 March 1942, in "With Our Boys in the Service," *Avondale Sun*, 24 March 1941, 16.

big."[63] Like other Eufaula servicemen during World War II, Nolin's thoughts often turned to his hometown. On one occasion, he thanked Carrie Snipes for sending a Christmas "care package" from the Eufaula Service Center, assuring her that such thoughtful gifts linked him to friends and relatives: "As long as we hear from home, we can face anything that confronts us."[64] Nolin also kept up with his high school classmates who were still civilians. In January 1942, he offered some very blunt advice to Monzie Alsobrook: "When are they going to catch up with you and jerk you in the army? Boy, you had better join the navy. When you are shot in this outfit, you, at least, have water to wash the blood off as you go down. *Phooey Bum joke*, eh."[65]

Alsobrook listened closely to his friend's suggestion. Like thousands of patriotic youngsters, Alsobrook had tried to enlist in the Navy the week following Pearl Harbor. Along with many other men, he was turned away from the recruiting station in Gadsden because the Navy already had surpassed its quota of volunteers. He returned to his training as a machinist at the Alabama School of Trades. While waiting to receive his Navy induction notice, he worked for about sixteen months as an aircraft machinist alongside his wife, Frances Starnes Alsobrook, at Brookley Field in Mobile. He was frequently embarrassed by the question from strangers: "Why aren't you in uniform?" After finally being inducted in autumn 1943, he left his wife with her parents in Eufaula and reported to Camp Peary, Virginia, the Navy "Seabees" training site for construction battalions.[66]

---

[63] Bill Nolin to "Miss Hallie" [Smith], 12 March 1941, in "William Nolin Likes Navy—But Prefers Eufalua [*sic*] to New York," *Avondale Sun*, 24 March 1941, 16.

[64] Bill Nolin to Carrie Snipes, n.d., c. 10 December 1943, in "Bill Nolin," *Avondale Sun*, 20 December 1943, 13; "Center Sends 161 Boxes to Soldiers," *Avondale Sun*, 4 October 1943, 14.

[65] Bill Nolin to "Hi Mate" [Thomas Alsobrook], 20 January 1942, in author's possession.

[66] Thomas N. Alsobrook's Report Ratings, Mechanic Learner, 5th US Civil Service Commission, 12 December 1941; P. J. Blattau to Thomas Alsobrook, 23 December 1941; War Department Report for Field Personnel Action, 29 December 1941, Probational Appointment for Thomas N. Alsobrook, Mechanic Learner, Brookley Field, Mobile, AL; all in author's possession; "Bridge Tea Shower Given For Recent Bride," *Eufaula Tribune*, n.d., c. September 1942; "Personals," *Avondale Sun*, 6 April 1942, 14; 21 September 1942, 5; 15 November 1943, 4; 18 September 1944, 16.

Alsobrook was amazed at the intensity and speed of Navy boot camp: "They really throw the training to you in a hurry."[67] Like his friend, Bill Nolin, and his brother-in-law, Earl Starnes, prior to induction, Alsobrook had never left the Southeast. But, after completing boot camp in mid-November 1943, he was aboard a troop train bound for Port Hueneme, California, for amphibious assault and weapons training. He informed his mother: "Well, we're still riding. Right now we are in the wide open spaces of Texas...west of Fort Worth. We've passed through West Va., Ken., Ill., Mo., Kan., Okala. [sic], and I reckon we'll go through about three more."[68]

With the conclusion of a rigorous course at Port Hueneme in beach assault techniques and marksmanship, Alsobrook proudly felt that he was now a full-fledged "Fighting Seabee." However, a week before Christmas 1943, he bitterly wrote home:

> I don't see anything left to do but take a boat ride.... The skipper told us the other day that he didn't think we would even need our guns where we are going. So you see we are not headed for action. In fact it looks like an old folks' home to me. You need not tell everybody that though. Let them think I'm fighting.[69]

He served until the end of the war in Hawaii, primarily on Johnston Island, an isolated, sandy atoll about 700 miles southwest of Honolulu. He later jokingly suggested that Eufaula was a more exciting location during the war than Hawaii.

Alsobrook accurately characterized life in Eufaula during those years. From 1942 until V-J Day, the Bluff City booked a heavy schedule of patriotic programs—War Bond rallies, scrap metal and rubber collection drives, parades, band concerts, flag ceremonies, and speeches. Southsiders actively participated in these events and organized elaborate flag and candle-lighting ceremonies in their churches to honor members in the military services. In 1943–1944, the Second Baptist Church had thirty-six members serving in the armed forces; Washington Street Methodist had fifty-two.[70]

---

[67] Thomas Alsobrook to Oma Alsobrook, 10 October 1943, in author's possession.

[68] Thomas Alsobrook to Oma Alsobrook, 13 November 1943, ibid.

[69] Thomas Alsobrook to Oma Alsobrook, 19 December 1943, ibid.

[70] "Salvage Committee Thanks Tribune," *Avondale Sun*, 1 June 1942, 5; "Scout Troop 10 of Eufaula," *Avondale Sun*, 13 December 1943, 14; "Band News," *Avondale Sun*, 21 February 1944, 4; "Bond Rally Held Thursday Night," *Eufaula Tribune*, 21 No-

The most dramatic, emotional public events in Eufaula were those that
allowed the community to honor their sons and daughters for their military
service. Furloughed combat officers and enlisted men were popular speakers
at churches, schools, civic clubs, and the Cowikee Community House. During summer 1942, naval aviator Tom Moorer and Colonel Heath Cowart, a
Troy native and commander of the 104th Artillery Battalion in New Guinea, addressed large, enthusiastic crowds. Because the Battery D soldiers were
serving under Cowart, his remarks were of particular interest to Eufaulians.
In response to a variety of questions from the audience about the current
combat situation in New Guinea and when their boys would be relieved,
Cowart emphasized that "the Japs are indomitable fighters," which has resulted in a prolonged war. He concluded by urging Eufaulians to keep writing letters to their boys to bolster their morale.[71]

A number of enlisted men on furlough left memorable impressions on
the Eufaula home front. Sailor Bill Gill, a former high school football star,
and Marine Avery Nolin, an Eagle Scout in Troop 10, devoted many of
their leave hours to visiting with Cowikee Band members and other children
at the Community House. Since Gill was a Pearl Harbor survivor and Nolin
had seen extensive action in the Pacific, Eufaula's youngsters looked up to
them with awe and admiration.[72]

But there was another Eufaula combat veteran who typified countless
"citizen soldiers" who were determined to do their part to win the war. The
son of a Wiregrass sharecropper, thirty-two-year-old Burnace Hobbs
worked in Cowikee Mill No. 1 before the war. In his disheveled, sun-
bleached khakis, with his protruding ears, bushy eyebrows, large nose, and
thin lips, Hobbs scarcely resembled a Hollywood-styled hero. Since he was
an older recruit and wore dentures, he had to persuade Army medical examiners that "he did not want to bite the Japs; he just wanted to fight them."

---

vember 1944, 1; "Dedication of Flags Sunday," *Avondale Sun*, 20 September 1943, 22;
Frances Alsobrook to Thomas Alsobrook, 18 November 1944; Thomas Alsobrook to
Oma Alsobrook, 8 October 1944; photograph of candles at Washington Street Method-
ist Church, 1944, all in author's possession.

[71] "Personals," *Avondale Sun*, 22 February 1943, 5; "Heroes Honored at Eufaula
with Special Event," *Columbus Daily Enquirer*, 19 July 1942, 19; Mrs. A. A. Couric,
"Eufaula Hears Pacific Officer," *Columbus Daily Enquirer*, 13 June 1942, 21 (quote).

[72] "Personals," *Avondale Sun*, 22 February 1943, 5; "Boy Scout News—Troop 10,"
Avondale Sun, 9 July 1945, 11.

Serving in an Army supply company on Guadalcanal in 1942, he lost an eye in combat and received a medical discharge in August 1943. After returning to Eufaula, Hobbs spoke at the Second Baptist Church Sunday school, Lee Theatre's Victory Prayer Service, and at Cowikee Band practice. He also chaperoned children's picnics and fishing expeditions to the Cowikee Mill Farm and Camp Rotary. He returned to his mill job, but he never fully recovered from the trauma of combat. Shuffled in and out of veteran's hospitals for the rest of his life, Hobbs suffered a fatal heart attack at age forty-two in April 1951.[73]

Hobbs and Eufaula's other troops who returned home after being discharged or furloughed were merely a trickle compared to the influx of soldiers on leave from Fort Benning and Camp Rucker. Situated only fifty miles south of Fort Benning, Eufaula was essentially an annex of one of the largest Army infantry and airborne training bases in the nation. On weekends, Fort Benning soldiers rode buses, borrowed vehicles, or hitchhiked to Eufaula. These troops were not seeking a hell-raising weekend of debauchery in the Bluff City; Phenix City, just across the river from Columbus, Georgia, provided plenty of that type of recreation. Soldiers who visited Eufaula desired to live normal civilian lives—if only for a few days—surrounded by reminders of their own homes and families. In return, Eufaulians saw their sons in these young soldiers' faces and opened their homes and hearts to them. Visiting troops who could not secure lodging in the Bluff City Inn seldom had any difficulty finding weekend accommodations with local families. D. F. "Doc" Barker, for example, rented rooms to soldiers and served wholesome family style meals on a large table in his hallway. As with other Southside families, Barker had plenty of fresh produce and eggs from his backyard garden and chicken coop.[74]

The Bluff City's three principal venues for entertaining the troops were the Cowikee Community House, the Crystal Club, and the Eufaula Service Center. This third organization—founded and staffed by local women—sent gift packages to Eufaulians serving in the military and furnished visiting

---

[73] B[urnace] Hobbs to Comer Jennings, n.d., c. November 1942, in "With Our Boys in Service," *Avondale Sun*, 22 December 1942, 13; "With Our Boys in Service," *Avondale Sun*, 5 October 1942, 13 (quote); 26 July 1943, 12; "Burnace Hobbs Given Honorable Discharge from the Army," *Avondale Sun*, 23 August 1943, 12; "Burnace Hobbs Succumbs to Heart Attack," *Avondale Sun*, 9 April 1951, 3.

[74] June Barker Clenney email to the author, 4 August 2015.

troops with refreshments, stationary, ink, pens, and shaving equipment. The Center's downtown building was provided free by the Masonic Lodge and included bath facilities, a dance floor, a Rock-Ola Nickelodeon, and reading tables. Dances were held there on Saturday afternoons and evenings.[75] Almost everyone who visited the Service Center raved about its amenities. However, Eufaula servicemen who read about it in the *Tribune* or *Avondale Sun* did not share this sentiment. In September 1944, Monzie Alsobrook informed his mother:

> Frances wrote me about keeping the Service Center again. She also told me that Aunt Carr[ie] told her she should be ashamed not to keep it since she isn't doing anything else. I've written you & Frances that I didn't want that to happen again so if you ever hear Carrie say any more to her you can tell her that I don't care to have my wife waiting on those "U.S.O. Commandoes."[76]

Despite Alsobrook's obvious jealousy over his wife being around other servicemen, the Center was universally popular with the 25,000 soldiers who patronized the facility between April 1942 and August 1945.[77]

The Community House also provided "a home away from home" for soldiers, but on a smaller scale than the Eufaula Service Center. Still, the servicemen's favorite hangout was the Crystal Club on Orange Street—in no small part because it attracted so many young women. By 1943, with the town's male population depleted by enlistments and the draft, the Crystal Club had become a magnet for women who loved to dance and socialize with men of their own age. Located in a renovated residence, the Club featured a dance floor, juke box, and an adjoining swimming pool. Bands per-

---

[75] "Eufaula Plans Quiet Season," *Columbus Daily Enquirer*, 20 December 1942, 20; "Center Sends 161 Boxes to Soldiers," *Avondale Sun* 4 October 1943, 14; "Eufaula Service Center Closes," *Eufaula Tribune*, 21 August 1945, 1; Flewellen, *Along Broad Street*, 338. Cowikee Mills employees and local citizens donated funds for the gift packages, which included two handkerchiefs, wash cloths, towel, soap, talcum powder, shoeshine kit, razor blades, one carton of cigarettes, and one can of smoking tobacco.

[76] Thomas Alsobrook to Oma Alsobrook, 4 September 1944, in author's possession.

[77] "Eufaula Service Center Closes," *Eufaula Tribune*, 21 August 1945, 1. Mrs. Sig Bloom, Carrie Snipes, and a large group of other Eufaula women were responsible for the Service Center's success.

formed at weekend dances.[78]

Inevitably, romances bloomed among the women and soldiers who met in Eufaula or at dances in Columbus, Georgia, or Ozark. In early February 1941, Oma Alsobrook noticed "quite a few weddings here over the weekend. Ellen Hatfield and Clinton Fussel[1], Ruby [Bigbee] & Mary Toler (G. W. Cutchens' sister in law) married soldiers from Ft. Benning. There is [sic] lots of soldiers here every weekend now."[79] During the war, the traditional length of courtships shrank considerably. Louise Smith, the daughter of mill operatives Emma and Will Smith, worked in the Cowikee offices in Eufaula. In February 1942, she married George DeSmet, age nineteen, a Fort Benning soldier from Chicago serving in the 2nd Armored Division. He shipped out to Europe a few months after their marriage. In October 1944, he was seriously wounded and returned to the United States for recuperation. Over the next eight months, his wife followed him as he underwent medical treatment at various Army hospitals. By summer 1945, however, they were divorced.[80]

Another young Southside woman, Dorriceil Hatfield, graduated from Eufaula High School in June 1943. Less than a month later, she married twenty-two-year-old David Carroll Parks, a native of Goree, Texas, who was a paratrooper in the 101st Airborne Division at Fort Benning.[81] Since the 101st was training intensively for combat, the couple only had a brief time together before Parks's deployment. On 17 September 1944, a friend of his wife's noted, "Paratroopers jumped in Holland today, and Dorriceil feels

---

[78] Mavis Barker McDonald, "Reminiscences of World War II in Eufaula," memoir, handwritten, n.d., c. 1991, copy provided to the author by Mavis and Roy McDonald; Flewellen, *Along Broad Street*, 336–37. By this time, Eufaula's adult male population had been reduced primarily to men who were deferred from the draft because of their age, physical or mental disabilities ("4-Fs"), or occupation (agriculture or an essential defense industry).

[79] Oma Alsobrook to Thomas Alsobrook, 7 February 1941, in author's possession.

[80] "Smith-DeSmet Marriage," *Avondale Sun*, 23 February 1942, 5; "Eufaula," photographs of Mr. And Mrs. George DeSmet, *Avondale Sun*, 23 March 1942, 13; "Second Battalion Wins 41st Infantry Bouts," *Columbus Daily Enquirer*, 24 January 1942, 10; Frances Alsobrook to Thomas Alsobrook, 30 October 1944; Thomas Alsobrook to Frances Alsobrook, 1 June 1945, in author's possession. Louise Smith's brothers were Tyson, Fred, Winston, and Earl Smith.

[81] "Hatfield-Parks Marriage Announced," *Columbus Daily Enquirer*, 8 July 1943, 8; "David Carroll Parks, Sr.," obituary, *Houston (TX) Chronicle*, 15 January 2004, n.p.

sure David jumped. She really does worry a lot and I can see why." Dorriceil finally received a letter from Parks six weeks later, indicating that he was safe in Holland. That Christmas he sent her mother a scarf sewn from the remnants of his parachute that bore burn holes from German bullets. Parks was wounded twice and earned two Bronze Stars during his service in World War II. But he never returned to his wife in Eufaula; instead, he went back to the Lone Star State.[82]

Other couples in Eufaula who fell in love during the war postponed their weddings until after V-J Day. Fifteen-year-old Mavis Barker first met her future husband, Louisiana-born Roy Thomas McDonald, age nineteen, during summer 1942. She later wrote, "Had it not been for the war and for Crystal Club, Roy and I probably would have never known each other."[83] She had noticed him dancing at the club, but McDonald paid little attention to this "little...young-looking girl." "As fate would have it," she recalled, "we finally came face to face late one Sunday afternoon under a big tree on North Randolph Street."[84] She and her mother were walking to their home on Cotton Avenue when McDonald asked them for directions to the Crystal Club. She offered to accompany him to Orange Street, but her mother intervened and said "No." Over the next year, Mavis and Roy danced together at the club, and he often visited in the Barker home on weekends.[85]

After McDonald was transferred from Fort Benning to Fort Jackson, South Carolina, and in 1943, overseas, the young couple stayed in touch by letter. Serving in Belgium during the frigid 1944–1945 winter with the 30th Division's 120th Infantry Regiment, McDonald fought at the Battle of the Bulge, where his feet were badly frozen. In September 1945, he was transferred to a military hospital in Hot Springs, Arkansas, for further treatment to his damaged feet. Mavis traveled for many hours by bus from Eufaula to

---

[82] Frances Alsobrook to Thomas Alsobrook, 17 September 1944 (quote); Frances Alsobrook to Thomas Alsobrook, 27 October 1944, in author's possession; Janet Hatfield Scroggins (Dorriceil Hatfield's niece) email to the author, 24 March 2016; "David Carroll Parks, Sr.," obituary, *Houston Chronicle*, 15 January 2004, n.p. The parachute jump into Holland launched Operation Market-Garden, the campaign to liberate Holland and drive a wedge into Germany. Due to a succession of troop deployment errors, the operation failed. See O'Neill, *A Democracy at War*, 365–66.

[83] McDonald, "Reminiscences of World War II."

[84] Ibid.

[85] Ibid.

be reunited with him. They were married in Hot Springs on 15 September 1945. Mavis and Roy Mcdonald returned to Eufaula, raised three children, and became proud grandparents and great-grandparents. In September 2015, they celebrated their seventieth wedding anniversary.[86]

These experiences reveal World War II's dramatic impact upon Eufaulians that reached from distant, horrific battlefields at the far ends of the earth into every corner of the home front. For those of "The Greatest Generation" who came of age during the war, it was an adrenaline-charged roller-coaster ride of emotional extremes—fear, terror, outrage, boredom, depression, despair, joy, and exhilaration. But whether overseas or at home, they were united by a shared common purpose—to win the war—and by an abiding belief that they were part of a cause far greater than their individual lives. And fifty years later, they looked back on the war as a pinnacle of their very existence—when they felt more intensely alive than at any time before or afterward. In the words of one Navy veteran who spoke for both servicemen and civilians, the war was "more exciting, more meaningful than anything I'd ever done."[87]

Each Eufaula serviceman who survived the war was affected differently by the experience. And like Southside's mill families, each had his own story. In March 1942, Earl Starnes, a lieutenant with the 141st Armored Signal Company, 1st Armored Division, wrote enthusiastically to his friend Hugh Comer in Sylacauga:

> All the army is new to me, but the armored forces is even newer. I am the company supply officer and division signal property officer.... You can realize the amount of planning and paper work involved in keeping the implements of communication.... It's a lot of work but I like it, don't think I would have gotten a job in a combat unit that I would have liked better, if I just had more time to put on it. We have lots of soldiering to do....[88]

---

[86] Ibid.; June Barker Clenney emails to the author, 14 January, 19 June 2016. Mavis Barker McDonald graduated from Eufaula High School in 1945. Her parents were Grady and Myrtle Poteat Barker, and her grandfather was D. F. "Doc" Barker. Roy McDonald was born in Livingston, LA, in 1922 and died at age ninety-three in Eufaula on 10 June 2016. He enlisted in the Army at age seventeen in 1940. I am indebted to the McDonalds and June Barker Clenney (Mavis McDonald's sister) for sharing their story.

[87] Benjamin Bradlee, editor of the *Washington Post*, quoted in Kennedy, *Freedom from Fear*, 712.

[88] Earl Starnes to Hugh Comer, n.d., c. 15 March 1942, in "With Our Boys in the

This letter reveals that the burden of his duties and the anticipation of going overseas were weighing heavily upon Starnes. A few weeks earlier, he briefly visited with his sister, Frances Starnes. After consuming a quart of Scotch in her presence, he said, "What the hell, I'm in the Army." Somewhat shocked at his new carefree attitude, she later remarked, "[H]e hopes he will be sent where the fighting is going on, so he says."[89] But on the eve of the 1st Armored Division's deployment to North Africa in May 1942, Starnes suffered a severe nervous breakdown and received a medical discharge.[90] Starnes was among several Eufaulians who were granted "Section Eight" psychological discharges. Noting this trend in early 1944, Monzie Alsobrook observed, "If boys around there don't stop coming home with M. D.'s [medical discharges], there won't be any left in the Service."[91]

As exemplified by the Battery D troops, World War II's enlistments were "for the duration," and lengthy tours of duty that exceeded two years were commonplace. By 1944, a number of Eufaula servicemen who had survived combat without suffering any physical wounds were still on active duty—such as eighteen-year-old Ranny Horace Johnson, with twenty-nine months in combat with the 2nd Marine Division, and Vassar Gordon, who had enlisted in the Navy before Pearl Harbor and had survived eight major sea battles.[92] An absence of Purple Hearts among their decorations did not mean that these men had not been wounded emotionally, however. Some had stared into the depths of hell itself. Ed Cochran reacted to the horrors of a liberated concentration camp in a letter to his mother in 1945, writing "I don't see how a man could treat another man like the Germans treated these people."[93] John "Handsome" Lockwood, who grew up at Cowikee Mills' Lone Oak Leghorn Farm and starred in high school football, served in an Army Graves Registration Company. Many years after the war, he was still

---

Service," *Avondale Sun*, 23 March, 1942, 5.

[89] Frances Starnes to Thomas Alsobrook, n.d., c. 10 March 1942, in author's possession.

[90] Wilson, *Manpower and Firepower* 184, 187, 195.

[91] Thomas Alsobrook to Oma Alsobrook, 24 January 1944, in author's possession.

[92] "Personals," *Avondale Sun*, 16 October 1944, 3; 13 November 1944, 7; Vassar A. Gordon to Oma Alsobrook, 22 May 1944; Thomas Alsobrook to Oma Alsobrook, 15 October 1944, in author's possession.

[93] Flewellen, *Along Broad Street*, 345.

haunted by nightmares of mangled, putrefied corpses.[94] Despite being exposed to such unfathomable horrors, these men returned to Eufaula and courageously tried to rebuild lives that were interrupted by war. Since medical treatment of combat stress disorders was in its infancy after the war, in retrospect, it seems astonishing that any of them were able to lead productive lives after their service.

Perhaps the most bizarre episode involving Eufaula's servicemen had nothing to do with what later would be termed post-traumatic stress disorder (PTSD). While the strange tale of airman Wilmer S. Thompson was harrowing, it also bespoke of courage, fortitude, and resourcefulness, and became the stuff of legends. Thompson, born in 1921, worked in Cowikee Mill No. 1 and played in the band. He enlisted in the Army Air Corps in 1941 and flew sixty-four missions as a B-17 bombardier-gunner over Sicily and Italy. On three separate occasions, he narrowly escaped death by bailing out of his crippled aircraft. In August 1943, his mother, Lillie Mathis Thompson, 530 South Eufaula Street, was notified by the War Department that he had died in combat in Italy. In an emotional memorial service at the Second Baptist Church in October 1943, Mayor Moss Moulthrop, Helen Mitchell Taylor, John B. DeVenny, First Baptist Pastor C. B. Price, and several other Eufaulians paid tribute to their deceased friend, "heroic flyer" Wilmer Thompson. The Cowikee Mills Band, directed by Red Beasley, provided the music for the service.[95]

Then, on 29 November 1943—a month after the memorial—the *Avondale Sun* printed this note under "Personals": "Appearing very much alive and in the best of health, Sgt. Wilmer Thompson, reported killed in action on Aug. 17th, is now at home in Eufaula visiting his mother...."[96] Thompson was dumbfounded to learn that he had been "dead" since August and in response paraphrased Mark Twain that the German Red Cross's report of his demise was "slightly exaggerated." The other twelve members of

---

[94] As a teenager, I once listened attentively as Lockwood described to my father in excruciating detail how his nightmares brought back the actual stench of the bodies he buried.

[95] "Barbour Countian, Reported Killed, Is Feted by Eufaulans [*sic*], in "With Our Boys in Service," *Avondale Sun*, 13 December 1943, 6; "Church Honors Sgt. Thompson," *Avondale Sun*, 18 October, 1943, 13.

[96] "Personals," *Avondale Sun*, 29 November 1943, 12; Flewellen, *Along Broad Street*, 342.

his bomber crew crashed and died near the Kasserine Pass in North Africa. He parachuted into the desert and found refuge with friendly Arab nomads. Camouflaged in the garb of "a Moslem woman," Thompson safely returned to the American lines on a borrowed horse. He suspected that the Army erroneously had assumed the entire bomber crew was lost based upon insufficient evidence found at the crash site.[97]

Others were less fortunate. Over the next two years, War Department telegrams blanketed Old Eufaula and Southside with notifications of servicemen who were killed, wounded, missing, or captured. From her desk at L. Y. "Yank" Dean III's Eufaula Bank and Trust Company, Frances Starnes Alsobrook meticulously recorded these developments in letters to her husband, Monzie. In late September 1944, she wrote:

> Lillian Luke's husband has been killed in France. I didn't know him. He was Lt. Calhoun. I feel so sorry for her—she has been here since he went overseas. Did I tell you about Lt. Daniel Roth's clothes and other personal belongings coming home? Well, you see Mr. Dean is administrator of the Roth estate, since Mrs. Roth's in the asylum, so they all came to the bank, and I had the queerest feeling when I saw them.[98]

Her comments throughout 1944 became a steady litany of depressing, heartbreaking news, interspersed with occasional rays of hope:

> Do you remember Hildred Braswell, Mr. Homer Braswell's boy? Anyway, he's missing in action and it's about to kill them. Isn't that awful? ...Leon Conner is missing in action. He is a pilot in the Navy air-corps—pilots a torpedo plane, and has been in the Pacific since January. Isn't that terrible? I just hope he is safe and not killed.... I heard that Bucky Davis had been freed from that prison camp in Slovakia. I don't know how true that is, but won't it be wonderful if he is out. He's lucky to still be alive.... I know Mr.

---

[97] "Eufaulian Rescues Three When Bus Sinks in Creek," *Avondale Sun*, 25 August 1952, 1, 6 (both quotes); "Barbour Countian, Reported Killed, Is Feted by Eufaulans [*sic*]," in "With Our Boys in Service," *Avondale Sun*, 13 December 1943, 6; "Religions Student Praised for Aid in Bus Accident," *(Baton Rouge, LA) Advocate*, 13 August 1952, 10. In August 1952, while studying for the priesthood in a Catholic order in Ligouri, MO, he heroically rescued three drowning passengers in an overturned bus that was swept off the highway by a flash flood. He died in 1968 and was buried at Fairview Cemetery.

[98] Frances Alsobrook to Thomas Alsobrook, 26 September 1944, in author's possession.

Claude and Miss Edna are happy....[99]

She did not confine her remarks to newly freed POWs, the dead and missing—every minute detail of daily life in Eufaula seemingly caught her perceptive eye. Extramarital affairs were on the rise, and she speculated as to which ones would lead to divorces and public scandals. Regarding wartime rationing of sugar, meat, gasoline, and luxury items, she focused primarily on Eufaula's lively black market and methods of skirting the restrictions. By opening a part-time barbershop in Ozark, near Camp Rucker, her father, Amos Starnes, was granted an additional emergency allotment of gasoline for commuting to the Wiregrass. When "a smuggler came through town," she, Myrtie Cade, and Frances Bondourant purchased gray squirrel coats, priced at $200 in stores, for $40 to $65.[100] She saved some of her harshest words for two Montevallo classmates, Sarah James Irby and Celia Higgins, whose husbands had not been drafted: "P. S. Dam[n] all these puny 4-F's like Ty and Charlie who still have their wives. I could s___ on them."[101]

These bitter comments undoubtedly resulted from the personal frustrations and jealousies that spread like a virus in Eufaula during the war. Such petty animosities were systemic in a small town like the Bluff City; they were greatly exacerbated and magnified by the war's extraordinary pressures.

From a larger perspective, beyond the minutiae of life on the home front, World War II placed a sharper, more focused edge on everything about Eufaula. The entire nation was fighting for its survival, and this small town was a full-fledged partner in this effort. Moreover, the final outcome of the war remained in doubt well into 1945, and this uncertainty further galvanized Americans' unity and fortitude during that last bloody year of combat. With such high stakes and everything on the line, the antiquated, moldering walls between the two Eufaulas fell away—never to arise again after the war.

And just as the Great Depression tossed them into the same boat, leveled, and democratized them, the people of Eufaula were transformed forev-

---

[99] Selections from Frances Alsobrook to Thomas Alsobrook, in order, 6 September, 8 November, 25 October, 2 November 1944, ibid.

[100] Frances Alsobrook to Thomas Alsobrook, 15, 18 November, 25 October 1944 (quote), ibid.; "Personals," *Avondale Sun*, 2 November 1942, 4.

[101] Frances Alsobrook to Thomas Alsobrook, 26 September 1944, in author's possession.

er by World War II. By September 1943, 134 men from Cowikee Mills No. 1 and No. 3 were in uniform. While this figure represented only about 22 percent of the two mills' total workforce, many of these were foremen. Therefore, although they were not formally promoted to these positions, for the first time in the mills' fifty-three-year history, women assumed supervisory roles.[102] Perhaps of equal historical significance, several of their daughters, including Doris Neal Higgins, Katie Lou Smith, Ila Mae Kelley, Dovie Conner, Mary Kate Braswell, Cleo Devlin, and Mildred Long, were the first women in Eufaula to enlist in auxiliary branches of the armed forces.[103] As in the case of the town's hundreds of men who served in World War II, these young women traveled far from the Bluff City and found themselves thrown together with other Americans of diverse economic backgrounds, religious beliefs, and social and political views. This experience significantly shaped how these Eufaulians looked upon themselves and their hometown. The war thus forced an entire generation to develop a more complex, introspective view of their hometown and the outside world.

Among Eufaula's servicemen who fought in Europe and the Pacific, one thought seemed to be predominant—relief that the war's destructive force had never reached the United States. Former Big Mill operative Clifford G. Mobley, a twenty-seven-year-old Army corporal, had landed in Normandy on D-Day plus one. In late September 1944, he wrote to Comer Jennings, "I am at present somewhere in Germany, helping to return some of the medicine that these Nazis dished out a few years ago. I am beginning to enjoy it now for what we destroy is now theirs for a change."[104] By May 1945, deeper in the heart of the devastated Third Reich, Mobley was personally stunned by the masses of refugees that the war had created:

> Everything is confused, almost chaotic. Thousands are homeless wandering about on the roads. Germans, Russians, and all. Others are trying to get home after 3 or 4 years of slave labor. They are traveling and carrying their

[102] "Honor Roll," "Eufaula," *Avondale Sun*, 15 September 1943, n.p.

[103] "Personals," *Avondale Sun*, 2 November 1942, 9; 19 April 1943, 14; "Doris Neal Higgins Completes Course," *Avondale Sun*, 20 March 1944, 12; "Miss Katie Lou Smith," *Avondale Sun*, 15 November 1943, 14; Flewellen, *Along Broad Street*, 342.

[104] Clifford G. Mobley to Comer Jennings, 21 September 1944, in "Letters from Our Men in Service," *Avondale Sun*, 16 October 1944, 10. Mobley served previously in the Army in the Philippines 1935–1938. He re-enlisted in 1940. "Word from Our Boys," *Avondale Sun*, 2 November 1942, 10.

few belongings on every type of wagon imaginable. I mean it is a pitiful sight, whole families from the ages of 60 to mere babies, but we are trying to round them up and ship them home. They aren't the only ones confused. I am too. God forbid this ever happening in America.[105]

During the bloody campaign from Normandy into Germany, Mobley lost several of his buddies, leaving him to contemplate the meaning of their deaths. Without any equivocation, he believed that his friends had given their lives to liberate the "oppressed people" of Europe, and he hoped these soldiers' families would take some solace in that. He told Comer Jennings that during the advance through liberated France, he was amazed at the outpouring of joy and gratitude from the people in each town and village. "I saw it," Mobley wrote, "and I can assure you it was both overwhelming and genuine."[106]

In 1944–1945, Mobley wrote several thoughtful letters to Jennings in which he articulated his views on many topics—the terrible European weather ("Hitler's Secret Weapon"), the necessity of deep fox holes, the tenacity of German soldiers, and postwar Germany's future. Celebrating Thanksgiving on the front lines in Germany in 1944, he broached "a delicate subject" with Jennings—"the question of the American Negro in postwar America." This topic had generated "quite a bit of argument among the troops," Mobley declared. He felt that Southerners in particular were "dodging the issue." He admitted that he had no idea how this issue would be resolved, but predicted that "whatever State or individual…clarifies their stand on the Negroes' status is the first to open a protest and a deluge of resentment on either side or both."[107]

The "Negro Question" dominated the thoughts and discussions of Eufaulians overseas and at home, even in the midst of the war. And their comments gave credence to Clifford Mobley's concerns. To news from his mother in February 1944 that Anniston had become an Army induction center for African Americans, Monzie Alsobrook responded: "It isn't fit for anything else. While we are on the subject about negroes. Some of the guys

---

[105] Clifford G. Mobley to Comer Jennings, 20 May 1945, in "Letters from Our Men in Service," *Avondale Sun*, 25 June 1945, 9.

[106] Clifford G. Mobley to Comer Jennings, 22 November 1944, in "Letters from Our Men in Service," *Avondale Sun*, 21 December 1944, 11.

[107] Ibid.

in here think nothing of living and mingling with them. I've had more arguments about negroes than any other thing. You'd be as shocked as I was to hear some of them. It's disgusting."[108]

Then, on 9 September 1944, racial violence erupted at home in Eufaula. Near the bus station on Broad Street, an African-American soldier allegedly grabbed a "Mrs. Jernigan" and said, "Come on, let's go have a good time." An unidentified white man stepped in and "almost killed him." Later in the day, several other white men brutally assaulted two more African Americans in a liquor store. The next day, Frances Starnes Alsobrook angrily wrote to her husband: "So you can see the Negroes still don't know their place here—it makes me so mad I could die—I wish they'd all get killed. You couldn't even get through town for them yesterday."[109] A year later, similar racial incidents were reported in Eufaula.[110]

With World War II winding down, the Bluff City's old tradition of racial violence resurfaced. Although the war had many dramatic, positive effects on Eufaula, in 1945, it remained clear that racial amelioration and reconciliation would be left up to the children and grandchildren of "The Greatest Generation." Only history would prove whether or not "Baby-Boomers" and their children were prepared for that monumental task. Regardless of its failure to resolve Eufaula's racial issues, World War II left many significant, historical legacies. The war empowered the Bluff City's women, particularly mill operatives, who embraced their new freedoms and opportunities and then fought tenaciously to keep them after the veterans returned in 1945. Although many of these men resumed working in the mills, a comparable number used the GI Bill to further their educations and launch new careers. Southsiders always hoped that their children would have better lives, and they saw this dream reach fruition in the postwar years. Very few of their children entered the mills; instead, they left Eufaula for college and professional careers in other towns and cities. With the steady departure of young Southsiders and the waning of the textile industry after the 1960s, Eufaula's mill village would soon become no more than a faded, sepia-toned memory.

It can be argued that a more diverse economy, greater educational op-

---

[108] Thomas Alsobrook to Oma Alsobrook, 7 February 1944, in author's possession.
[109] Frances Alsobrook to Thomas Alsobrook, 10 September 1944, ibid.
[110] Thomas Alsobrook to Oma Alsobrook, 19 June 1945, ibid.

portunities, and a highly mobile population in the postwar era hastened Eufaula's decline as a cotton mill town, but the most dynamic legacy of World War II for Eufaula was that it touched every family. From the early months of 1942 through V-J Day, Blue Star Service Flags appeared in windows all over Eufaula and across the county. By the war's end, about forty-five of those emblems would be replaced with gold stars, honoring men killed in action.

From 1941–1945, as during the Great Depression, shared sacrifices united the town in a common bond. The shattered families buried their dead sons at Fairview Cemetery and alongside lonely, rural church yards and gently embraced the wounded who were broken physically and emotionally. Then, the Reverend Wharton's statue, "The Man with his Backside to Southside," became just another historic monument in the Bluff City, marking what once was true (a demonstrable symbol of the lines between Southside and Old Eufaula) and what had ceased to be.

Epilogue

Images of Southside

*Why,... us people will go on livin' when all them people is gone,
Why,... we're the people that live. They ain't gonna wipe us out. Why,
we're the people—we go on.*
—John Steinbeck, *The Grapes of Wrath*, 1939

As revealed in the prologue, visitors to Eufaula today will find little physical evidence that the cotton mills and Southside ever existed or that multiple generations of men, women, and children worked and dwelled there. Moreover, prior to World War II, coverage of Southside in Eufaula's newspapers of record—the *Daily and Weekly Times*, the *Daily Citizen*, and the *Tribune*—perhaps could most charitably be described as sporadic. In contrast, the *Montgomery Advertiser*, *Columbus Enquirer*, and *Macon Telegraph* historically devoted more pages to Southside. Florida Dewar's short-lived *Southside News*, in 1920–1921, provided a fleeting glimpse inside the mill village. Around 1923, the *Avondale Sun* began publishing special features about each of the Comer mill villages, including Southside. Over the next sixty years, the *Avondale Sun* faithfully recorded the story of Eufaula's mill settlement supplemented with a rich array of photographs.

While the *Avondale Sun* is an invaluable chronicle of daily life in Southside, a variety of public documentation adds texture to our existing knowledge of individual citizens—United States Census and Social Security records, poll and property tax receipts, draft registrations for both world wars, claims for veteran's medical and burial benefits, and Barbour County probate court filings. The Census records' specific details as to dates and states of birth, home ownership, and literacy are particularly vital to even the most rudimentary historical analysis of Southside.

The Census records indicate that Southsiders generally were literate in varying degrees, dependent largely upon how many years they attended school before entering the work force in the mills or elsewhere. Many Southsiders, such as Tom Alsobrook, Mallie Parish, and Amos Starnes, with only a few years of formal education, were "self-taught" or tutored by their wives.

As a general rule, while they rarely wrote personal diaries, journals, or other introspective accounts of their lives, Southsiders dutifully inscribed the dates of births, deaths, marriages, and other family events in their Bibles. As working people with a dearth of leisure time, Eufaula's mill villagers reserved their handwritten communications almost exclusively for relatives and friends. These letters' predominant topics included sickness and health, the weather, local gossip, and personal family business.

Since Southsiders were neither historians nor archivists, they seldom preserved their personal correspondence. They frequently moved and routinely discarded anything considered extraneous, such as large bundles of letters. Even sentimental attachments to caches of personal correspondence did not guarantee their preservation. For example, sometime in the 1920s after she had retrieved any accompanying photographs, Oma Parish Alsobrook burned all of her letters to and from her beloved husband, Ernest. Likewise, after his parents died in the 1980s, Wendell Franklin Wentz tossed a sizable volume of family records that predated World War I, including several Southside account books from his grandfather's market. However, Wentz saved his family's photograph collection.

Dating back to their arrival in Eufaula in the late 1880s, Southsiders obviously placed a great deal of value in their family photographs. During the 1880s and 1890s, mill villagers actively patronized two photographers in downtown Eufaula—J. W. Taylor and J. W. Flournoy—both specialists in portraiture. By the early 1900s, native Ohioan Harry Ellsworth Maugans had become Eufaula's principal photographer. For over fifty years, Maugans produced iconic, panoramic scenes of the Bluff City and the surrounding countryside and intimate portraits of families and individual Eufaulians. He photographed several generations of Southsiders (including the author in 1947) in his studio at 206 East Broad Street or in their homes.

With the widespread popularity of inexpensive, hand-held cameras and paper film marketed by Eastman Kodak and other companies in the late nineteenth century, many Eufaulians became amateur photographers. Southsiders also pursued the popular "Kodaking" hobby and took hundreds of shots—church gatherings, front porch socials, parties, picnics, and excursions on the bluffs overlooking the river and into Georgia, at Lake Cherokee and Providence Canyon. Although they occasionally snapped pictures of mill operatives outside plants No. 1 and No. 3, Southsiders primarily gravitated toward scenes of the bluffs, river, and railroad trestles. In short, Southsiders' photographs captured the most important elements in their lives—families, friends, and leisure time spent away from the mills.

Some of the more intriguing images serve as an historical portal, opening Southsiders' lives for viewing and scrutiny. March 1907, as depicted in chapter 3, was undoubtedly the cruelest time for the Parish and Dunaway families. Turner Parish, while released from jail on bond for murder, attacked Chewalla Mills superintendent Dan Poole, who, in self-defense, shot and killed his young operative. That month William Dunaway also killed himself with a morphine overdose. A few months later, three-year-old O. V. Parish died after suffering severe burns.

In 1909, two years after so much death and sorrow, the Parishes and Dunaways posed for a family photograph, probably at Almarine and Epsie Parish's home on Dale Road. This photograph, which is the only surviving image of both families, provides a haunting glimpse into their lives. The unknown photographer—possibly Harry Maugans—formally arranged everyone in two rows, and with the exception of six-year-old J. T. Dunaway, standing rigidly at attention in front, they all appear comfortable and relaxed. Based on their facial expressions, the photographer had just directed them to "smile." Almarine and Epsie are seated prominently in the front row with the hands folded almost identically upon their laps. The fifty-five-year-old Parish matriarch, with only the slightest trace of a smile on her lips, stares straight ahead with her striking, pale blue eyes. Her husband, Almarine, two years her senior, squints at the camera. A year after sitting for this portrait, he died at age fifty-eight. Oma Parish, age ten, stands between her grandmother, Epsie, and her aunt, Allie Dunaway. Oma's parents, Jessie and Mallie Parish, are behind her. The seven surviving children of Epsie and Almarine Parish—six in the back row—range in age from fifteen to thirty-five, born between 1874 and 1894. At least nine of the twenty people in the photograph had worked in the mills at one time or would do so in the future. Those who entered the mills as children look much older than their years. Cliff Parish, on the left end of the back row, is barely twenty-one; his sister, Carrie Parish, on his left, is nineteen. They both appear to be well into their thirties.

Like the characters in Thornton Wilder's *Our Town*, the Parishes and Dunaways cannot foresee what the future holds for them. This photograph encapsulated a rare moment in their lives when they were all together and

appear to be happy and content. They have suffered through the twin cruci-
bles of loss and grief and have emerged sadder but more resilient. Many of
them have endured exhausting, seemingly endless days and nights in the
mills. They are weary but not broken in body or spirit—somewhat reminiscent of the long-suffering fictional Joad clan immortalized by John Steinbeck
in *The Grapes of Wrath*. They are Southsiders. As long as we remember them
and tell their stories, they will never die.

Bibliography

Manuscripts and Records
Archives and Libraries
10th US Census, 1880, Inhabitants Schedule, 1140th Militia District, Early County, Georgia, NARA, Washington, DC.
12th–16th US Census, 1900–1940, Schedule No. 1: Population, Barbour County, Alabama, NARA, Washington, DC.
13th–14th US Census, 1910–1920, Schedule No. 1: Population, Clay County, Alabama, NARA, Washington, DC.
13th–15th US Census, 1910–1930, Schedule No. 1: Population, Montgomery County, Alabama, NARA, Washington, DC.
14th–15th US Census, 1920–1930, Schedule No. 1: Population, St. Clair County, Alabama, NARA, Washington, DC.
15th US Census, 1930, Schedule No. 1: Population, Jefferson County, Alabama, NARA, Washington, DC.
Booker T. Washington Papers, Manuscript Division, Library of Congress, Washington, DC (LC)
Clergy File, Franklin D. Roosevelt Papers, President's Personal File (PPF), Franklin D. Roosevelt Presidential Library and Museum, Hyde Park, New York.
Compiled Service Records, War Department Collection of Confederate Records, Record Group 109, NARA, Washington, DC.
Federal Writers' Project Papers, Southern Historical Collection, Wilson Library, University of North Carolina, Chapel Hill, North Carolina (SHC, UNC).
Harry L. Hopkins Papers, Franklin D. Roosevelt Presidential Library and Museum, Hyde Park, New York.
James McDonald Comer's Avondale Mill Office Files, Department of Archives and Manuscripts, Birmingham Public Library, Birmingham, Alabama (BPLA).
Lou Henry Hoover Papers, White House General Files, Requests for Assistance, Herbert Hoover Presidential Library, West Branch, Iowa.
Miscellaneous Birth and Death Certificates, State of Alabama, Bureau of Vital Statistics, State Board of Health, Montgomery, Alabama (ABVS)
Records of the Adjutant General's Office, US Army, Record Group 94, NARA, Washington, DC.
Records of the US District Courts, Record Group 21, Middle District of Georgia, NARA Regional Branch, Morrow, Georgia.
State Guide File, Barbour County, Alabama, Works Progress Administration Rec-

ords, Manuscript Division, Library of Congress, Washington, DC (LC).
World War I Draft Registration Cards, 1917–1918, Record Group 163, National
Archives and Records Administration, Morrow, Georgia.

Alabama Department of Archives and History, Montgomery, Alabama (ADAH)
Works Progress Administration Files
Governor Bibb Graves Administrative Files
Governor Benjamin M. Miller Administrative Files
Governor William Dorsey Jelks Biographical File
Reuben Francis Kolb Biographical File
Tuskegee University Publications File
John W. Tullis to G. Gunby Jordan, 31 October 1898, SPR 744
Alabama Confederate Pension and Service Records

Personal Collections
Author's Collection, Mobile, Alabama
Hallie Taylor Dalon Collection, Eufaula, Alabama
Ginny Dunaway Young Collection, Willis, Texas

Newspapers
Alabama
Avondale Sun, 1924–1962
Birmingham Age-Herald, 1896–1897, 1934
Birmingham News, 1934, 1938, 1983
Clayton Record, 1929
Dothan Eagle, 1911, 1936, 1944
Eufaula Daily Citizen, 1929
(Eufaula) Southside News, 1921
Eufaula Weekly Times and News, 1881–1882
Eufaula Tribune, 1940–1945, 1978, 1994, 2002–2014
Huntsville Times, 1986
Mobile Daily Herald, 1905
Montgomery Advertiser, 1893, 1902–1923
(Montgomery) Southern Courier, 1965
Tuscaloosa News, 1931

Georgia
Atlanta Constitution, 1906–1907, 1911–1912, 1921–1922

BIBLIOGRAPHY

Augusta Chronicle, 1920
Columbus Daily Enquirer, 1888–1889, 1899, 1901, 1911, 1914, 1917–1918, 1929, 1934–1944
Columbus Ledger, 1903, 1913, 1917, 1919
Macon Telegraph, 1884, 1888, 1893, 1905, 1921, 1930
Macon Weekly Telegraph, 1869–1870, 1875, 1880–1881, 1884, 1888, 1893, 1905

Other Locations
(Baton Rouge LA) Advocate, 1952
(Biloxi MS) Daily Herald, 1922, 1930, 1938
Boston Herald, 1922, 1929
Bryan (TX) Eagle, 1907
Charlotte (NC) News, 1891, 1910–1911, 1921
Charlotte (NC) Observer, 1893, 1903, 1907, 1910, 1921
(Findlay, OH) Republican-Courier, 1963
(Franklin, PA) News-Herald, 1924–1925
Greensboro (NC) Daily News, 1920
(Greenwood, SC) Index-Journal, 1921
Houston (TX) Chronicle, 2004
Jefferson City (MO) Post-Tribune, 1929
Kansas City (MO) Times, 1893
Kingsport (TN) Times, 1929
Manitowoc (WI) Herald-Times, 1929
Miami (FL) Herald, 1921
Miami (OK) Daily News-Record, 1929
(New Orleans, LA) Times-Picayune, 1888, 1910
New York Age, 1929
New York Herald, 1879, 1881
(Newport News, VA) Daily Press, 1907
Pittsburgh (PA) Courier, 1929
Reading (PA) Times, 1929
Richmond (VA) Times-Dispatch, 1929
Salisbury (NC) Evening Post, 1916
(St. Petersburg, FL) Independent, 1940
Winston-Salem (NC) Journal, 1920–1921

Published Reports
Alabama Official and Statistical Register, 1911. Montgomery, AL: Brown Printing

Company, 1912.

Alabama Official and Statistical Register, 1915. Montgomery, AL: Brown Printing Company, 1915.

Alabama Official and Statistical Register, 1923. Montgomery, AL: Brown Printing Company, 1923.

Alabama Official and Statistical Register, 1951. Alexander City, AL: Outlook Publishing Co., n.d.

Examples of Welfare Work in the Cotton Industry: Conditions and Progress, New England and in the South. New York: Woman's Department, The National Civic Federation, 1910.

Hart, Hastings H. *Social Problems of Alabama: A Study of the Social Institutions and Agencies of the State of Alabama as Related to Its War Activities*. Montgomery, AL: State of Alabama, 1918.

Oates, W. H. *Annual Report of the Factory Inspector of the State of Alabama for the Year Ending December 31st, 1912*. Montgomery, AL: Brown Printing Company, 1913.

US Department of Labor. Bureau of Labor Statistics, *Welfare Work for Employees in Industrial Establishments in the United States*. Bulletin No. 250. Washington DC: Government Printing Office, 1919.

Court Cases and Legal Documents

United States v. Powell. 112 US564 (1908) affg.151Fed.648 (CCND Ala. 1907).

United States of America v. E. M. Alsobrook, et al., #2268, 1920–1921, Boxes 51–52, Record Group 21, Records of US District Court, Middle District of Georgia, Macon Division, National Archives and Records Administration, Morrow, Georgia.

Books

Allen, Frederick Lewis. *The Big Change: America Transforms Itself, 1900–1950*. New York: Harper and Brothers, 1952.

Arsenault, Raymond, and Orville Vernon Burton, editors. *Dixie Redux: Essays in Honor of Sheldon Hackney*. Montgomery, AL: New South Books, 2013.

Blight, David W. *Race and Reunion: The Civil War in American Memory*. Cambridge, MA: Harvard University Press, 2011.

Brewer, Willis. *Brief Historical Sketches of Military Organizations Raised in Alabama during the Civil War*. Montgomery: Alabama Department of Archives and History, 1966.

Bunn, Mike. *Civil War Eufaula*. Charleston, SC: The History Press, 2013.

Cash, W. J. *The Mind of the South*. New York: Alfred A. Knopf, 1941.

Cohen, Adam. *Nothing to Fear: FDR's Inner Circle and the Hundred Days That Created Modern America*. New York: Penguin Books, 2009.

Cox, Karen C. *The United Daughters of the Confederacy and the Preservation of Confederate Culture*. Gainesville: University of Florida Press, 2003.

Feldman, Glenn. *The Irony of the Solid South: Democrats, Republicans, and Race, 1865–1944*. Tuscaloosa: University of Alabama Press, 2013.

Flewellen, Robert H. *Along Broad Street: A History of Eufaula, Alabama, 1823–1984*. Eufaula: City of Eufaula, 1991.

Flynt, Wayne. *Poor but Proud: Alabama's Poor Whites*. Tuscaloosa: University of Alabama Press, 1989.

Foster, Gaines M. *Ghosts of the Confederacy: Defeat, the Lost Cause, and the Emergence of the New South, 1865 to 1913*. New York: Oxford University Press, 1987.

Frost, David, Jr. Edited by Louise Westling. *Witness to Injustice*. Jackson: University Press of Mississippi, 1995.

Gallager, Gary, and Alan T. Nolan, editors. *The Myth of the Lost Cause and Civil War History*. Bloomington: Indiana University Press, 2000.

Gibson, Maria Layng. Edited and completed by Sara Estella Haskin. *Memories of Scarritt*. Nashville, TN: Cokesbury Press, 1928.

Goldfield, David. *Still Fighting the Civil War: The American South and Southern History*. Baton Rouge: Louisiana State University Press, 2002.

Grantham, Dewey W. *Southern Progressivism: The Reconciliation of Progress and Tradition*. Knoxville: University of Tennessee Press, 1983.

Hall, Jacquelyn Dowd, James Leloudis, Robert Korstad, Mary Murphy, LuAnn Jones, and Christopher B. Daley. *Like a Family: The Making of a Southern Cotton Mill World*. Chapel Hill: University of North Carolina Press, 1987.

Handbook for Scoutmasters. New York: Boy Scouts of America, 1913.

Hardman, J. B. S., editor. *American Labor Dynamics: In the Light of Post-War Developments*. New York: Harcourt, Brace and Company, 1928.

Harlan, Louis R. *Booker T. Washington: The Making of a Black Leader, 1856–1901*. London: Oxford University Press, 1975.

———. *Booker T. Washington: The Wizard of Tuskegee, 1901–1915*. New York: Oxford University Press, 1983.

Haws, Robert, editor. *The Age of Segregation: Race Relations in the South, 1890–1945*. Jackson: University Press of Mississippi, 1978.

Herring, Harriet L. *Welfare Work in Mill Villages: The Story of Extra-mill Activities in North Carolina*. Chapel Hill: University of North Carolina Press, 1929.

Howard, Robert West, editor. *This is the South*. Chicago: Rand McNally & Company. 1959.

Jacoway, Elizabeth, Dan T. Carter, Lester C. Lanon, and Robert C. McMath, Jr., editors. *The Adaptable South: Essays in Honor of George Brown Tindall*. Baton Rouge: Louisiana State University Press, 1991.

Janney, Caroline. *Burying the Dead, but not the Past: Ladies Memorial Associations and the Lost Cause*. Gainesville: University of Florida Press, 2003.

Kellogg, Charles Flint. *NAACP: A History of the National Association for the Advancement of Colored People*. 2 vols. Baltimore: Johns Hopkins University Press, 1973.

Kennedy, David M. *Freedom from Fear: The American People in Depression and War, 1929–1945*. New York: Oxford University Press, 1999.

MacDonald, Lois. *Southern Mill Hills: A Study of Social and Economic Forces in Certain Textile Mill Villages*. New York: Alex L. Hillman Publishers, 1928.

Mayfield, James J. *The Code of Alabama*. 3 vols. Nashville, TN: Marshal & Bruce Company, 1907.

McElvaine, Robert S, editor. *Down and Out in the Great Depression: Letters from the Forgotten Man*. Chapel Hill: University of North Carolina Press, 1983.

———. *The Great Depression: America, 1929–1941*. New York: New York Times Book Co., 1984.

McGovern, James R., *Anatomy of a Lynching: The Killing of Claude Neal*. Baton Rouge: Louisiana State University Press, 1982.

McMurry, Linda O. *To Keep the Waters Troubled: The Life of Ida B. Wells*. New York: Oxford University Press, 1998.

Meier, August, *Negro Thought in America, 1880–1915: Racial Ideologies in the Age of Booker T. Washington*. Ann Arbor: University of Michigan Press, 1969.

Meier, August and Elliott Rudwick. *From Plantation to Ghetto*. New York: Hill and Wang, 1970.

Mills, Cynthia, and Pamela Simpson, editors. *Monuments to the Lost Cause: Women, Art, and the Landscapes of Southern Memory*. Knoxville: University of Tennessee Press, 2003.

Mitchell, Broadus. *The Rise of Cotton Mills in the South*. Baltimore: Johns Hopkins University Press, 1921.

Mitchell, Broadus and George Sinclair Mitchell. *The Industrial Revolution in the South*. Baltimore: Johns Hopkins University Press, 1930.

Moore, Albert Burton. *History of Alabama*. Tuscaloosa: Alabama Book Store, 1951.

O'Neill, William. *A Democracy at War: America's Fight at Home and Abroad in World War II*. New York: The Free Press, 1993.

Osterweis, Rollin G. *The Myth of the Lost Cause*. Hamden, CT: Archon Books, 1973.

Owen, Thomas McAdory. *History of Alabama and Dictionary of Alabama Biography.* 4 vols. Chicago: S. J. Clarke Publishing Co., 1921.

Perrett, Geoffrey. *America in the Twenties: A History.* New York: Simon & Schuster, 1982.

Rabinowitz, Howard N. *Race Relations in the Urban South, 1865–1899.* New York: Oxford University Press, 1978.

Rauchway, Eric. *The Great Depression and the New Deal: A Very Short Introduction.* New York: Oxford University Press, 2008.

Rhyne, Jennings J. *Southern Cotton Mill Workers and Their Villages.* Chapel Hill: University of North Carolina Press, 1930.

Rogers, William Warren. *The One-Gallused Rebellion: Agrarianism in Alabama, 1865–1896.* Baton Rouge: Louisiana State University Press, 1970.

Rogers, William Warren, Robert David Ward, Leah Rawls Atkins, and Wayne Flynt. *Alabama: The History of a Deep South State.* Tuscaloosa: University of Alabama Press, 1994.

Savage, Kirk. *Standing Soldiers, Kneeling Slaves: Race, War, and Monument in Nineteenth-century America.* Princeton: Princeton University Press, 1997.

Simkins, Francis Butler. *A History of the South.* New York: Alfred A Knopf, 1963.

Smartt, Eugenia Persons. *A History of Eufaula, Alabama.* Birmingham, AL: Roberts & Sons, 1933.

Sobel, Robert. *The Great Bull Market: Wall Street in the 1920s.* New York: Norton, 1968.

The Cokesbury Worship Hymnal. Nashville, TN: Abington Press, 1966; orig. pub. 1938.

Thompson, Mattie Thomas. *History of Barbour County, Alabama.* Eufaula, AL: Privately printed, 1939.

Towns, W. Stuart. *Enduring Legacy: Rhetoric and Ritual of the Lost Cause.* Tuscaloosa: University of Alabama Press, 2012.

Trout, Steven. *On the Battlefield of Memory: The First World War and American Remembrance, 1919–1941.* Tuscaloosa: University of Alabama Press, 2010.

Walker, Anne Kendrick. *Backtracking in Barbour County: A Narrative of the Last Alabama Frontier.* Richmond, VA: Dietz Press, 1941.

Watkins, T. H. *The Hungry Years: A Narrative History of the Great Depression in America.* New York: Henry Holt and Company, 1999.

Webb, Samuel L. and Margaret E. Armbrester, editors. *Alabama Governors: A Political History of the State.* Tuscaloosa: University of Alabama Press, 2001.

Wiebe, Robert H. *Businessmen and Reform.* Chicago, IL: Quadrangle Paperbacks, 1962.

———. *The Search for Order, 1877–1920.* New York: Hill and Wang, 1967.

Wilson, John B. *Maneuver and Firepower: The Evolution of Divisions and Separate Brigades.* Army Lineage Series. Washington, DC: Center of Military History, United States Army, 1998.

Young, Marjorie W., editor. *Textile Leaders of the South.* Columbia, SC: R. L. Bryan Company, 1963.

Articles

Alsobrook, David E. "Mobile's Solitary Sentinel: U. S. Attorney William H. Armbrecht and the Richard Robertson Lynching Case of 1909." *Gulf South Historical Review* 20/1 (Fall 2004): 6–27.

———. "William D. Jelks (1901–1907)." *Encyclopedia of Alabama* (online). http://www.encyclopediaofalabama.org/article/h-1438.

———. "Southside and Eufaula's Cowikee Mills Village, 1910–1945." *Alabama Heritage* 119 (Winter 2016): 16–27.

Ashby-Macfayden, Irene M. "The Fight Against Child Labor in Alabama." *American Federationist* 8 (May 1901): 150–57.

Boroughs, G. C. "Rival Textiles and Substitutes." *The Clothing Designer & Manufacturer* 13/5 (August 1918): 245–46.

Breedlove, Michael A. "Donald Comer." *Encyclopedia of Alabama* (online). http://www.encyclopediaofalabama.org/face/Article.jsp?=h-2616.

Bunn, Mike. "'Equality in the Union, or Independence Out of It.'" *Alabama Heritage* 121 (Summer 2016): 23-27.

Bunn, Mike, and Douglas Clare Purcell. "Eufaula to Host Annual Meeting." *Alabama Historical Association 66th Meeting* 28/1 (Spring 2013): 5–8.

Cone, Bernard M. "Some Phases of Welfare Work." *Southern Textile Bulletin* 3/18 (4 July 1912): 4–5.

"Confederate Monument at Eufaula, Ala." *Confederate Veteran* 13/1 (January 1905): 12.

DeSantis, Vincent P. "The Great and Devastating Depression." *Notre Dame Magazine* (Winter 1987–1988): 25–28.

Douglas, O. W. "Industrial Recreation and Welfare." *Southern Textile Bulletin* 16/4 (26 September 1918): 1.

Draper, E. S. "Community Work in Southern Mill Villages." *Southern Textile Bulletin* 18/10 (8 May 1919): 31–32.

Dumenil, Lynn. "American Women and the Great War." *Organization of American Historians Magazine of History* 17/1 (October 2002): 35–37.

Haynes, Edmund. "Conditions Among Negroes in the Cities." *Annals of the Ameri-*

BIBLIOGRAPHY

can Academy of Political and Social Science 49 (September 1913): 105–119.

Janney, Caroline E. "The Lost Cause." *Encyclopedia Virginia.*
http://www.encyclopediavirginia.org/lost_cause_the.

Jelks, William Dorsey. "The Acuteness of the Negro Question: A Suggested Remedy." *North American Review* 184 (15 February 1907): 389–95.

Keller, Pat. "The End of an Era: Milltown Life from 1914 to 1978," *Alabama Life* 1/1 (June—July 1978): 40–43.

McLaron, Louise. "Workers' Education in the South." *Vassar Quarterly* 20/2 (1 May 1935): 100–106.

Michaels, George V. S. "Safegaurding [*sic*] Textile Employees." *Southern Textile Bulletin* 1 (20 April 1911): 5, 17.

Otey, Elizabeth L. "Women and Children in Southern Industry." *Annals of the American Academy of Political and Social Science* 153 (January 1931): 163–69.

Perry, Mark. "Dissecting the Myth of the Lost Cause in Montgomery, Alabama." *Politico Magazine* (August 2015).
http://www.politico.com/magazine/story/2015/08/south-lost-cause-confederacy-alabama-120914.

Rogers, William Warren. "Reuben F. Kolb: Agricultural Leader of the New South." *Agricultural History* 32/4 (1958): 109–119.

Rutherford, Karen. "Ida B. Wells-Barnett." The Mississippi Writers Page.
http://mwp.olemiss.edu//dir/wells-barnett_ida/.

Smyth, Lena Rivers. "Welfare Work Accomplishing Results." *Southern Textile Bulletin* 12/10 (2 November 1916): 1, 6–7.

Snow, Whitney Adrienne. "Cotton Mill City: The Huntsville Textile Industry, 1880–1989." *Alabama Review* 63/4 (October 2010): 243–81.

Speiser, Matthew A. "Origins of the Lost Cause: The Continuity of Regional Celebration in the White South, 1850–1872." In *Essays in History.* Corcoran Department of History. University of Virginia, 2011.
http://www.essaysinhistory.com/articles/2011/6.

Steptoe, Tyina. "Barnett, Ida Wells (1862–1931). The Black Past: Remembered and Reclaimed." http://www.blackpast.org/aah/barnett-ida-wells-1862-1931.

Tannenbaum, Frank. "The South Buries Its Anglo-Saxons." *Century* 106 (June 1923): 205–15.

"The Plant that runs on Happiness." *Look* (2 August 1949): 26–31.

"The Year Brings Many Changes to the Mountain Brook Home Development." *The Jemison Magazine* 21 (January 1930): 3–5.

Tindall, George B. "Business Progressivism: Southern Politics in the Twenties." *South Atlantic Quarterly* 62 (Winter 1963): 92–106.

"University Treats Soldiers' Garments of Vermin." *The Iowa Alumnus* 15/6 (Marc 1978): 168-69.

"War and Reunion—The Lost Cause in Southern Memory." Tennessee Virtual Archive. Tennessee State Library and Archives. http://teva.contentdm.oclc.org/cdm/landingpage/collection/p15138coll4.

Williams, David S. "Lost Cause Religion." New Georgia Encyclopedia, 5 May 2005 (revised 14 April 2016). http://www.georgiaencyclopedia.org /articles/history-archaeology/lost-cause-religion.

Dissertations, Theses, and Other Unpublished Papers

Adams Family History: "Joseph Decalve Adams and Descendants." Copy in author's possession.

Akin, Edward. "Avondale's Welfare Programs for Youth: The Programs and the People Who Made Them Work." Paper presented at the Organization of American Historians Meeting, 11 April 1980. Copy in author's possession.

———. "'Mr. Donald's Help': Donald Comer, Avondale's Birmingham Operatives and the United Textile Workers, 1933–34." Paper presented at the Southern Historical Association Meeting in 1980. Copy in author's possession.

Alsobrook, David Ernest. "William Dorsey Jelks: Alabama Editor and Legislator." MA Thesis, West Virginia University, 1972.

———. "Alabama's Port City: A Study of Mobile during the Progressive era, 1896–1917." PhD diss., Auburn University, 1983.

Alsobrook, Oma Parish. "A Brief History of Washington Street Methodist Church." 1956 typescript. Original in author's possession.

Breedlove, Michael Alan. "Donald Comer: New Southerner, New Dealer." PhD diss., The American University, 1990.

Butler, Larry Scott. "Diary of an Alabama SCOPE Volunteer—Larry Butler," Summer 1965. Copy in author's possession.

———. "A Short History of the Freedom Movement in Barbour County, Alabama," 10 December 1965. Copy in author's possession.

DeVenny, Jeanine Smith. "My Thoughts on the Cowikee Community House in Eufaula." 2015 typescript. Copy in author's possession.

———. "Granddaddy DeVenny's Life." 2000 typescript. Copy in author's possession.

———. "Hymns from my Childhood." 2016 typescript. Copy in author's possession.

Grimshaw, Allen Day. "A Study in Social Violence: Urban Race Riots in the United States." PhD diss., University of Pennsylvania, 1959.

Hrabe, John Allen. "William (Billy) Hrabe." 2014 typescript biographical sketch. Copy in author's possession.

Laurence, Jacob. "'Their Names Liveth for Evermore.' Remembering the Great War in Mobile." Paper presented at the Alabama Historical Association Meeting, Mobile Bay's Eastern Shore, 16 April 2011. Copy in author's possession.

McDonald, Mavis Barker. "Reminiscences of World War II in Eufaula." c. 1991 handwritten manuscript. Copy in author's possession.

"Parkview Baptist Church Centennial, 1895–1995." 1995 typescript. Copy in author's possession.

Purcell, Douglas Clare. "A History of Eufaula First Methodist Church, 1834–1989." 1989 typescript. Copies of selected pages in author's possession.

"Service Record Book of Men and Women in Eufaula, Alabama and Community." n.d. typescript. VFW Post No. 5850, Eufaula Carnegie Library, Eufaula, AL. Copy in author's possession.

Wentz, Wendell Franklin. "Favorite Hymns of Childhood." 2016. Copy in author's possession.

Young, Ginny Dunaway. "Ancestors of David Ernest Alsobrook." 2013 typescript family history. Copy in author's possession.

———. "Descendants of Almarine Parish." 2013 typescript family history. Copy in author's possession.

Miscellaneous Websites

Alabama Confederate Pension and Service Records. http://interactive.ancestry.com /1593/31335_b00261–00063/13.

Alabama High School Football History Association (AHSFHA). http://ljwvbly.ahstha.org/teams2/coach_stop1.asp?

Goldsmith, Earl D. "The Spirit of the American Doughboy." http://doughboysearchers.weebly.com/thespirit-of-the-american-doughboy.html.

"Otha Burnett Carter." http://treesancestrylibrary.com/tree/71462450/person/30238100216.

"O. V. Parrish [*sic*] (1905–1907)-Find A Grave Memorial" #52673767, http://www.findagrave.com.

Index

* 9 7 8 0 8 8 1 4 6 6 0 8 9 *